CAT'S Café

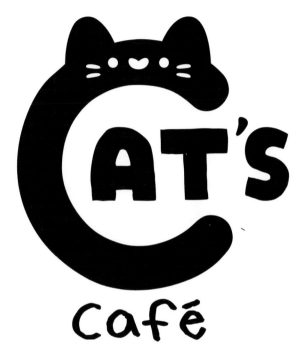

CAT'S café

a comics collection by

MATT TARPLEY

Andrews McMeel
PUBLISHING®

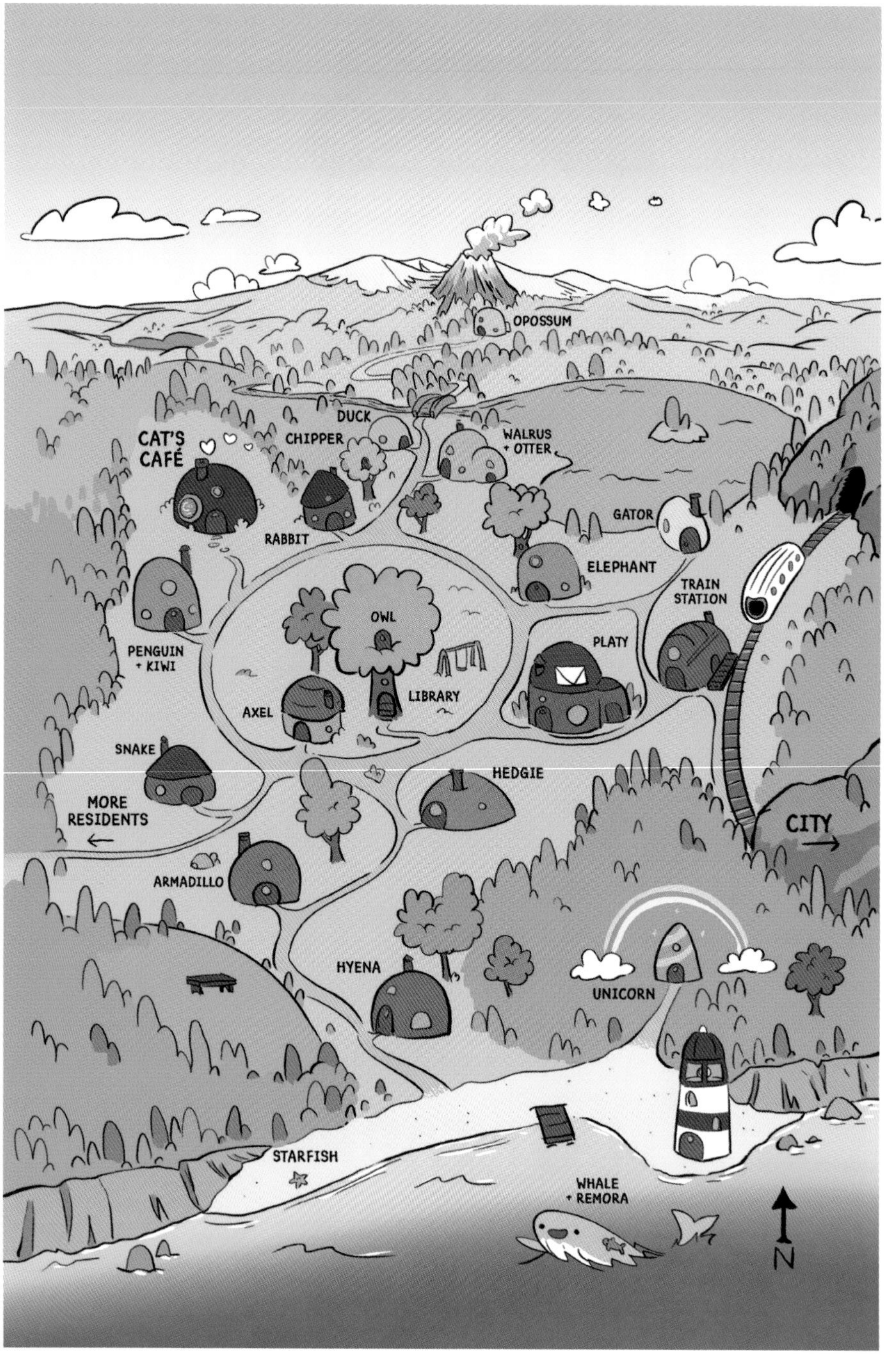
OPOSSUM
DUCK
CAT'S CAFÉ
CHIPPER
WALRUS + OTTER
GATOR
RABBIT
ELEPHANT
TRAIN STATION
OWL
PLATY
PENGUIN + KIWI
LIBRARY
AXEL
SNAKE
HEDGIE
MORE RESIDENTS
CITY
ARMADILLO
HYENA
UNICORN
STARFISH
WHALE + REMORA
N

For Mom and Dad

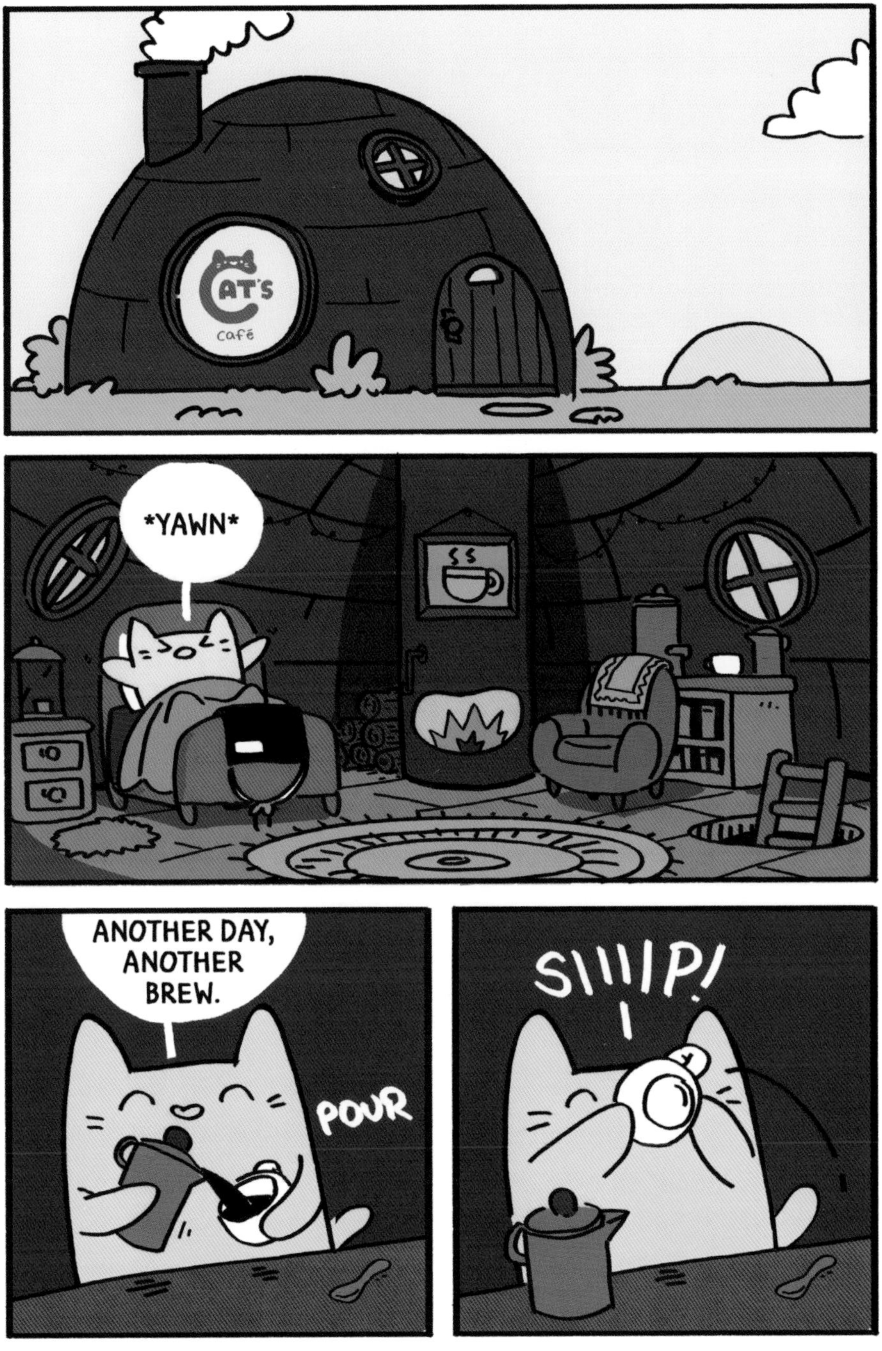
CAT'S
café
YAWN
ANOTHER DAY, ANOTHER BREW.
POUR
SIIIIP!

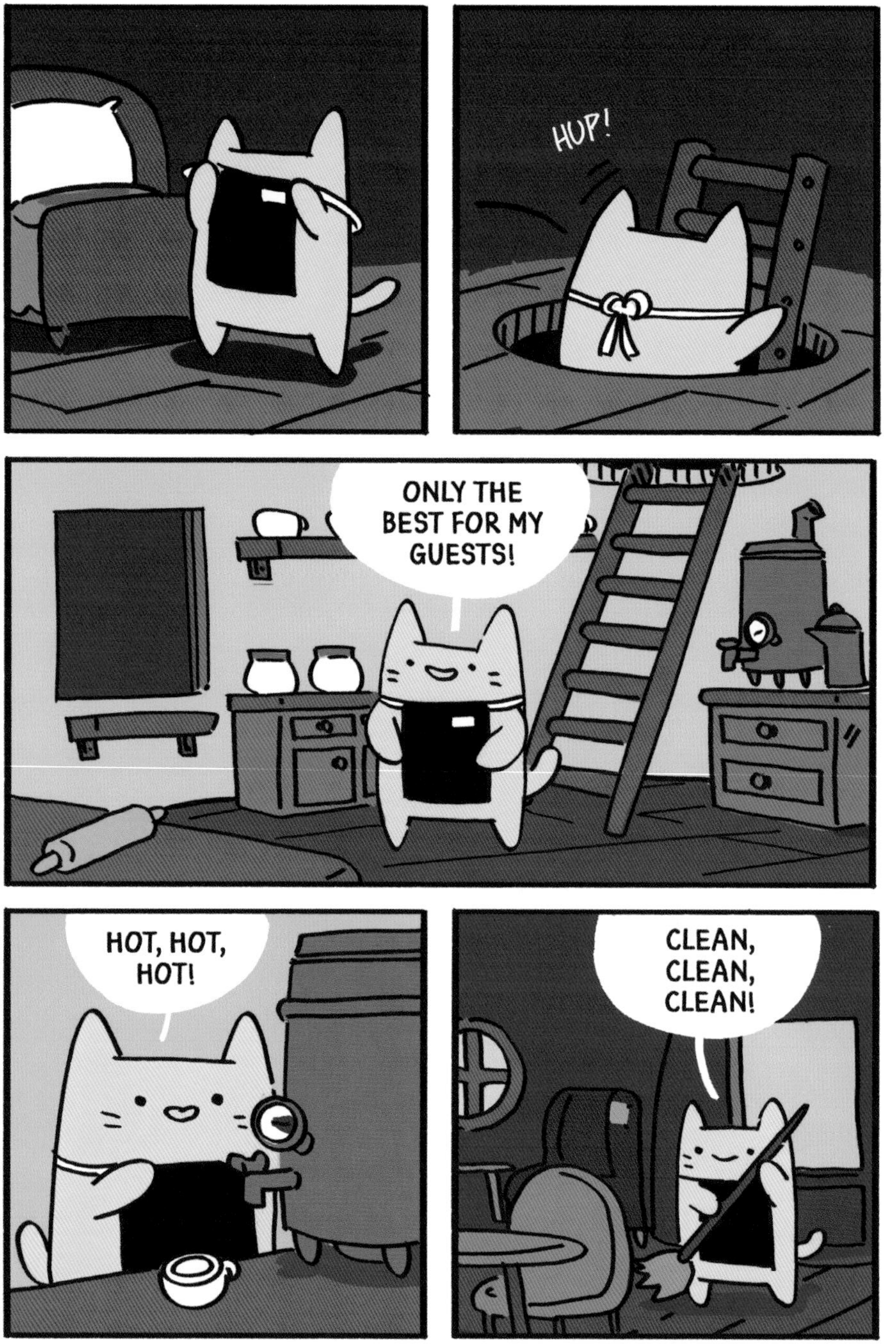
HUP!
ONLY THE BEST FOR MY GUESTS!
HOT, HOT, HOT!
CLEAN, CLEAN, CLEAN!

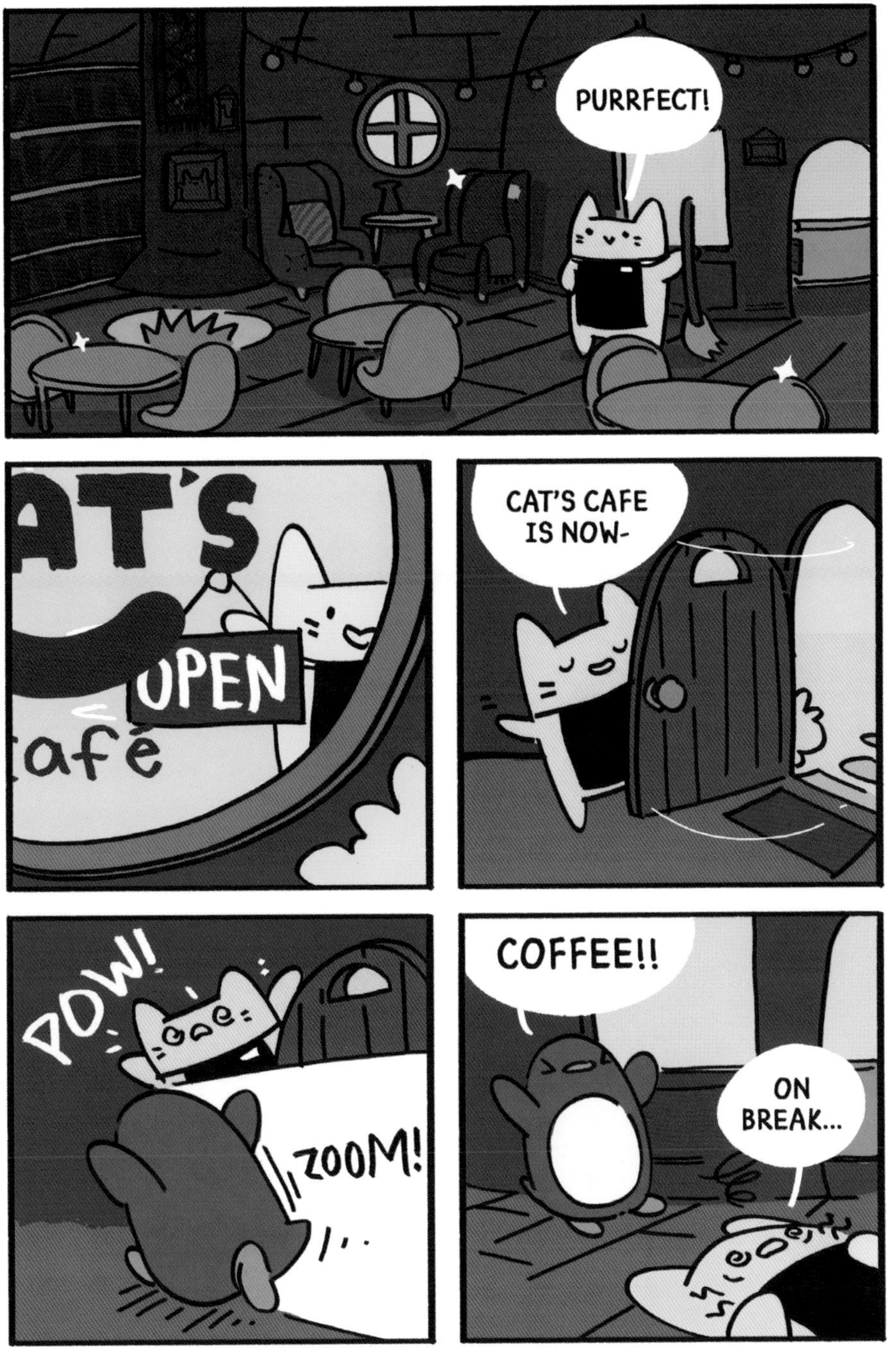
PURRFECT!
AT'S
OPEN
afé
CAT'S CAFE IS NOW-
POW!
ZOOM!
COFFEE!!
ON BREAK...

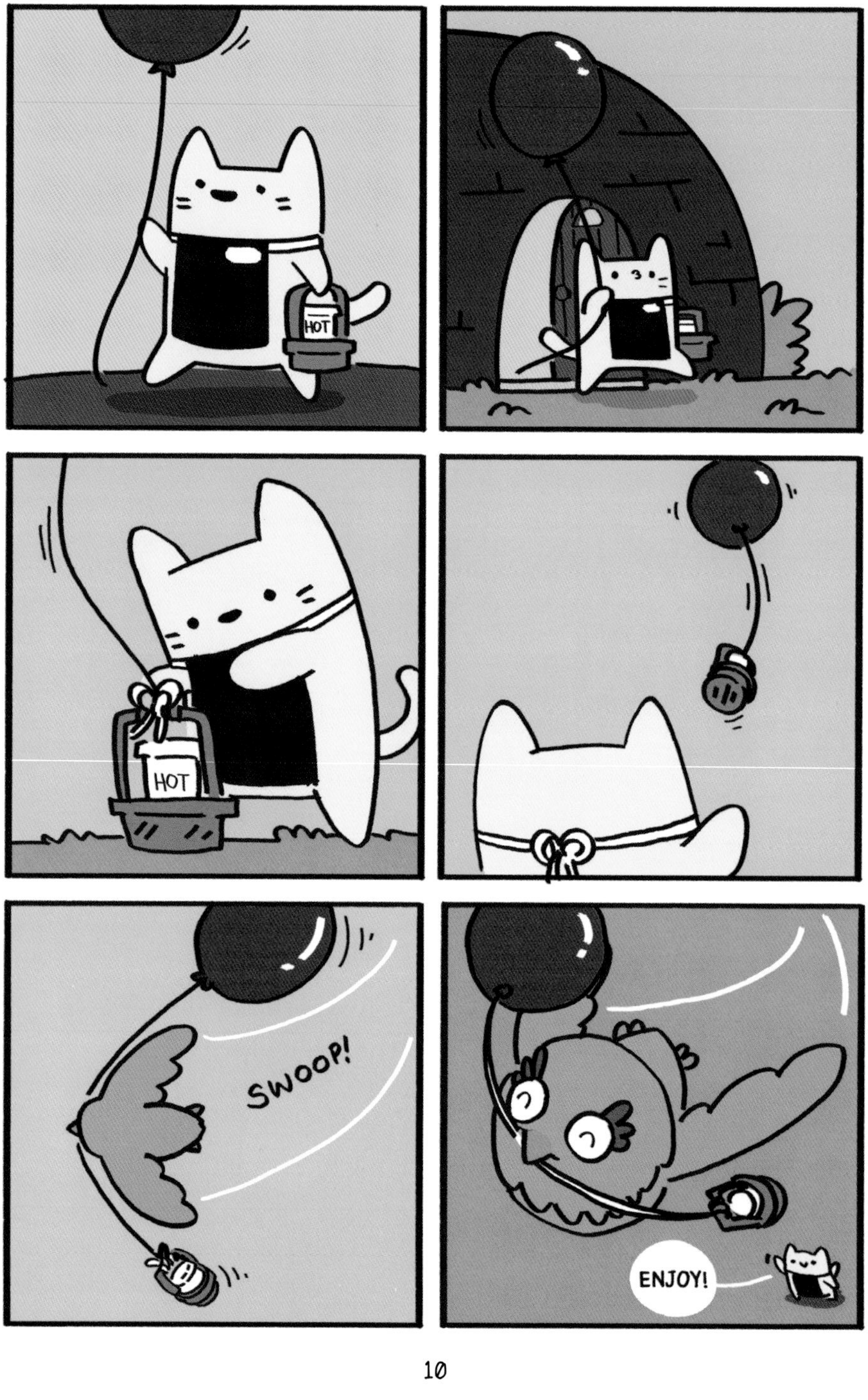
HOT
HOT
SWOOP!
ENJOY!

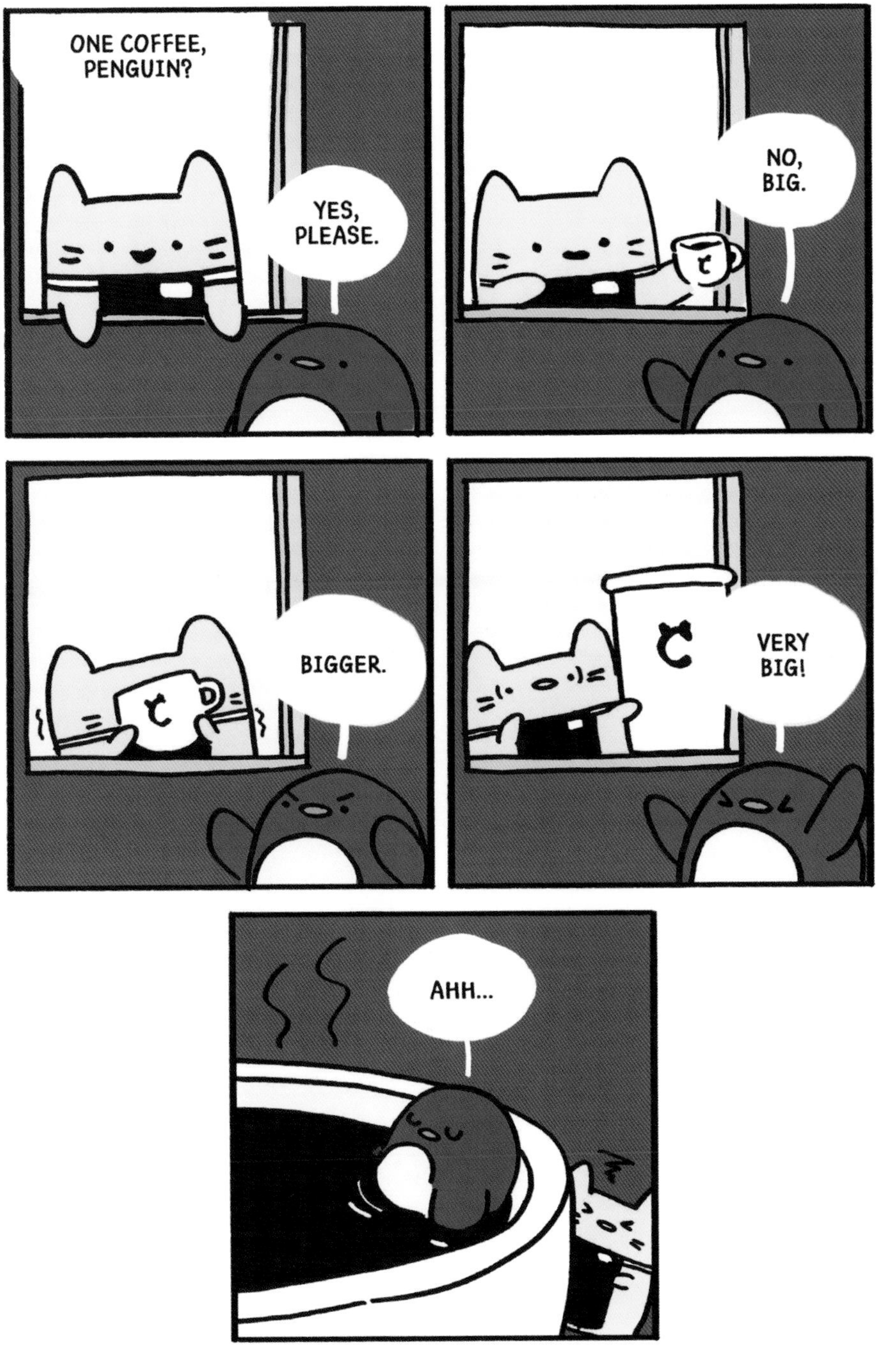
ONE COFFEE, PENGUIN?
YES, PLEASE.
NO, BIG.
BIGGER.
VERY BIG!
AHH...

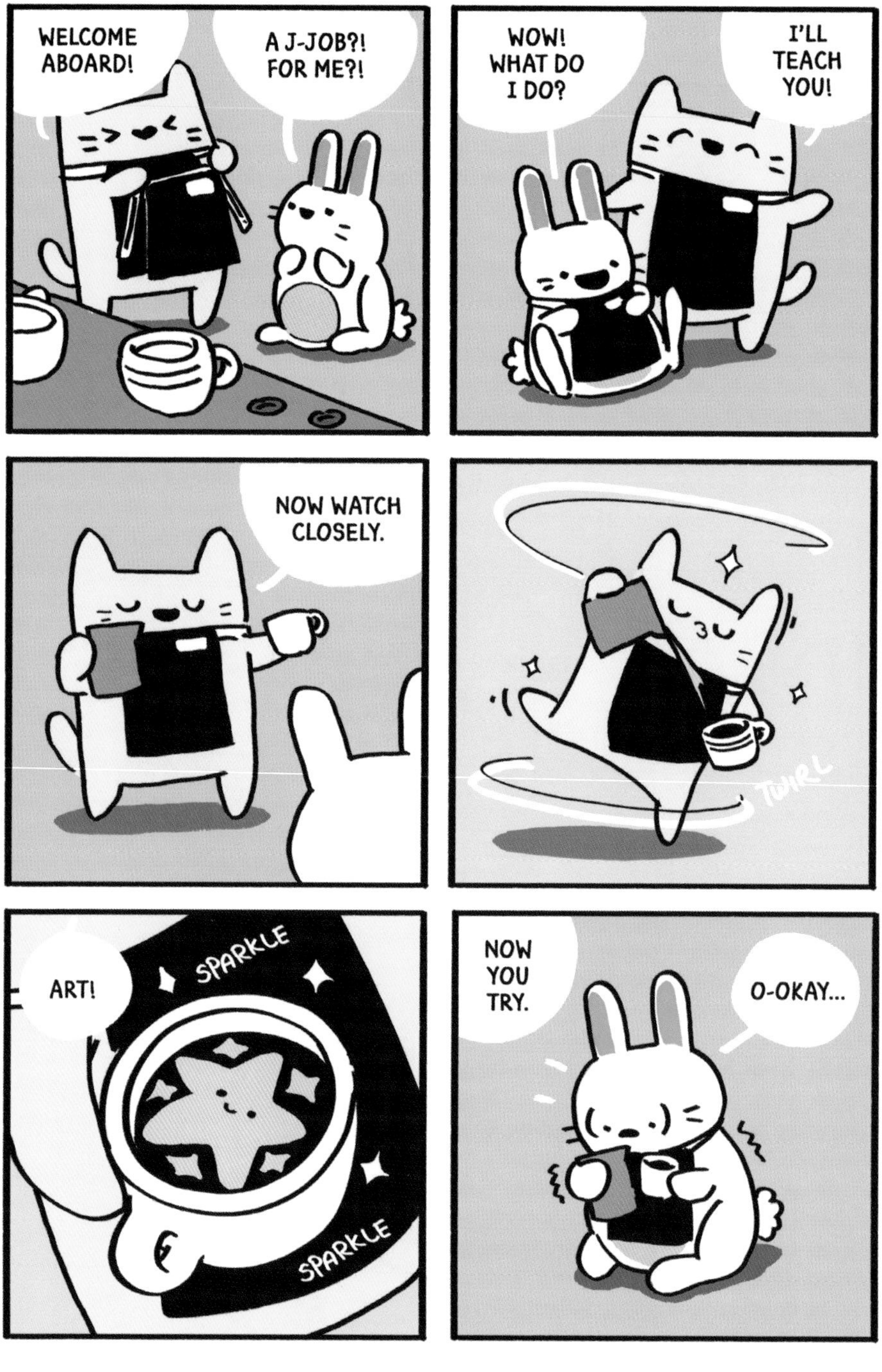
WELCOME ABOARD!
A J-JOB?! FOR ME?!
WOW! WHAT DO I DO?
I'LL TEACH YOU!
NOW WATCH CLOSELY.
TWIRL
ART!
SPARKLE
SPARKLE
NOW YOU TRY.
O-OKAY...

FWIP
FUMP
SPLAT!
NOW THAT'S ART!

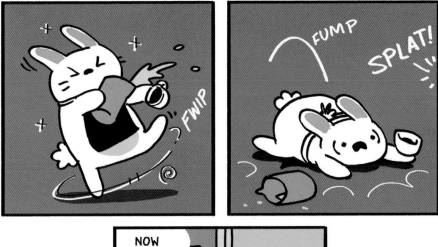

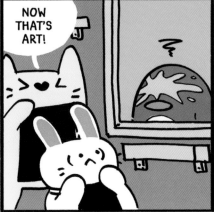

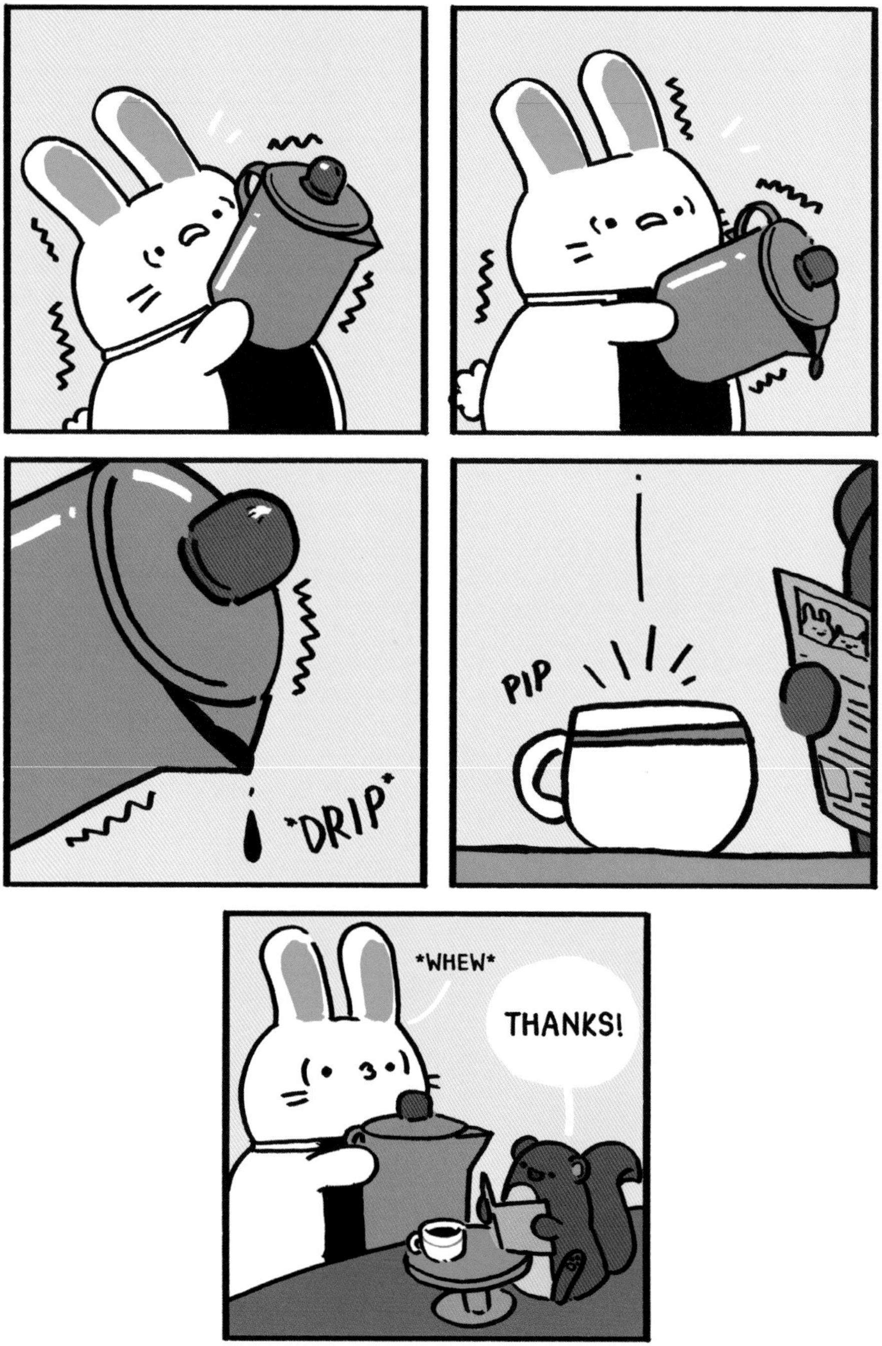
DRIP
PIP
WHEW
THANKS!

MIND IF I USE MY OWN MUG, CAT?
NOT AT ALL!
POUR
POUR POUR
POUR POUR POUR
?!
PENGUIN!
WAT DIS?

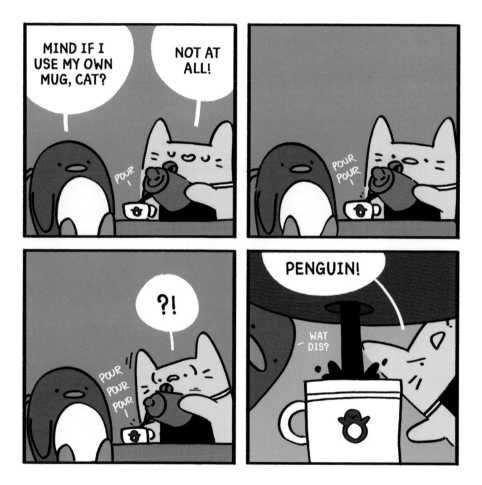

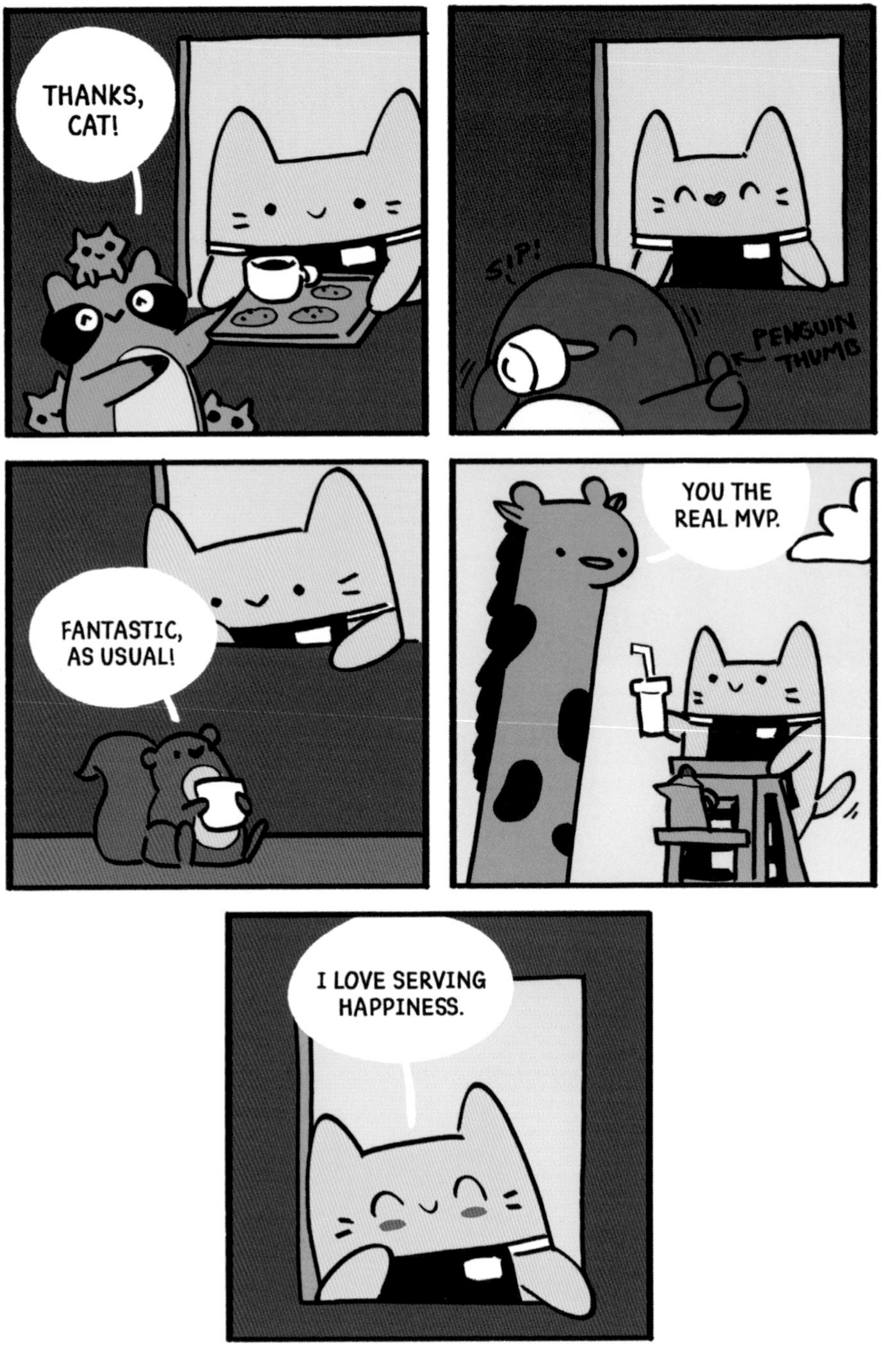
THANKS, CAT!
SIP!
PENGUIN THUMB
FANTASTIC, AS USUAL!
YOU THE REAL MVP.
I LOVE SERVING HAPPINESS.

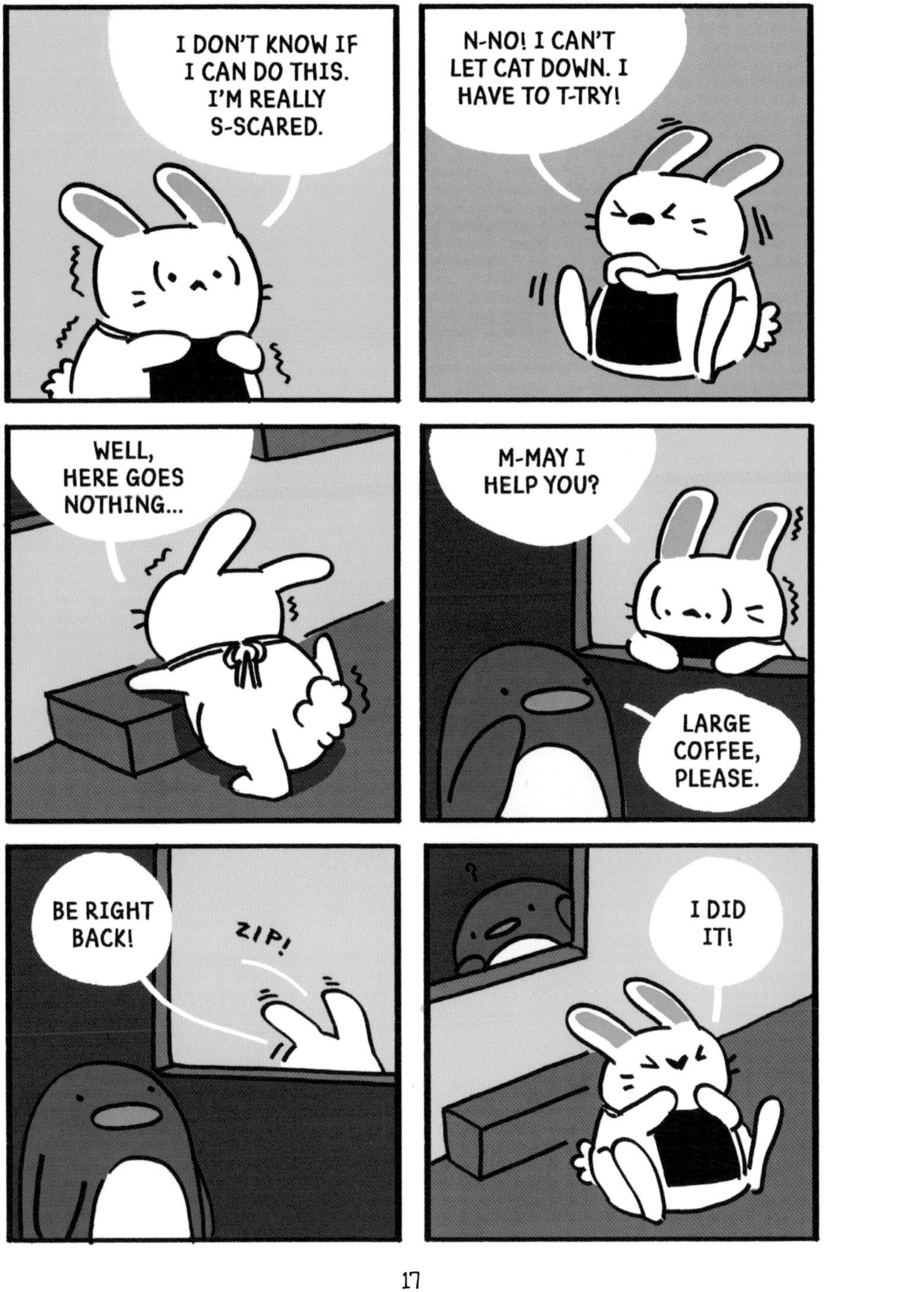
I DON'T KNOW IF I CAN DO THIS. I'M REALLY S-SCARED.
N-NO! I CAN'T LET CAT DOWN. I HAVE TO T-TRY!
WELL, HERE GOES NOTHING...
M-MAY I HELP YOU?
LARGE COFFEE, PLEASE.
BE RIGHT BACK!
ZIP!
I DID IT!

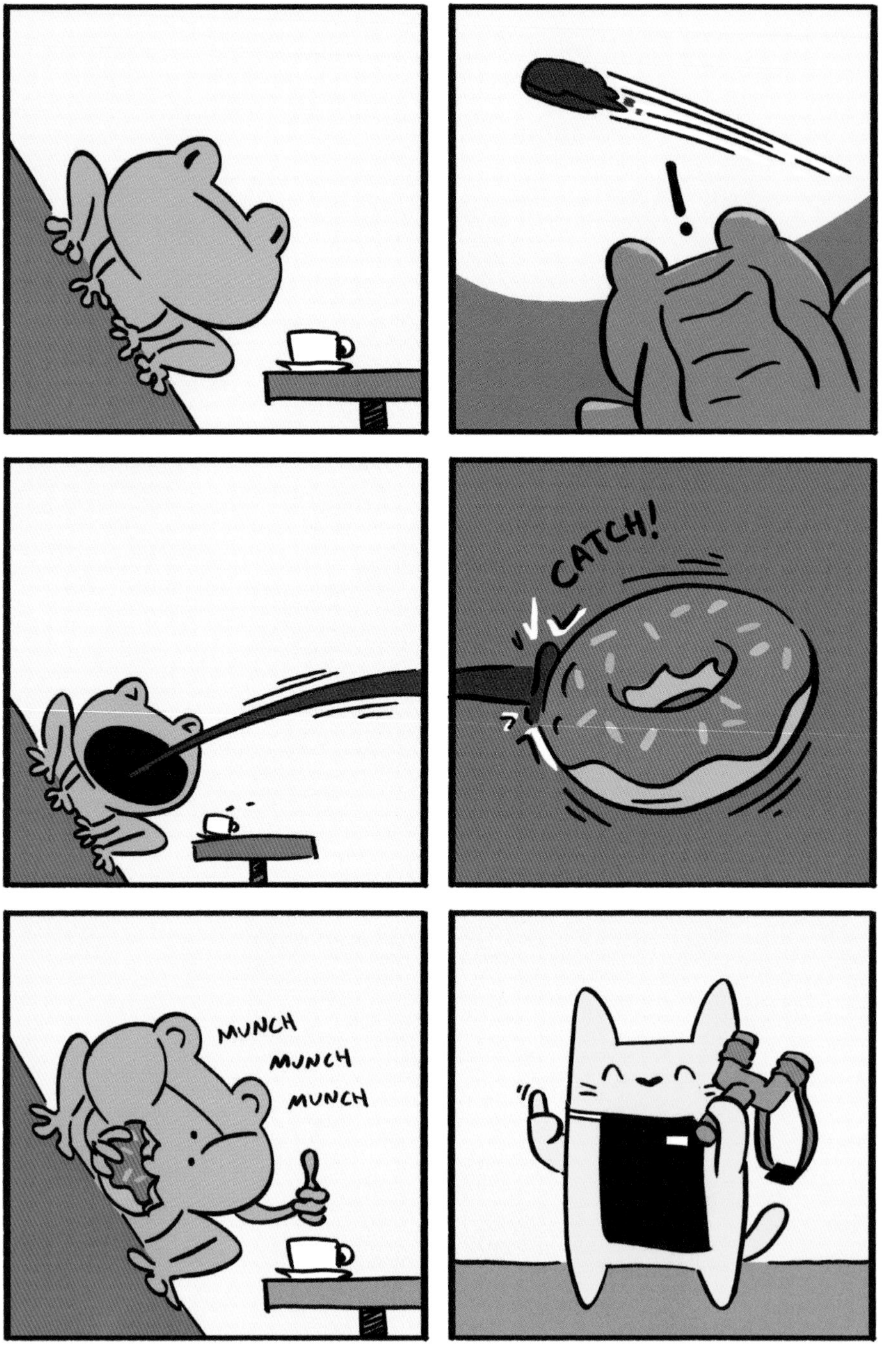
!
CATCH!
MUNCH
MUNCH
MUNCH

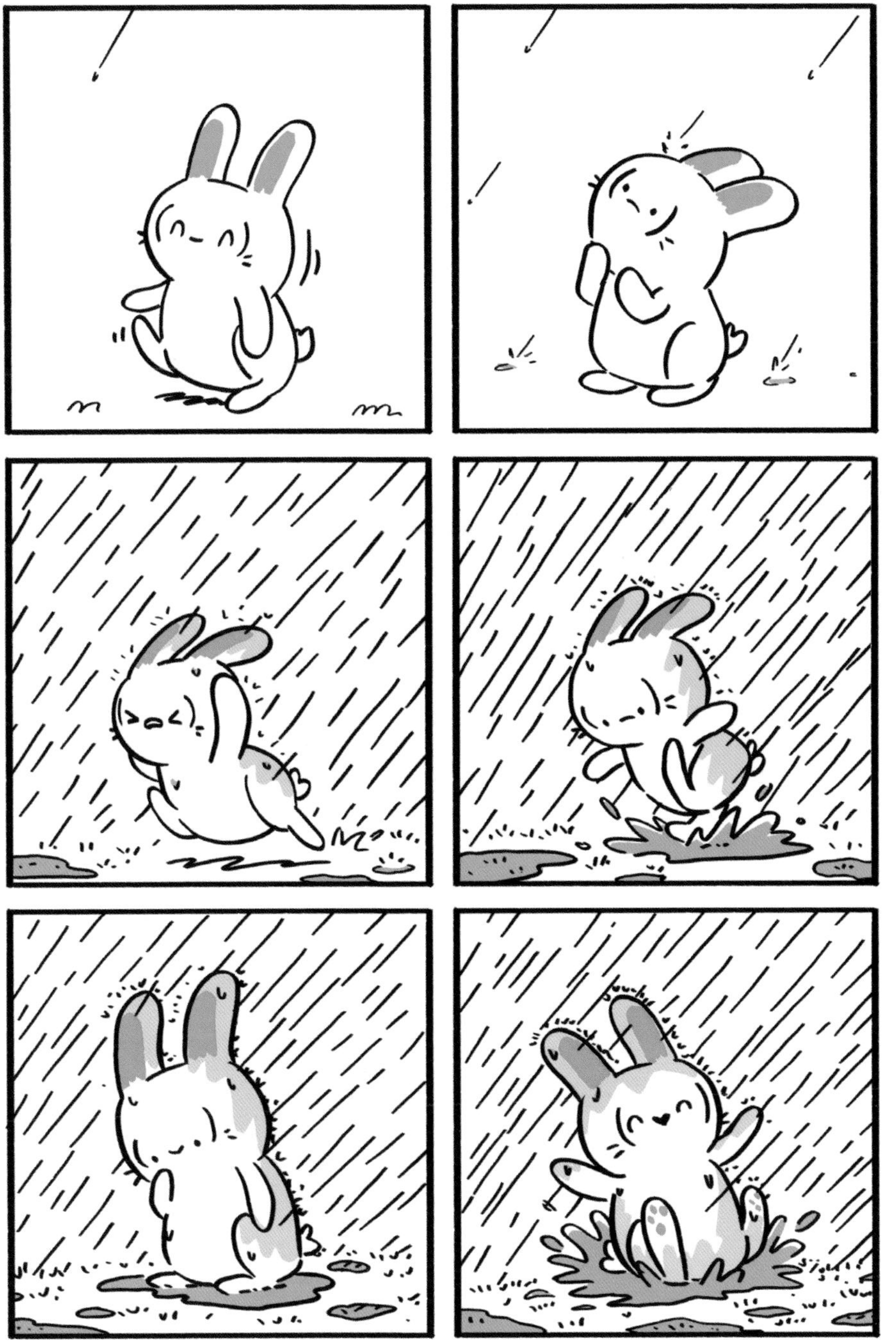

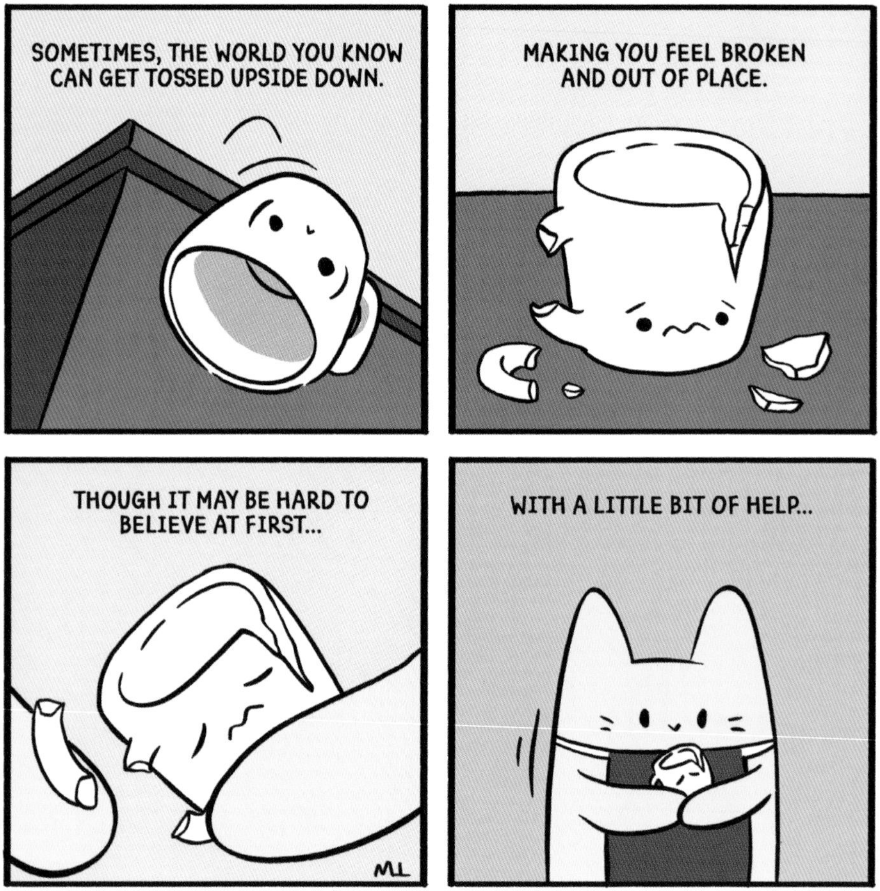
SOMETIMES, THE WORLD YOU KNOW CAN GET TOSSED UPSIDE DOWN.
MAKING YOU FEEL BROKEN AND OUT OF PLACE.
THOUGH IT MAY BE HARD TO BELIEVE AT FIRST...
ML
WITH A LITTLE BIT OF HELP...

IT'S POSSIBLE TO FEEL RIGHT AGAIN.

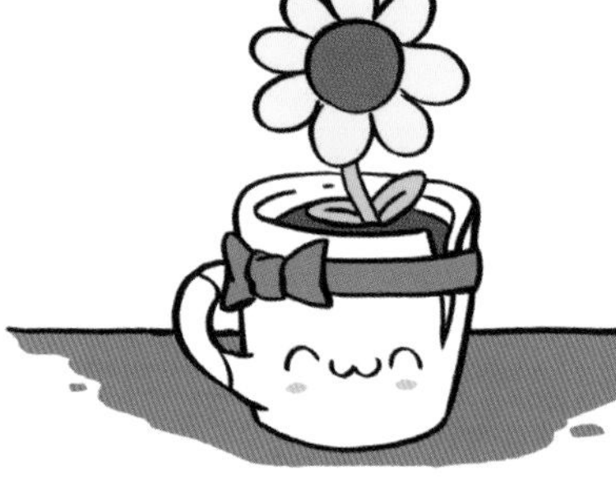

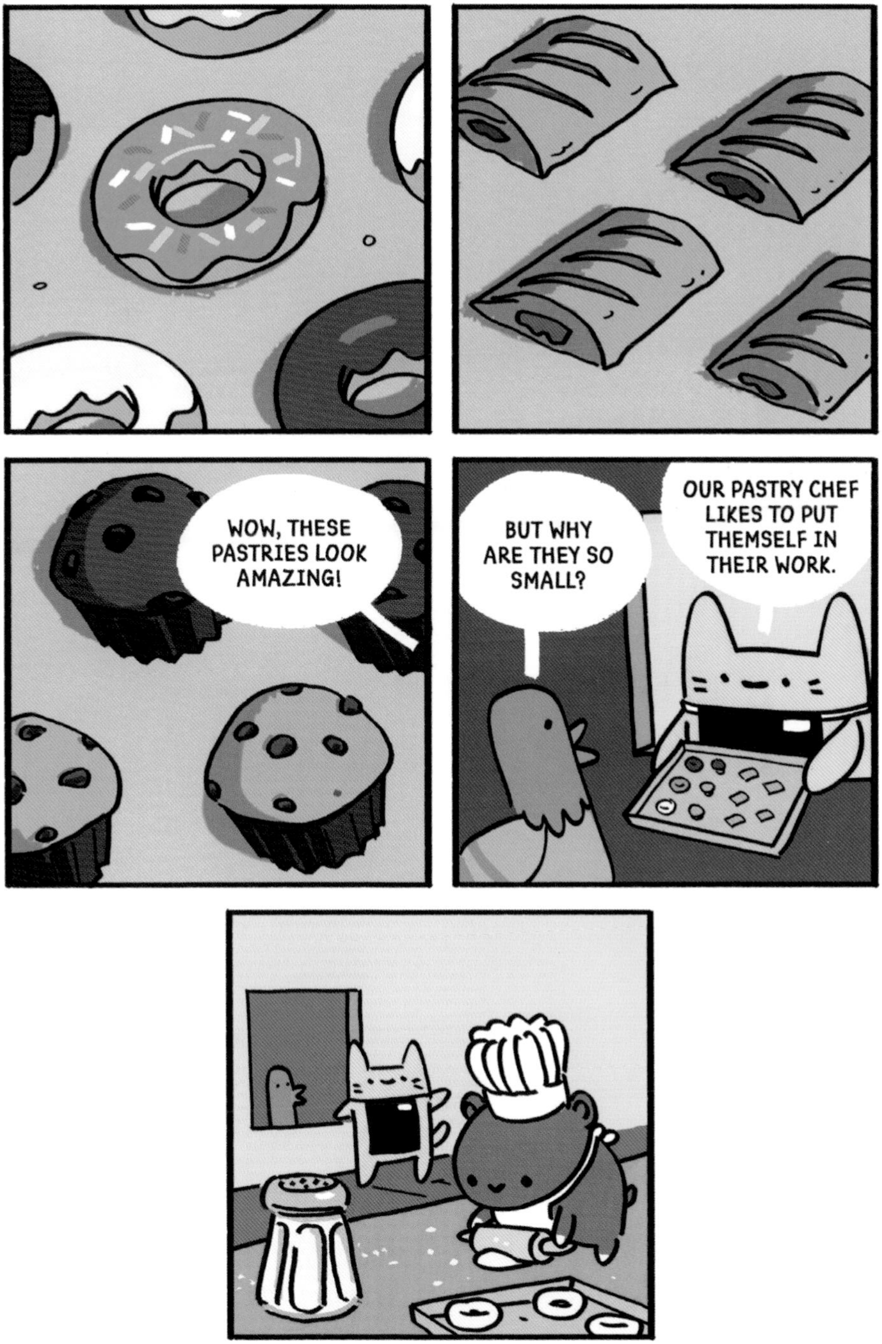
WOW, THESE PASTRIES LOOK AMAZING!
BUT WHY ARE THEY SO SMALL?
OUR PASTRY CHEF LIKES TO PUT THEMSELF IN THEIR WORK.

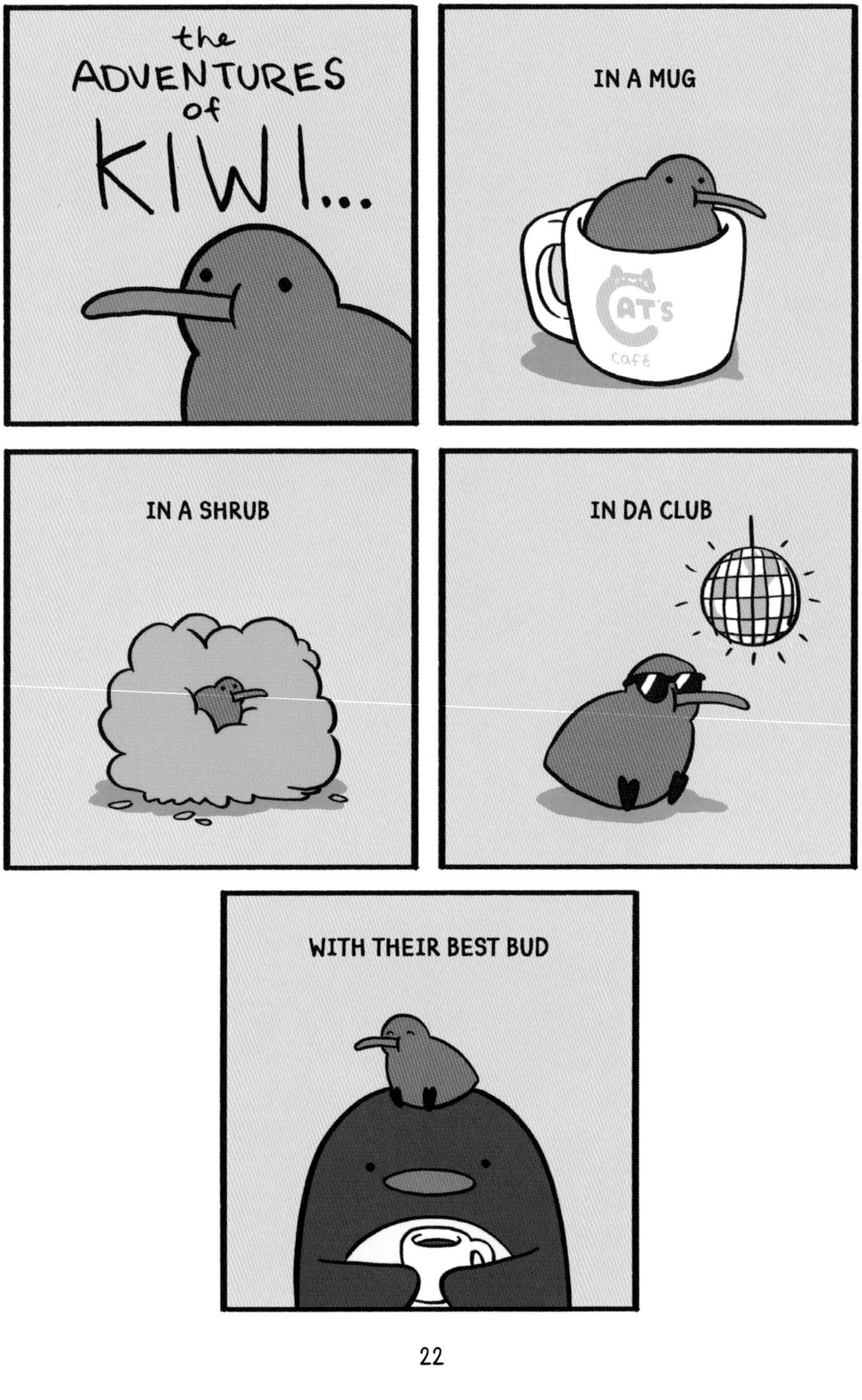
the ADVENTURES of KIWI...
IN A MUG
CAT'S
café
IN A SHRUB
IN DA CLUB
WITH THEIR BEST BUD

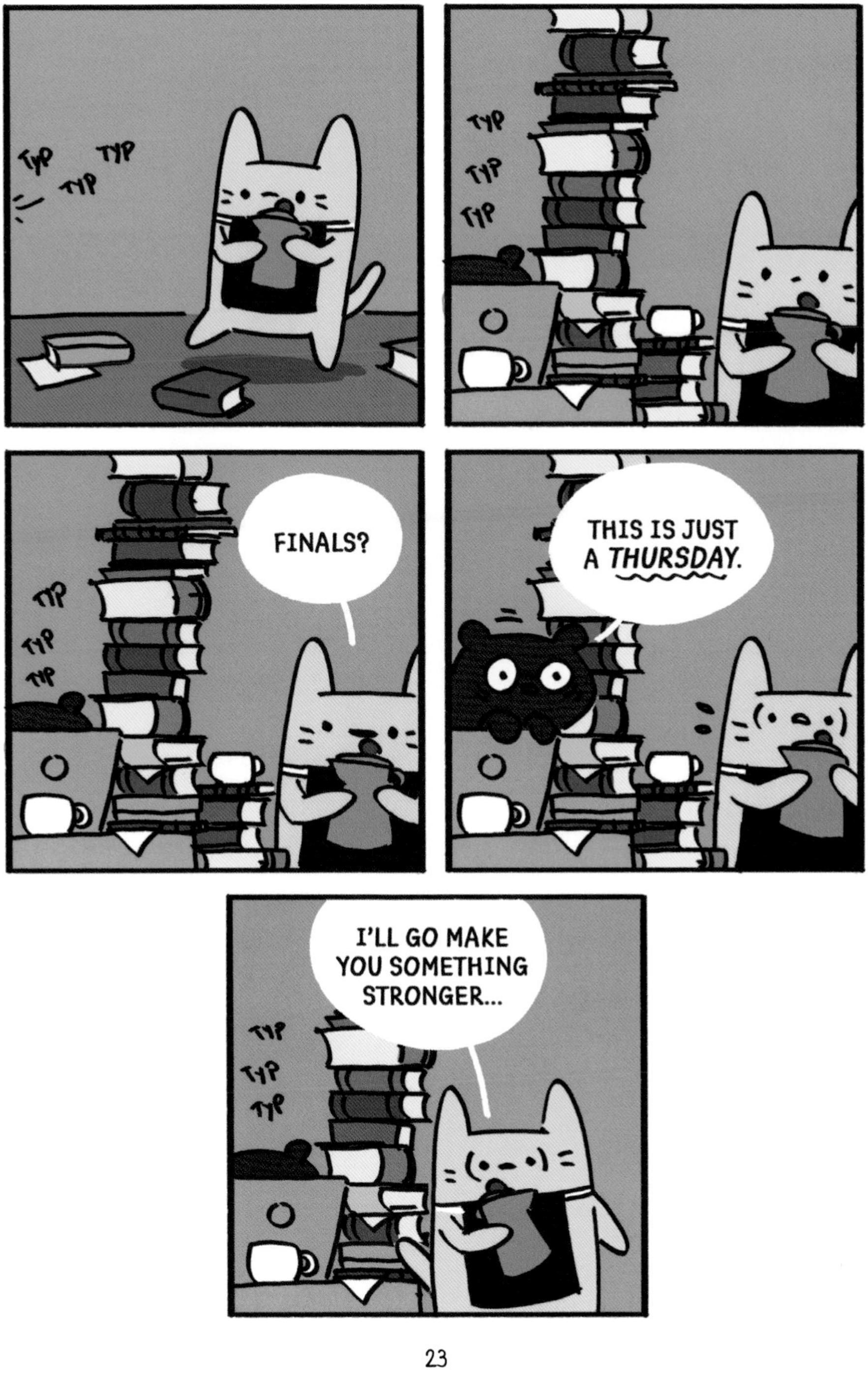
TYP TYP TYP
TYP TYP TYP
TYP TYP TYP
FINALS?
THIS IS JUST A THURSDAY.
I'LL GO MAKE YOU SOMETHING STRONGER...
TYP TYP TYP

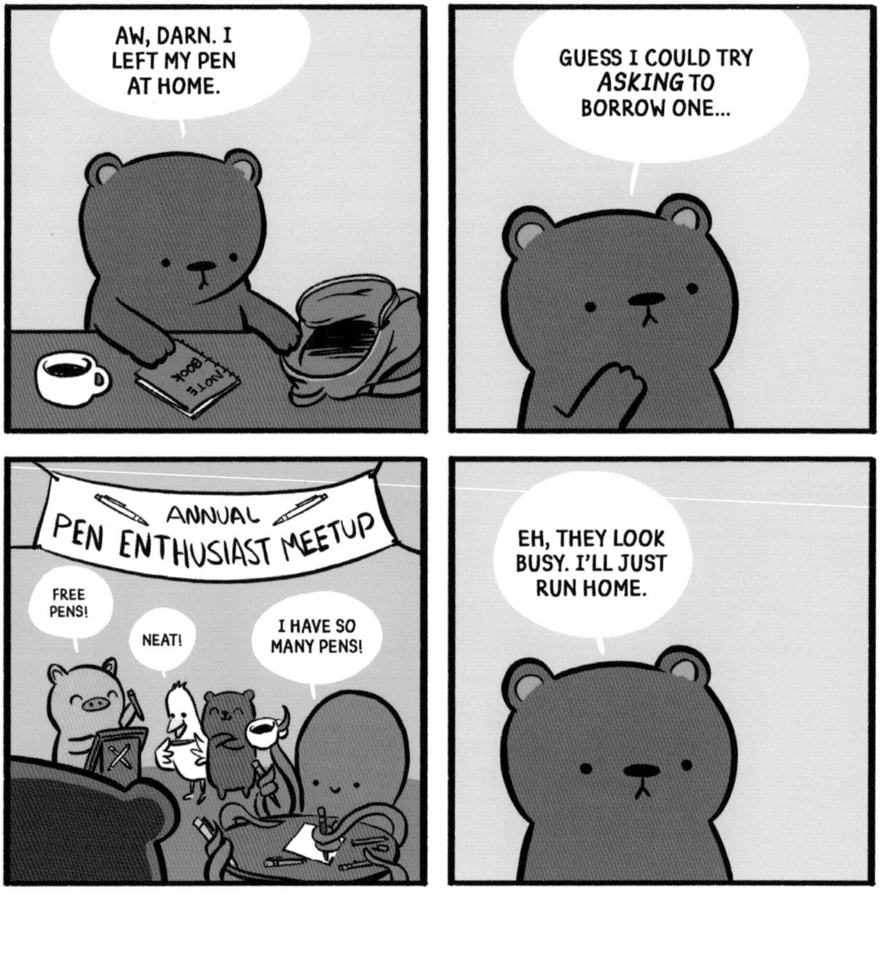
AW, DARN. I LEFT MY PEN AT HOME.
GUESS I COULD TRY *ASKING* TO BORROW ONE...
ANNUAL PEN ENTHUSIAST MEETUP
FREE PENS!
NEAT!
I HAVE SO MANY PENS!
EH, THEY LOOK BUSY. I'LL JUST RUN HOME.

WHY DO YOU DRINK COFFEE?

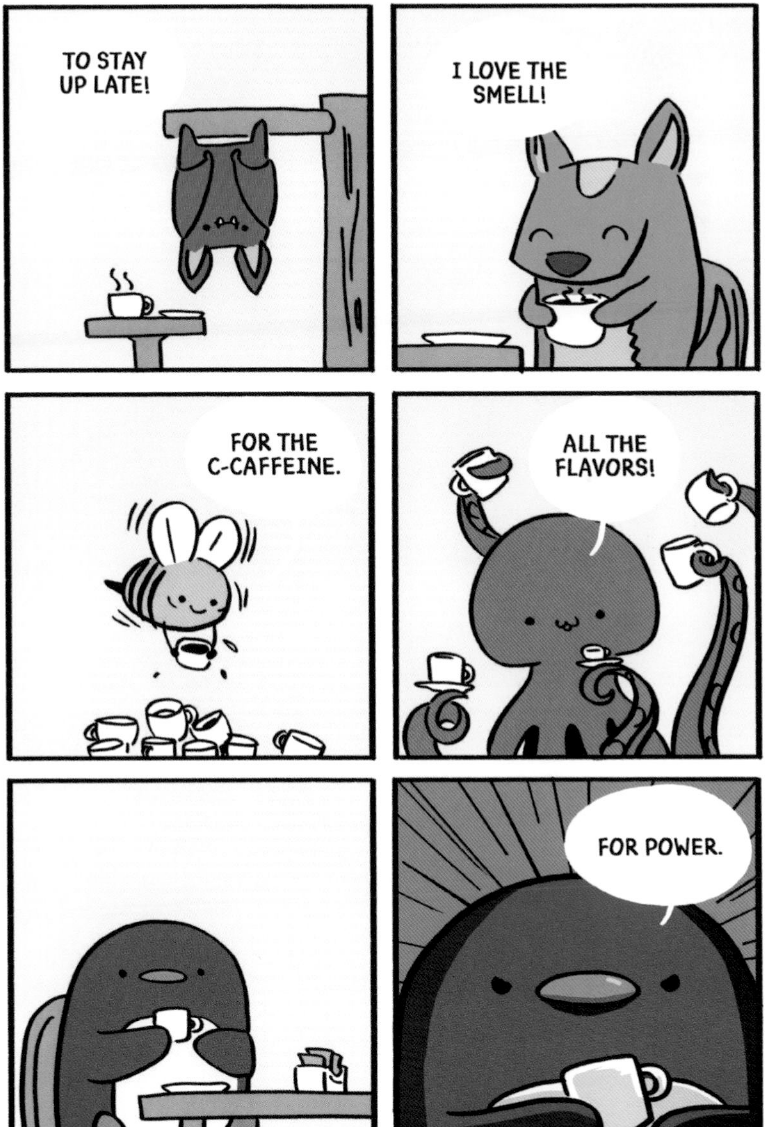
TO STAY UP LATE!
I LOVE THE SMELL!
FOR THE C-CAFFEINE.
ALL THE FLAVORS!
FOR POWER.

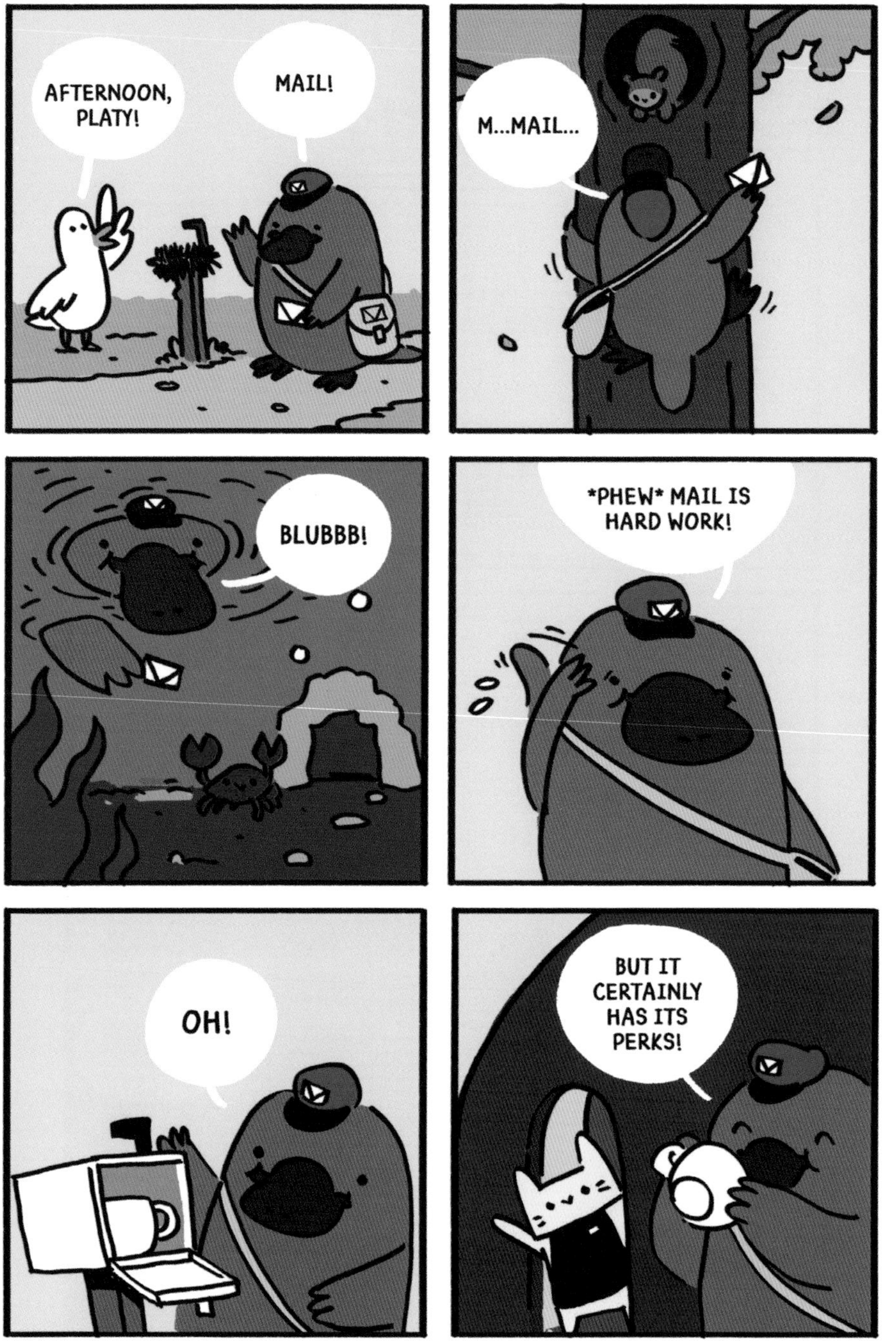
AFTERNOON, PLATY!
MAIL!
M...MAIL...
BLUBBB!
PHEW MAIL IS HARD WORK!
OH!
BUT IT CERTAINLY HAS ITS PERKS!

HELP PENGUIN GET TO THE COFFEE!

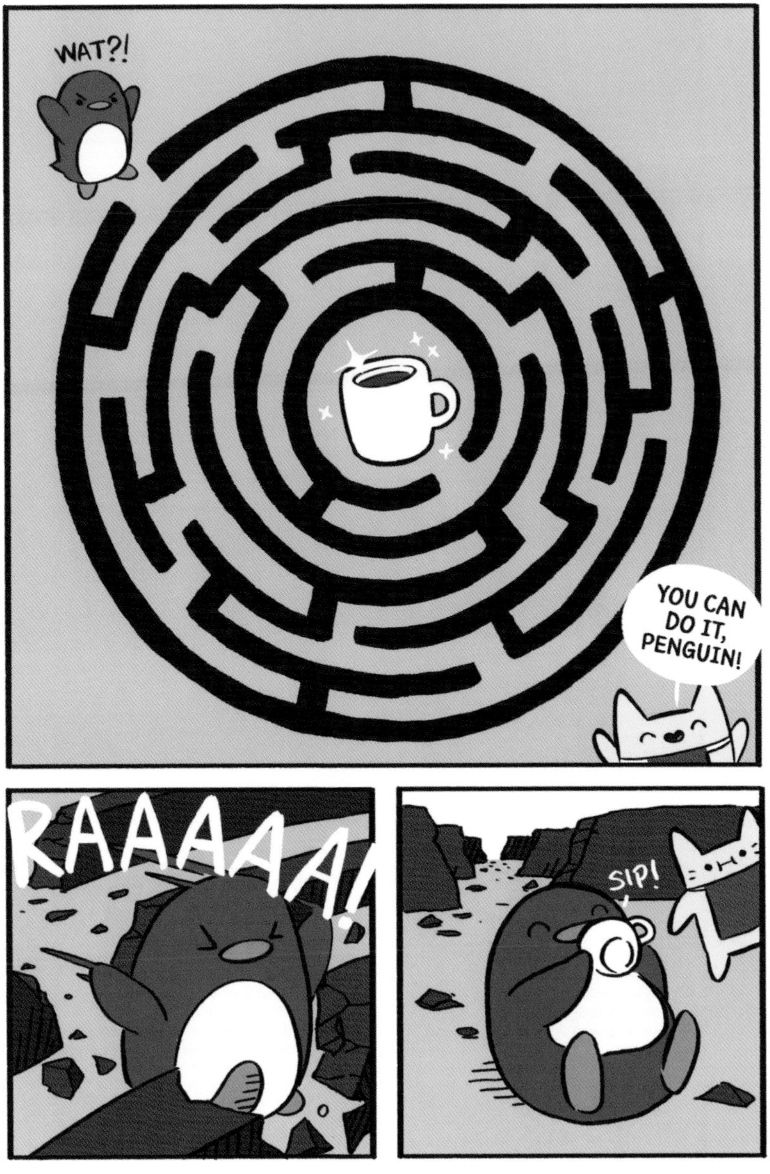
WAT?!
YOU CAN DO IT, PENGUIN!
RAAAAA!
SIP!

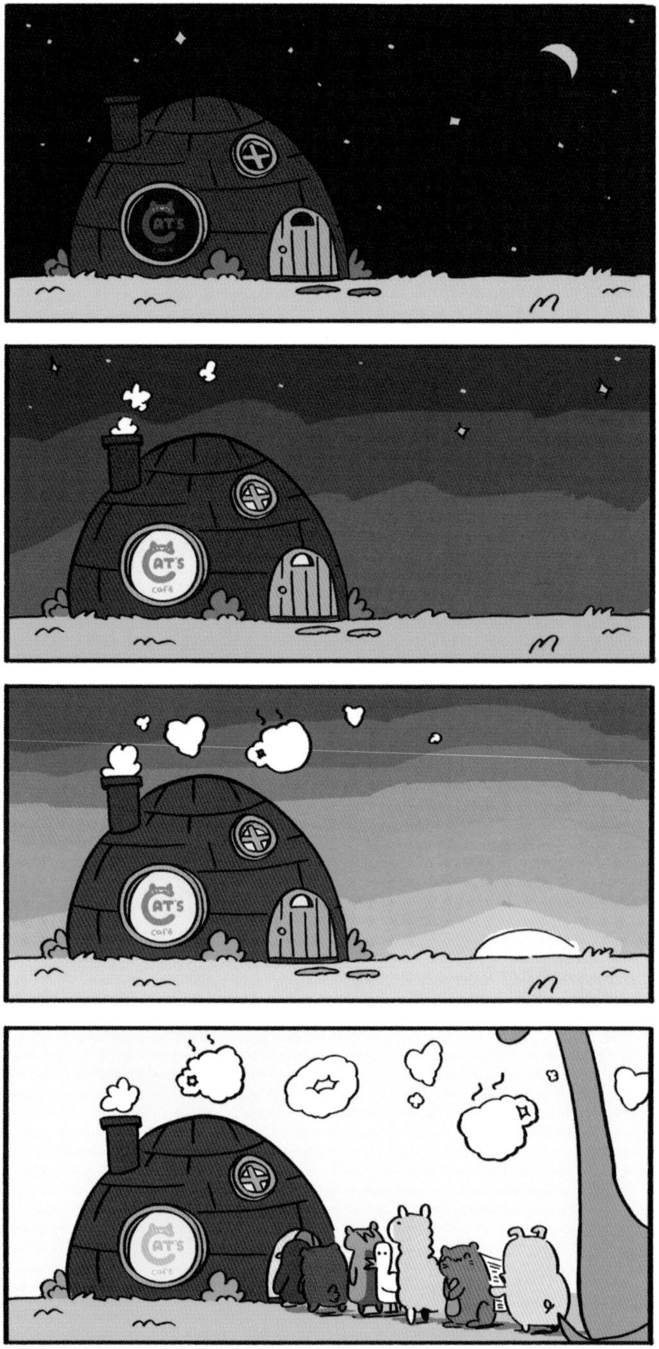
CAT'S
café

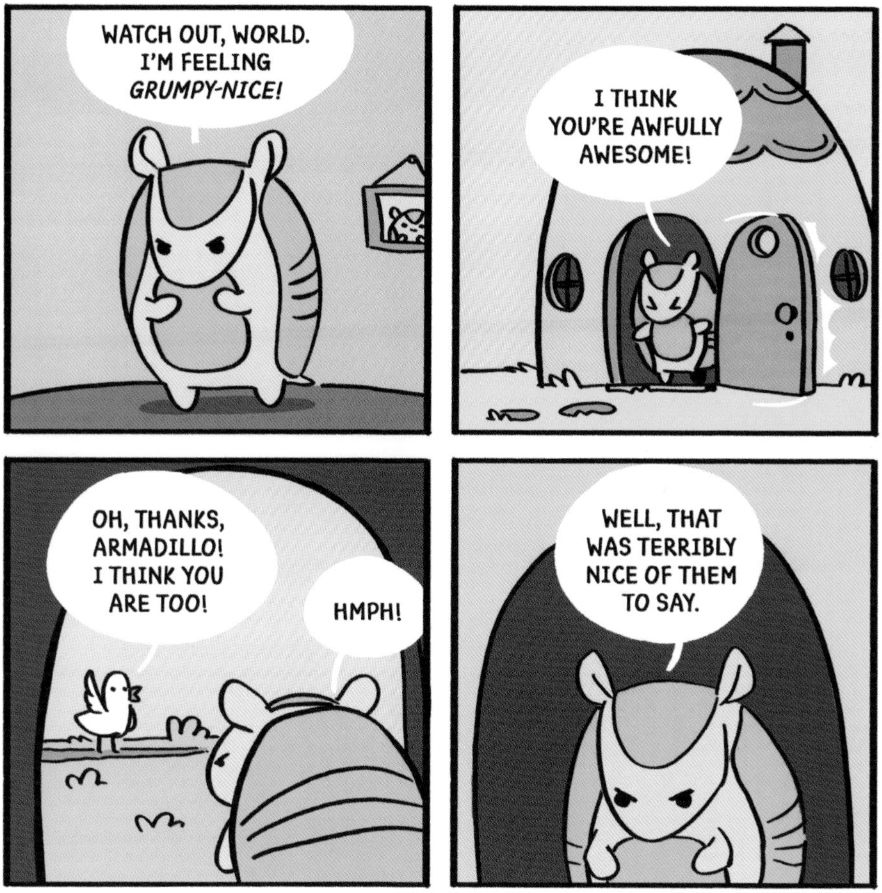
WATCH OUT, WORLD. I'M FEELING *GRUMPY-NICE!*
I THINK YOU'RE AWFULLY AWESOME!
OH, THANKS, ARMADILLO! I THINK YOU ARE TOO!
HMPH!
WELL, THAT WAS TERRIBLY NICE OF THEM TO SAY.

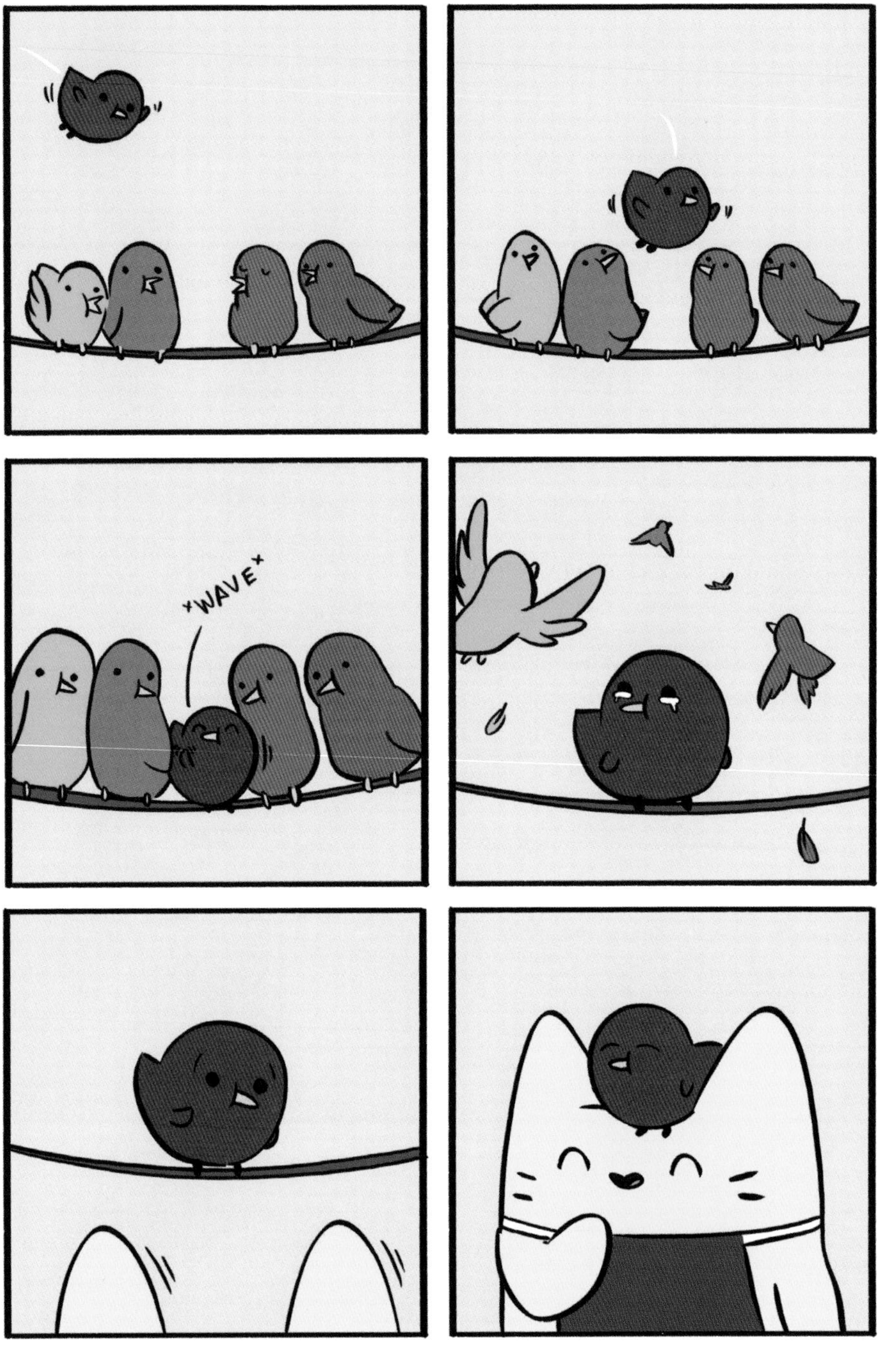
WAVE

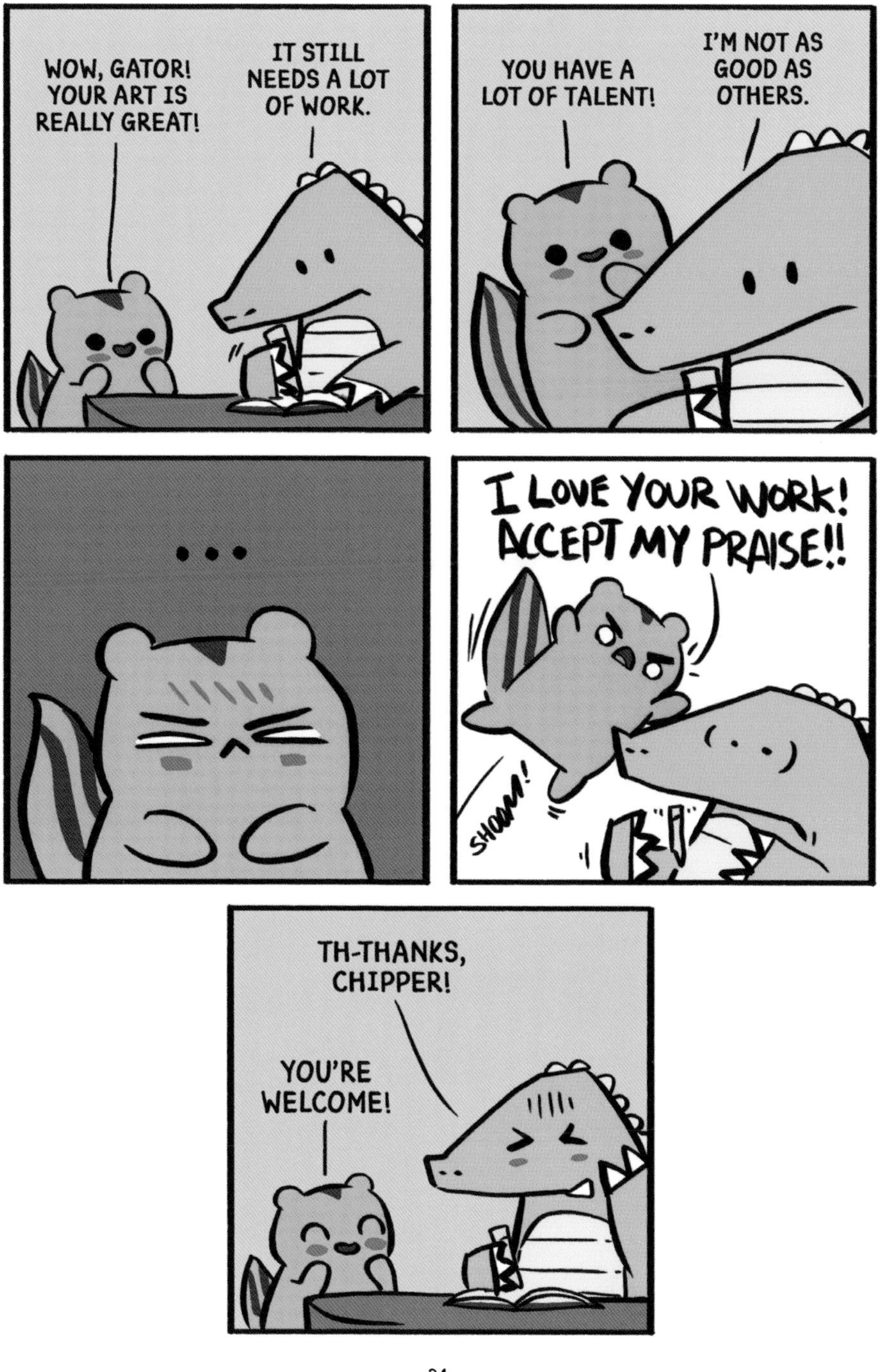
WOW, GATOR! YOUR ART IS REALLY GREAT!
IT STILL NEEDS A LOT OF WORK.
YOU HAVE A LOT OF TALENT!
I'M NOT AS GOOD AS OTHERS.
...
I LOVE YOUR WORK! ACCEPT MY PRAISE!!
SHOOM!
TH-THANKS, CHIPPER!
YOU'RE WELCOME!

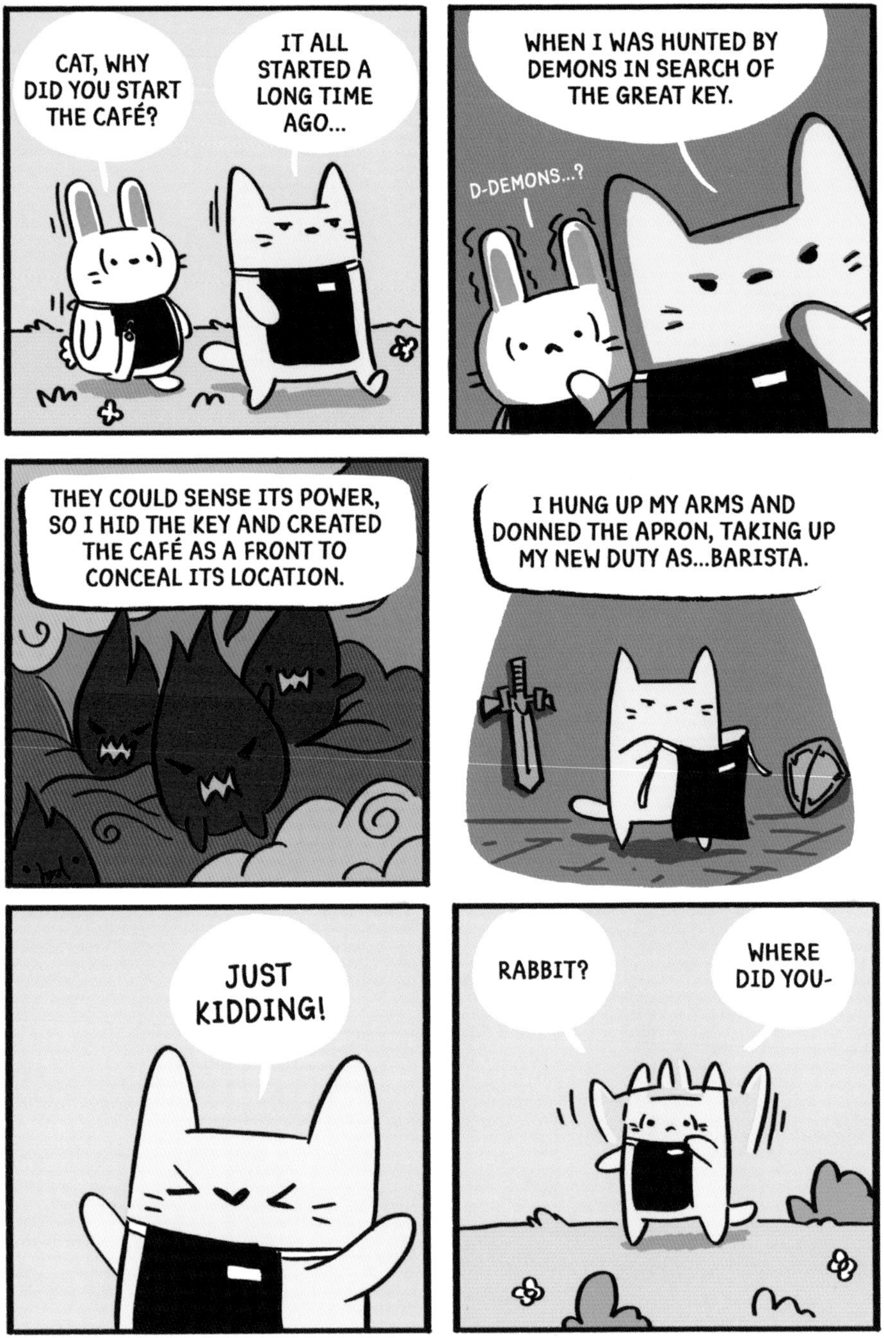
CAT, WHY DID YOU START THE CAFÉ?
IT ALL STARTED A LONG TIME AGO...
WHEN I WAS HUNTED BY DEMONS IN SEARCH OF THE GREAT KEY.
D-DEMONS...?
THEY COULD SENSE ITS POWER, SO I HID THE KEY AND CREATED THE CAFÉ AS A FRONT TO CONCEAL ITS LOCATION.
I HUNG UP MY ARMS AND DONNED THE APRON, TAKING UP MY NEW DUTY AS...BARISTA.
JUST KIDDING!
RABBIT?
WHERE DID YOU-

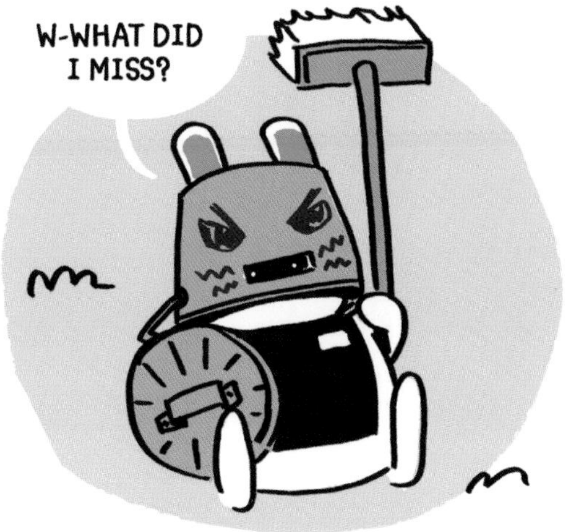
W-WHAT DID I MISS?

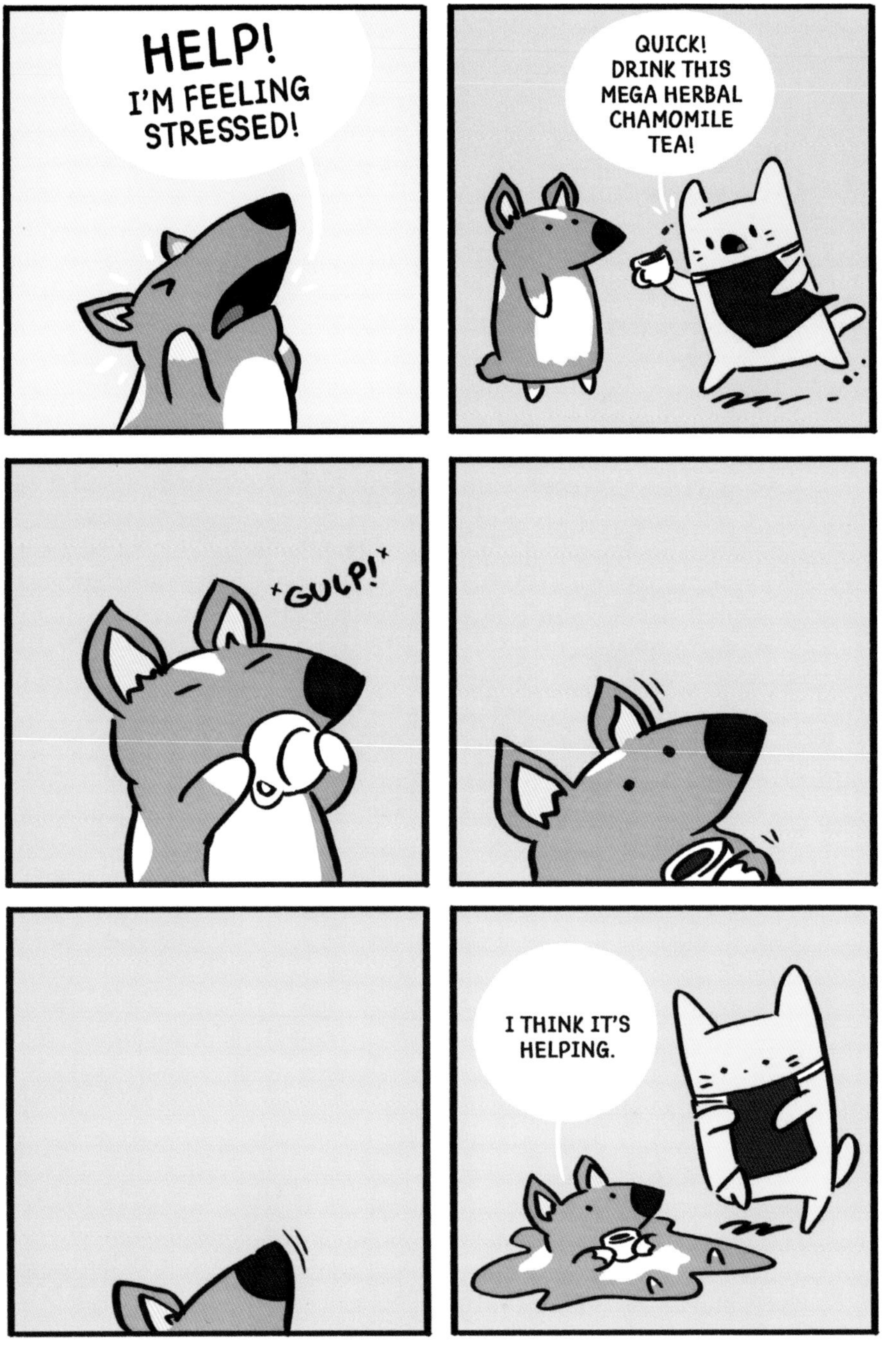
HELP!
I'M FEELING STRESSED!
QUICK! DRINK THIS MEGA HERBAL CHAMOMILE TEA!
GULP!
I THINK IT'S HELPING.

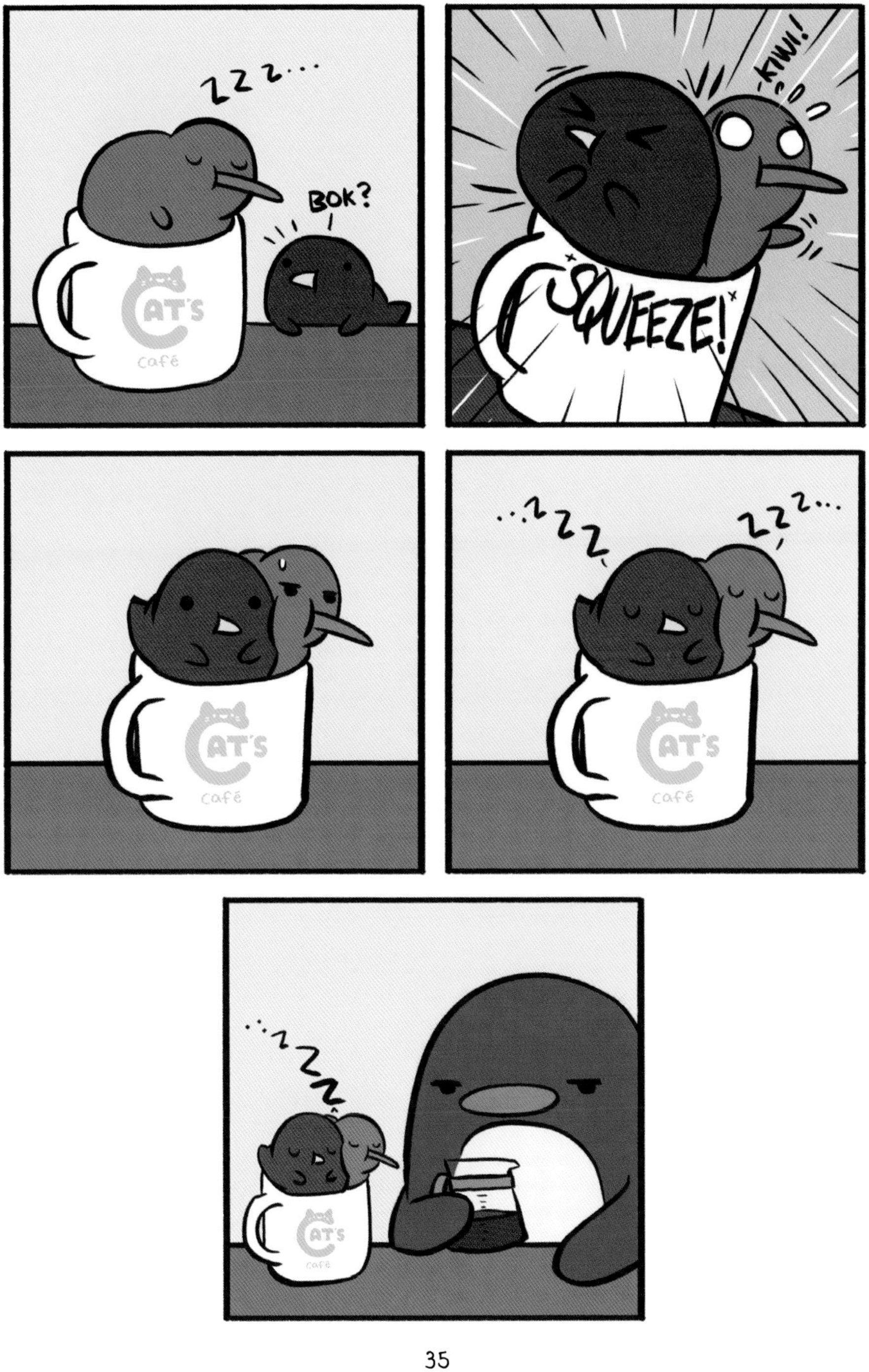
Z Z Z...
BOK?
KIWI!
SQUEEZE!
CAT'S
café
...ZZZ
ZZZ...
...ZZZ

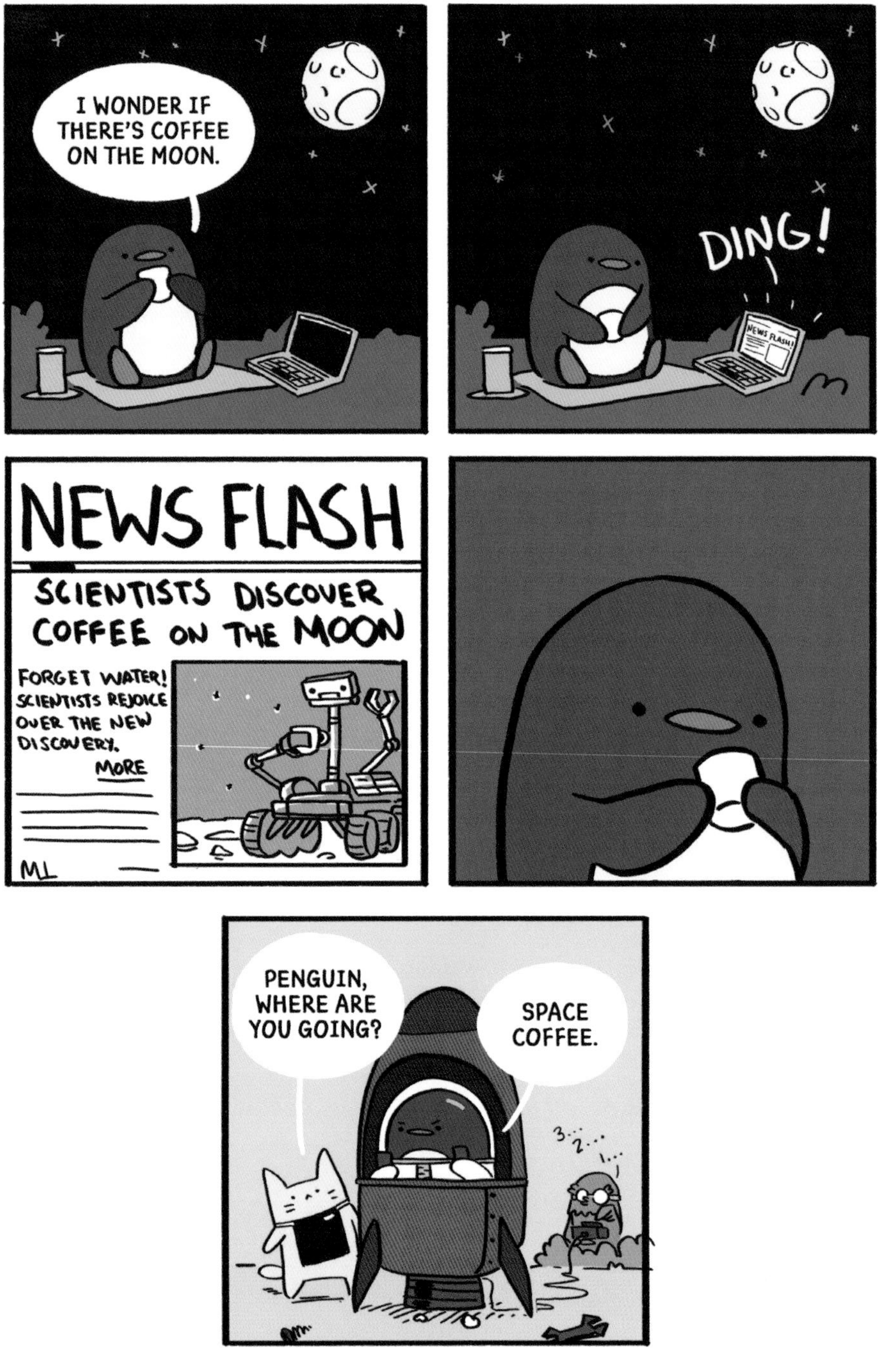
I WONDER IF THERE'S COFFEE ON THE MOON.
DING!
NEWS FLASH!
NEWS FLASH
SCIENTISTS DISCOVER COFFEE ON THE MOON
FORGET WATER! SCIENTISTS REJOICE OVER THE NEW DISCOVERY.
MORE
ML
PENGUIN, WHERE ARE YOU GOING?
SPACE COFFEE.
3...
2...
1...

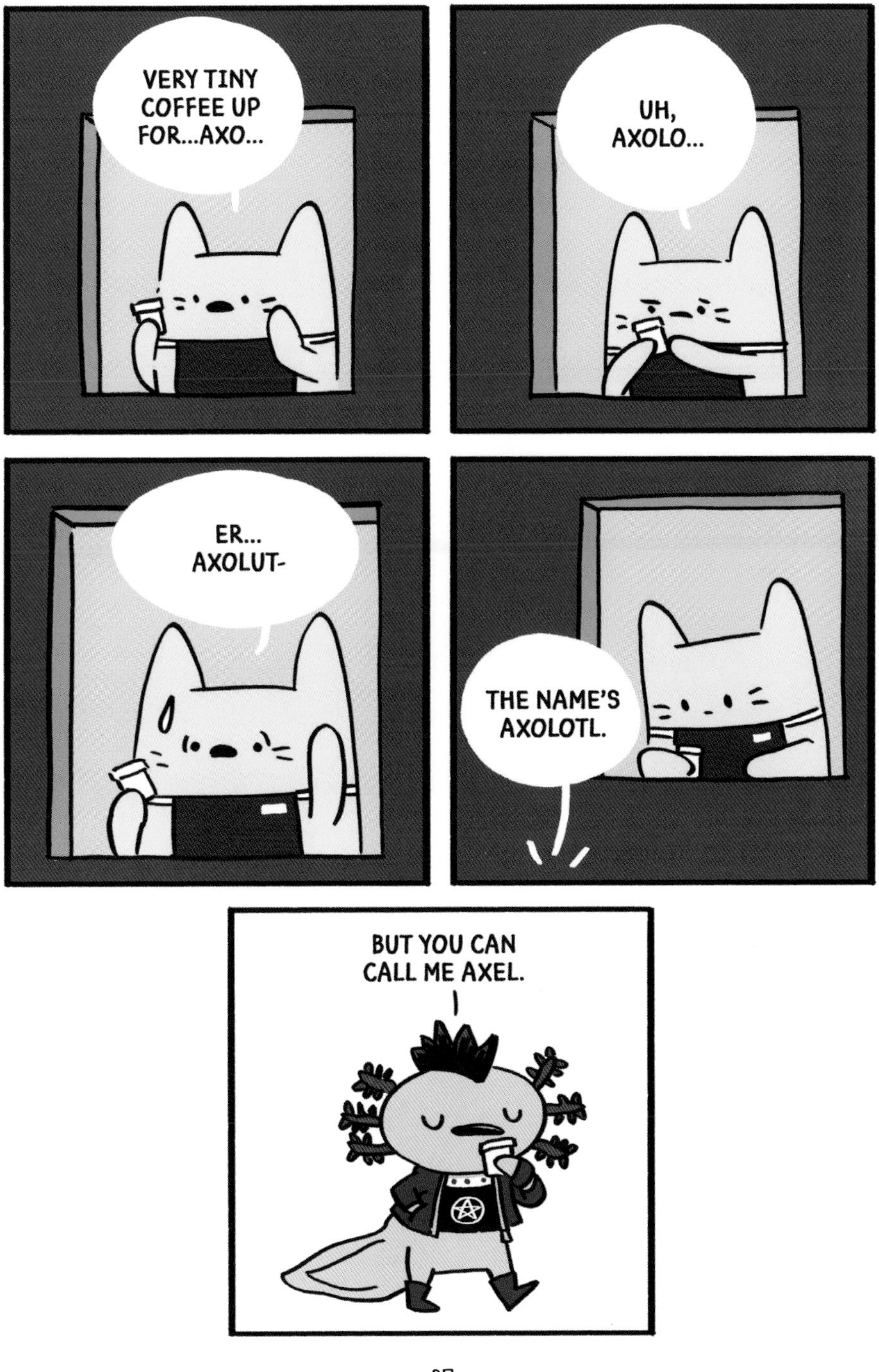
VERY TINY COFFEE UP FOR...AXO...
UH, AXOLO...
ER... AXOLUT-
THE NAME'S AXOLOTL.
BUT YOU CAN CALL ME AXEL.

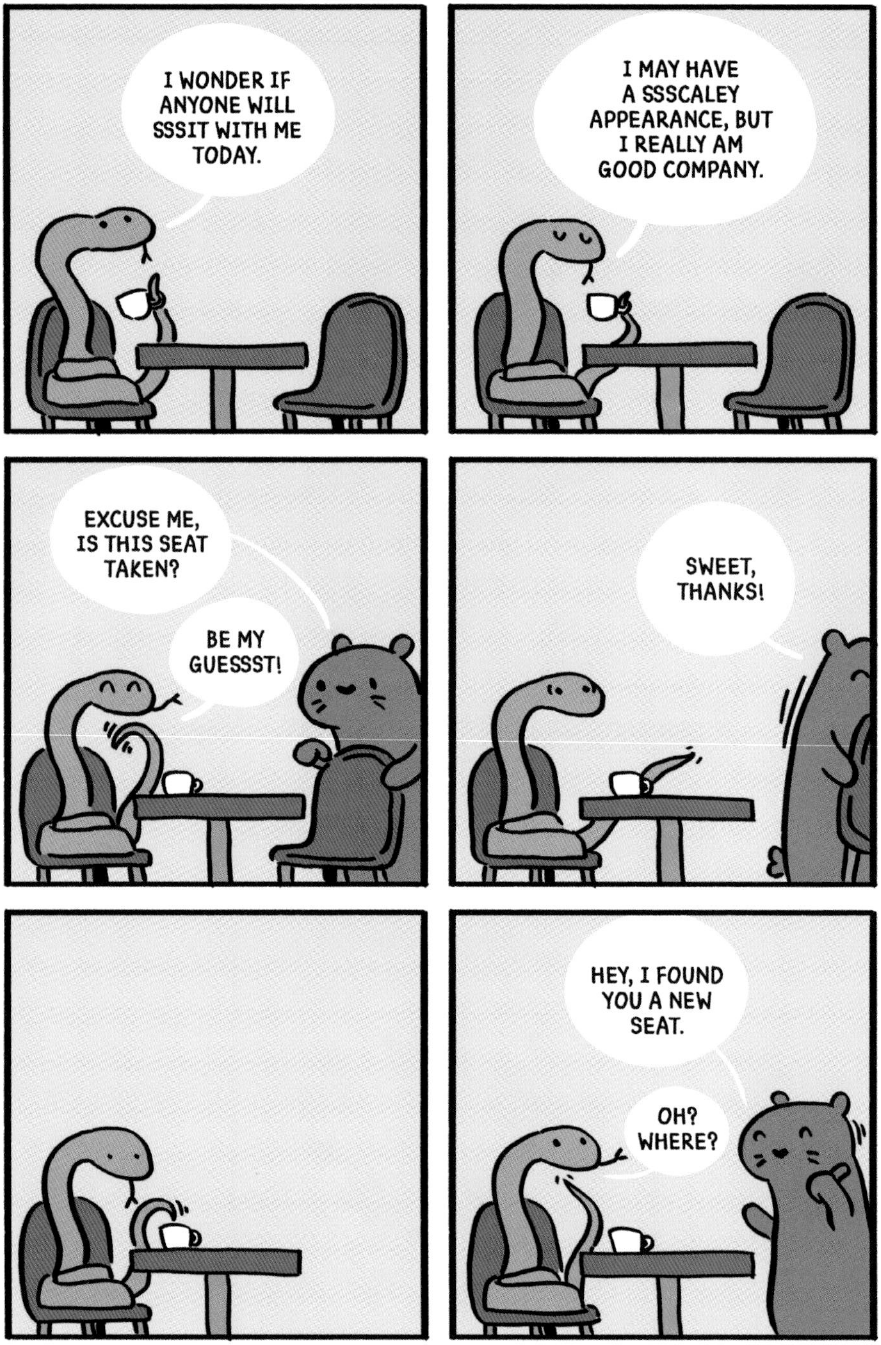
I WONDER IF ANYONE WILL SSSIT WITH ME TODAY.
I MAY HAVE A SSSCALEY APPEARANCE, BUT I REALLY AM GOOD COMPANY.
EXCUSE ME, IS THIS SEAT TAKEN?
BE MY GUESSST!
SWEET, THANKS!
HEY, I FOUND YOU A NEW SEAT.
OH? WHERE?

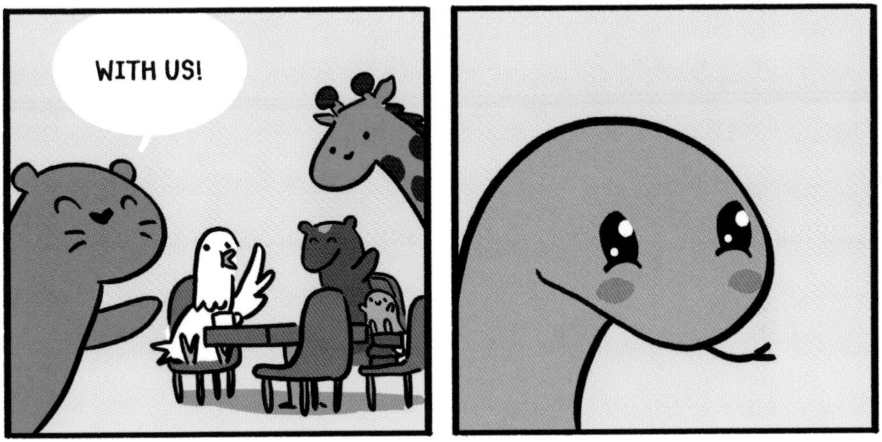
WITH US!

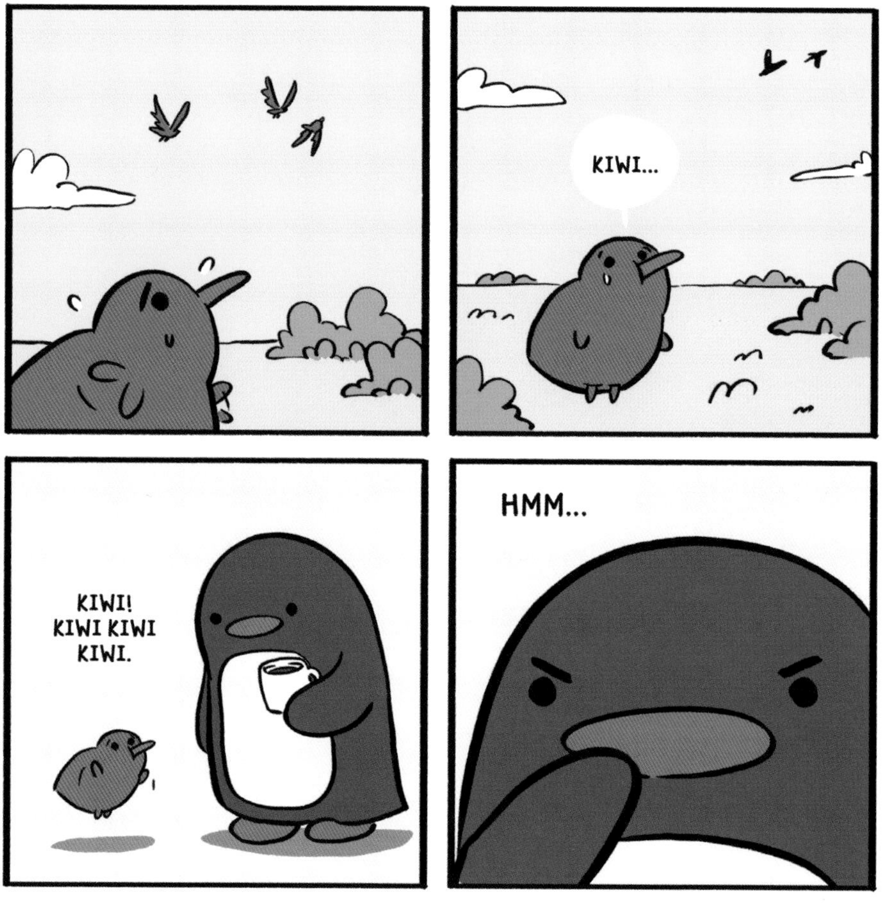
KIWI...
KIWI!
KIWI KIWI
KIWI.
HMM...

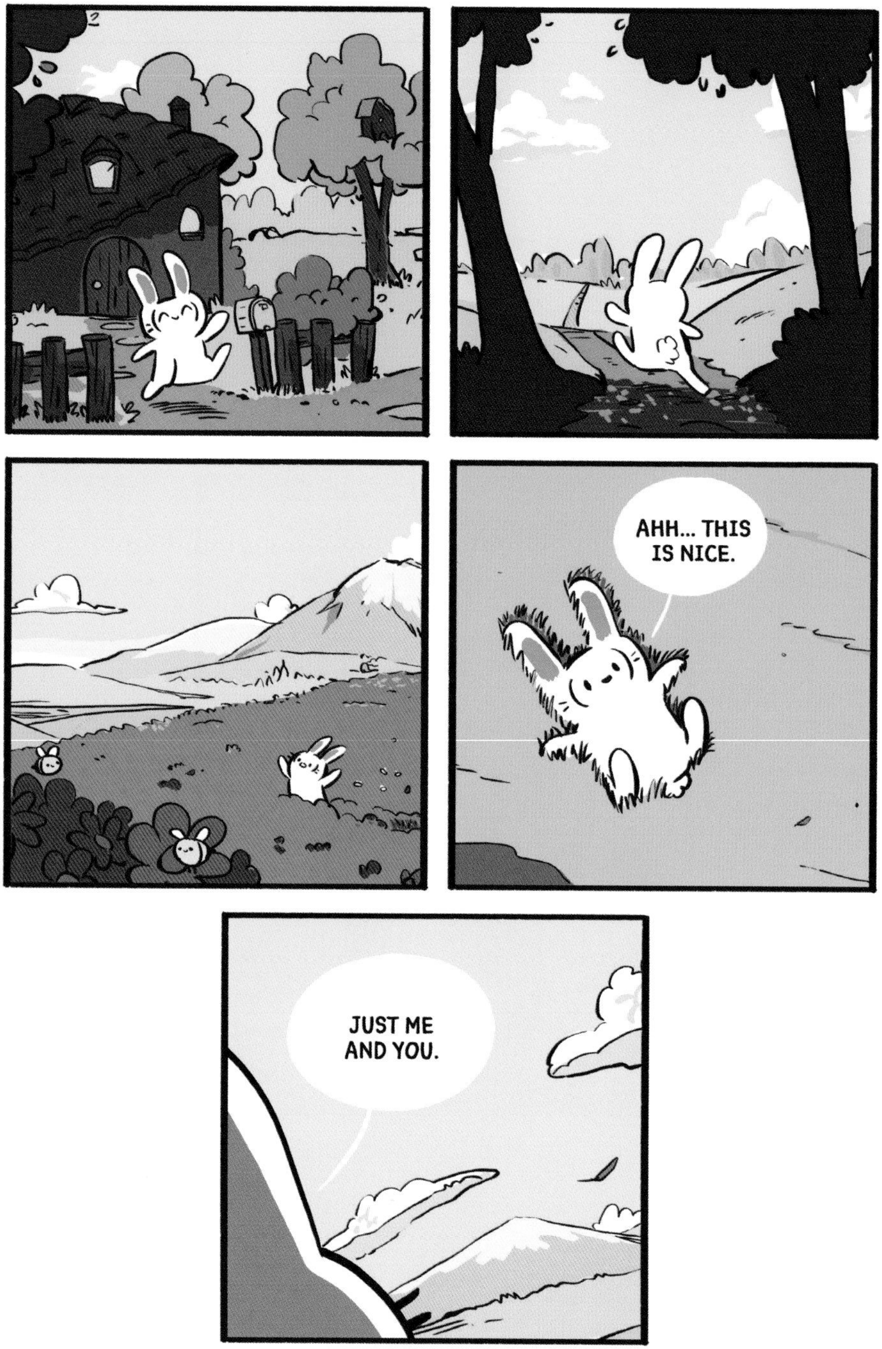
AHH... THIS IS NICE.
JUST ME AND YOU.

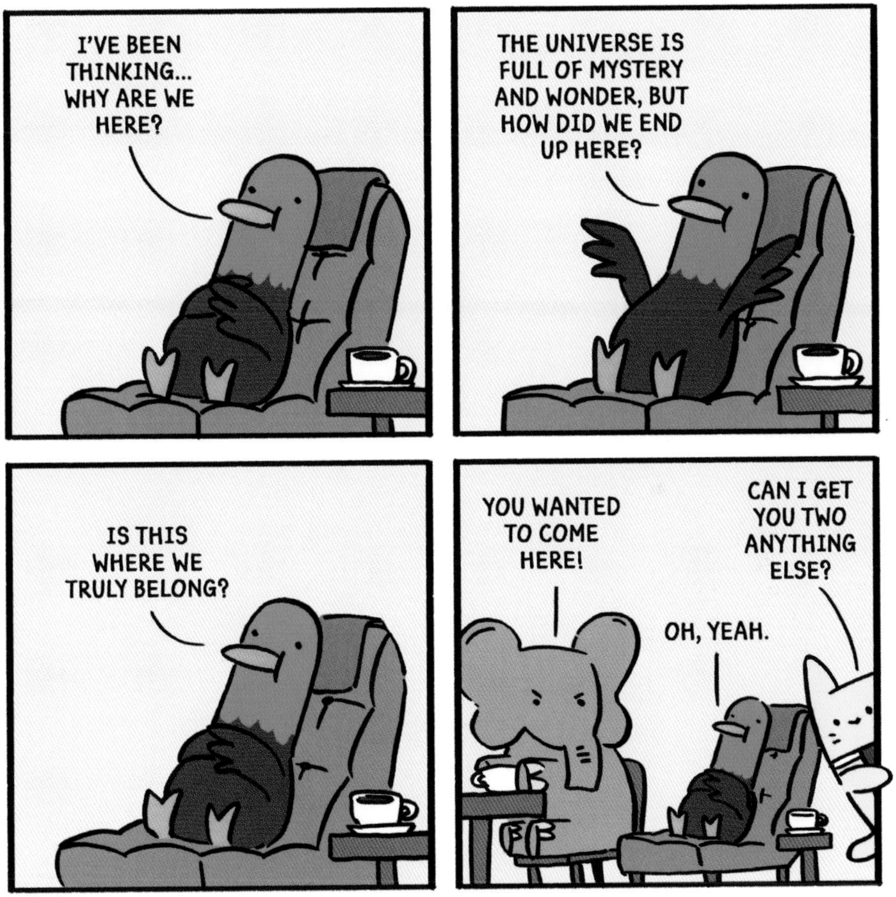
I'VE BEEN THINKING... WHY ARE WE HERE?
THE UNIVERSE IS FULL OF MYSTERY AND WONDER, BUT HOW DID WE END UP HERE?
IS THIS WHERE WE TRULY BELONG?
YOU WANTED TO COME HERE!
CAN I GET YOU TWO ANYTHING ELSE?
OH, YEAH.

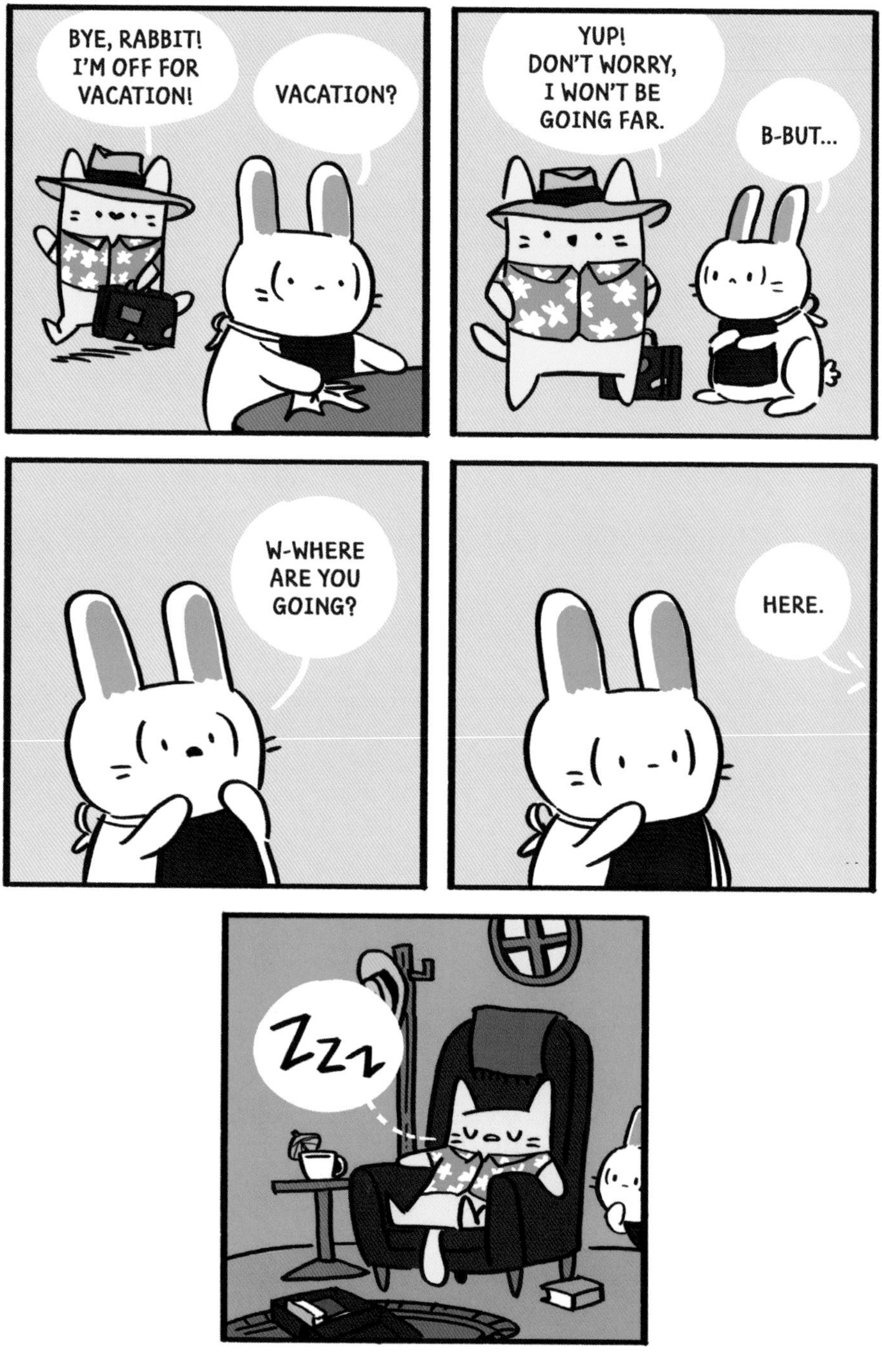
BYE, RABBIT! I'M OFF FOR VACATION!
VACATION?
YUP! DON'T WORRY, I WON'T BE GOING FAR.
B-BUT...
W-WHERE ARE YOU GOING?
HERE.
ZZZ

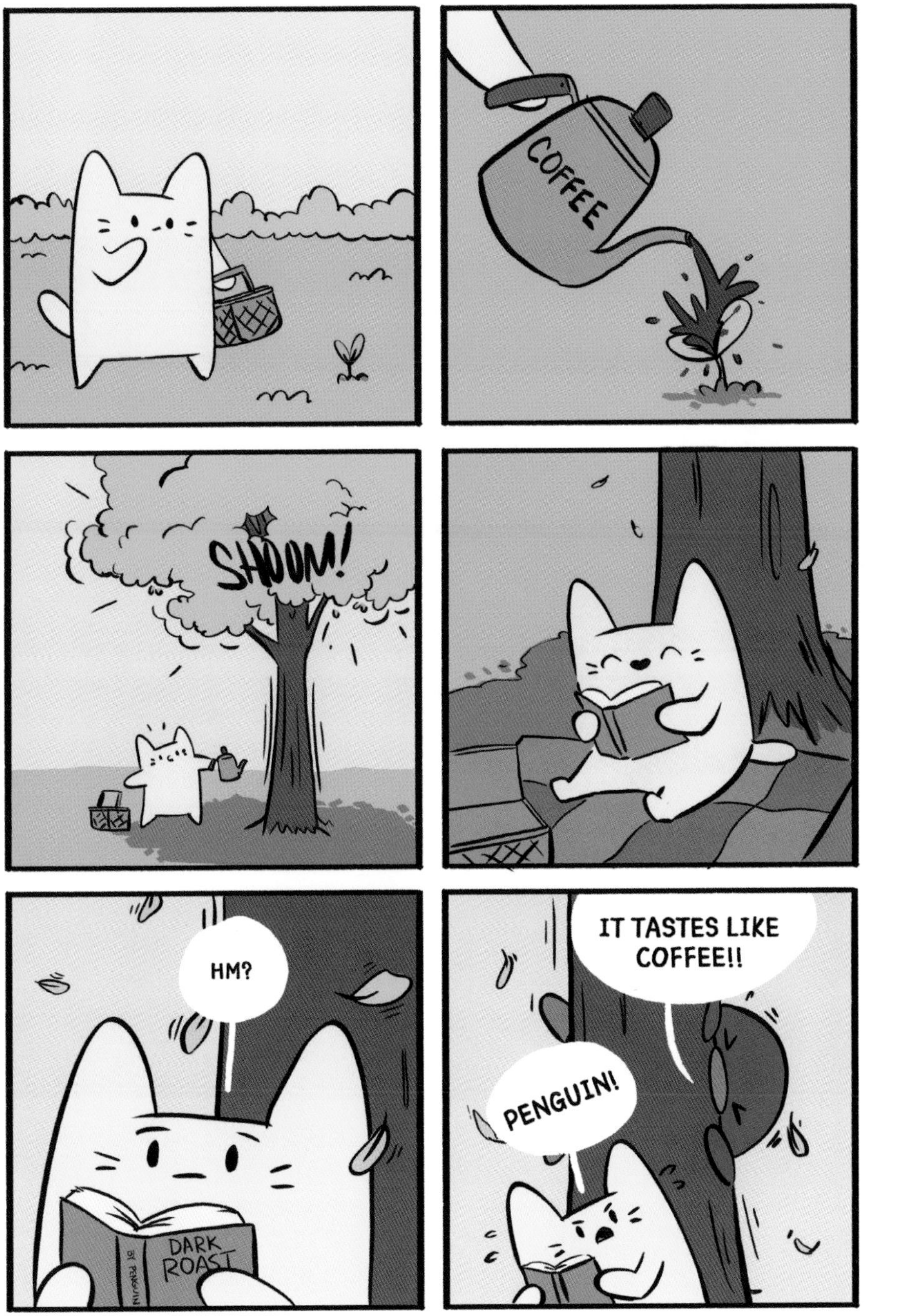
COFFEE
SHOOM!
HM?
DARK ROAST
BY PENGUIN
IT TASTES LIKE COFFEE!!
PENGUIN!

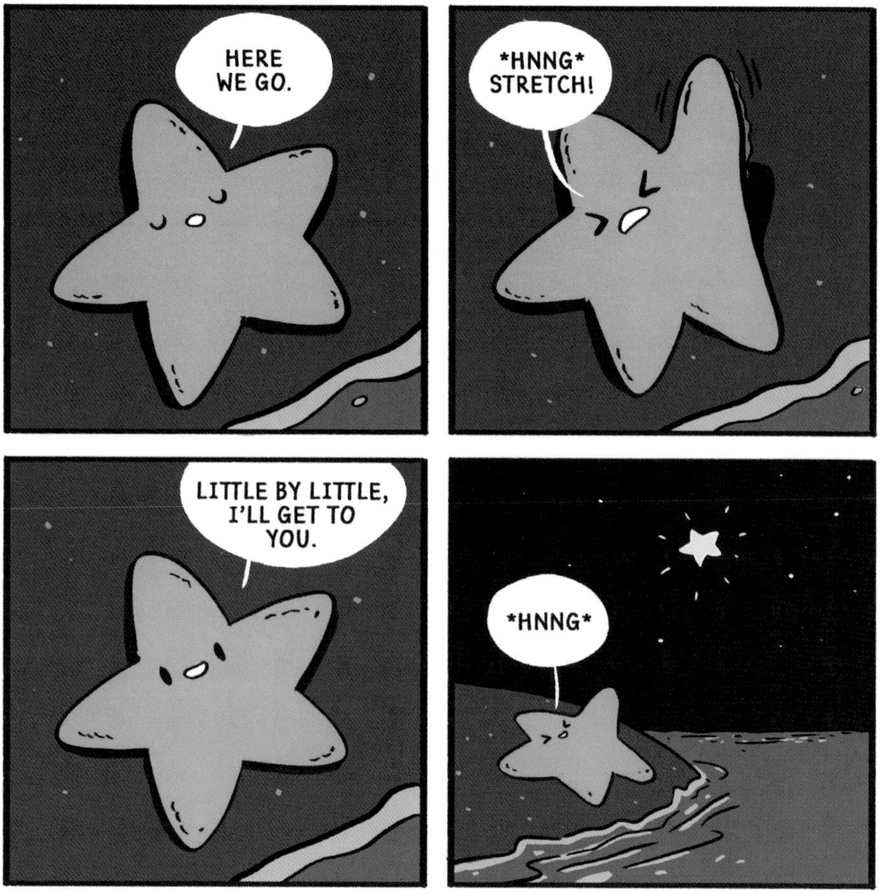
HERE WE GO.
HNNG STRETCH!
LITTLE BY LITTLE, I'LL GET TO YOU.
HNNG

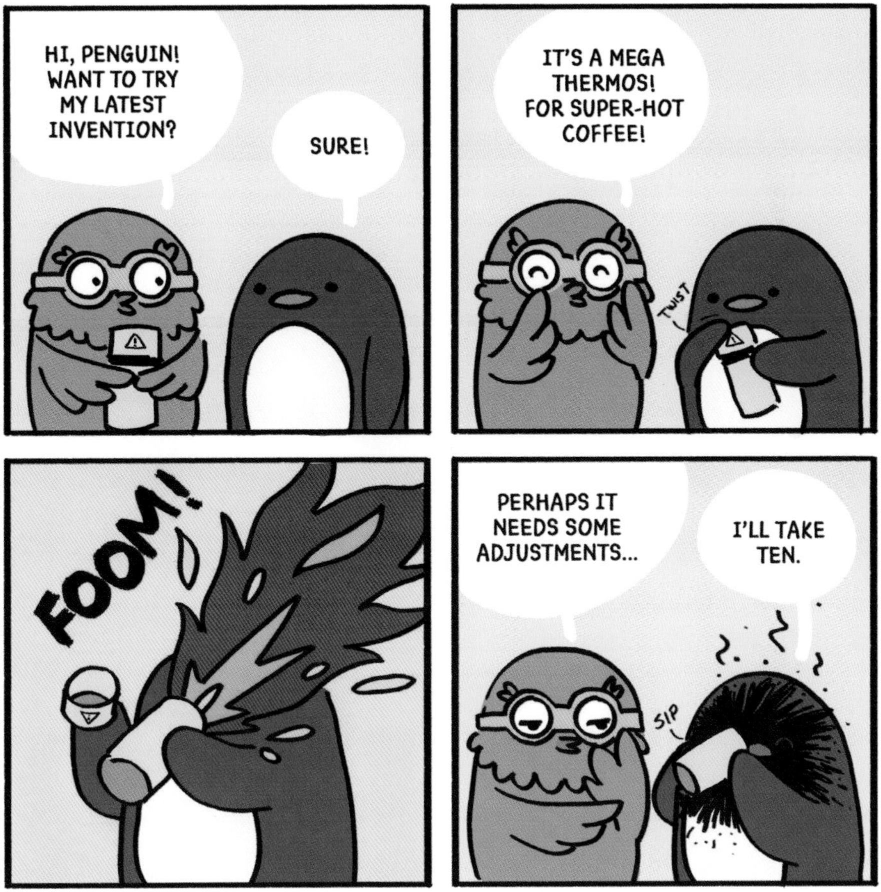
HI, PENGUIN! WANT TO TRY MY LATEST INVENTION?
SURE!
IT'S A MEGA THERMOS! FOR SUPER-HOT COFFEE!
TWIST
FOOM!
PERHAPS IT NEEDS SOME ADJUSTMENTS...
I'LL TAKE TEN.
SIP

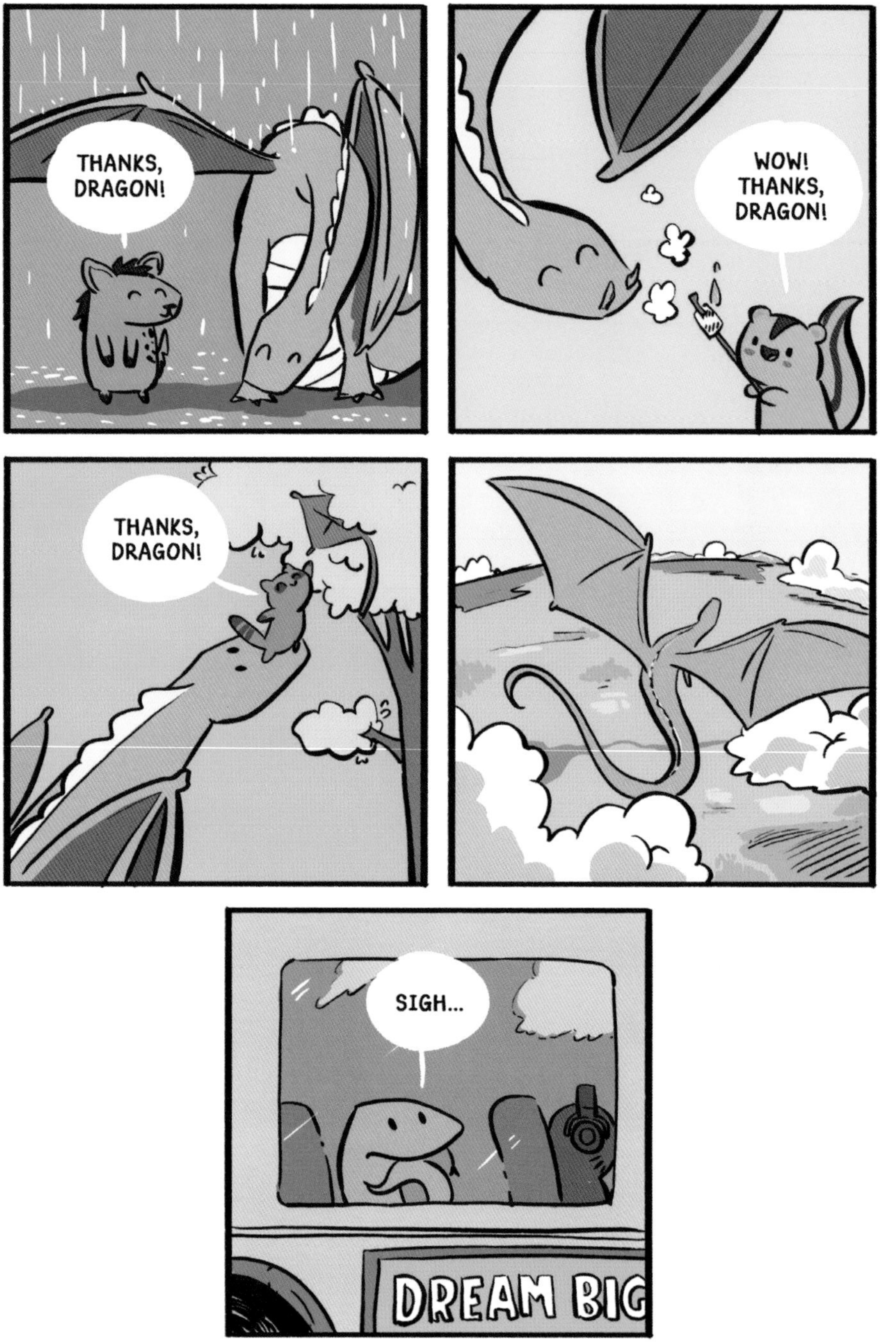
THANKS, DRAGON!
WOW! THANKS, DRAGON!
THANKS, DRAGON!
SIGH...
DREAM BIG

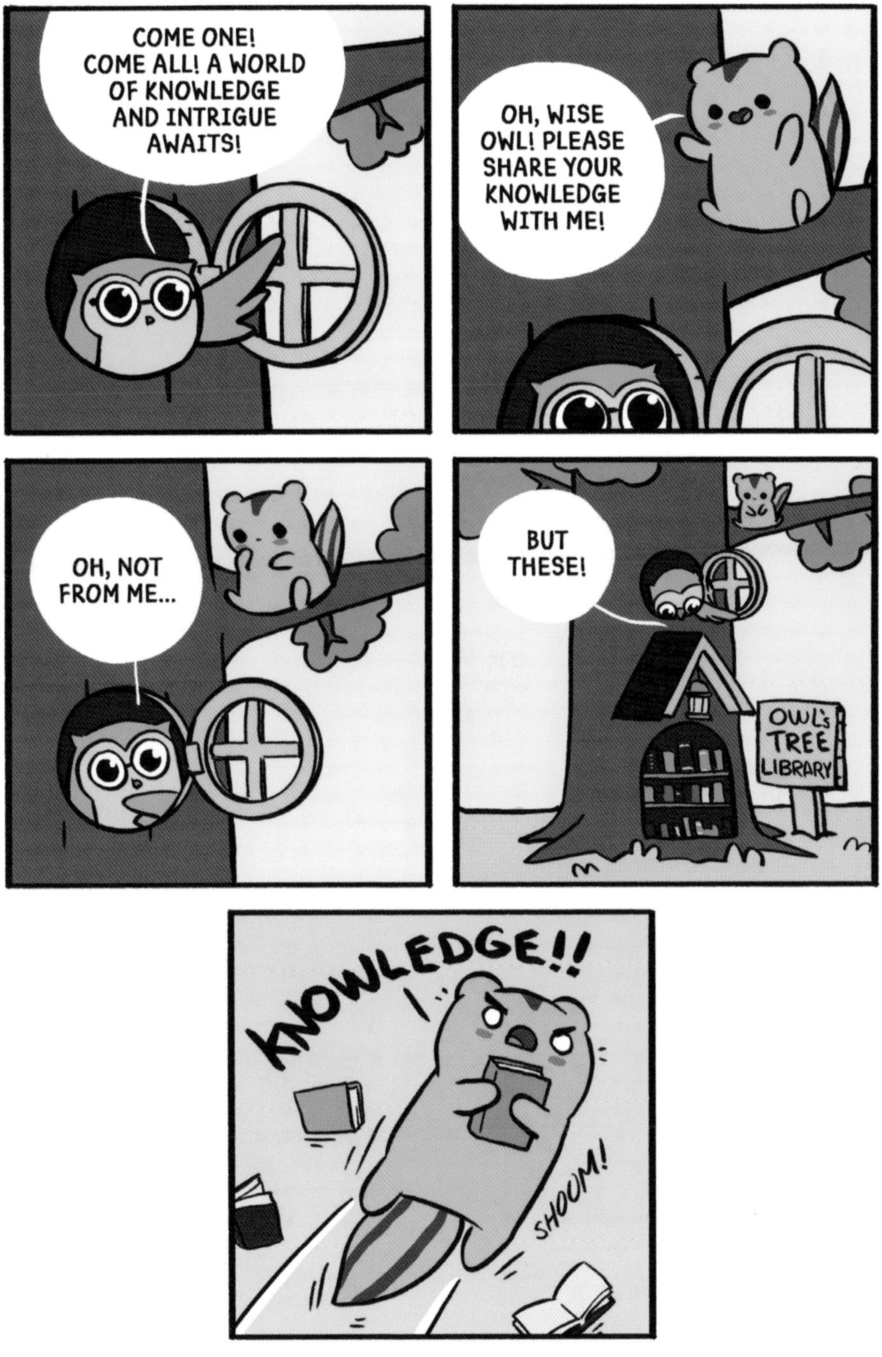

COME ONE! COME ALL! A WORLD OF KNOWLEDGE AND INTRIGUE AWAITS!
OH, WISE OWL! PLEASE SHARE YOUR KNOWLEDGE WITH ME!
OH, NOT FROM ME...
BUT THESE!
OWL's TREE LIBRARY
KNOWLEDGE!!
SHOOM!

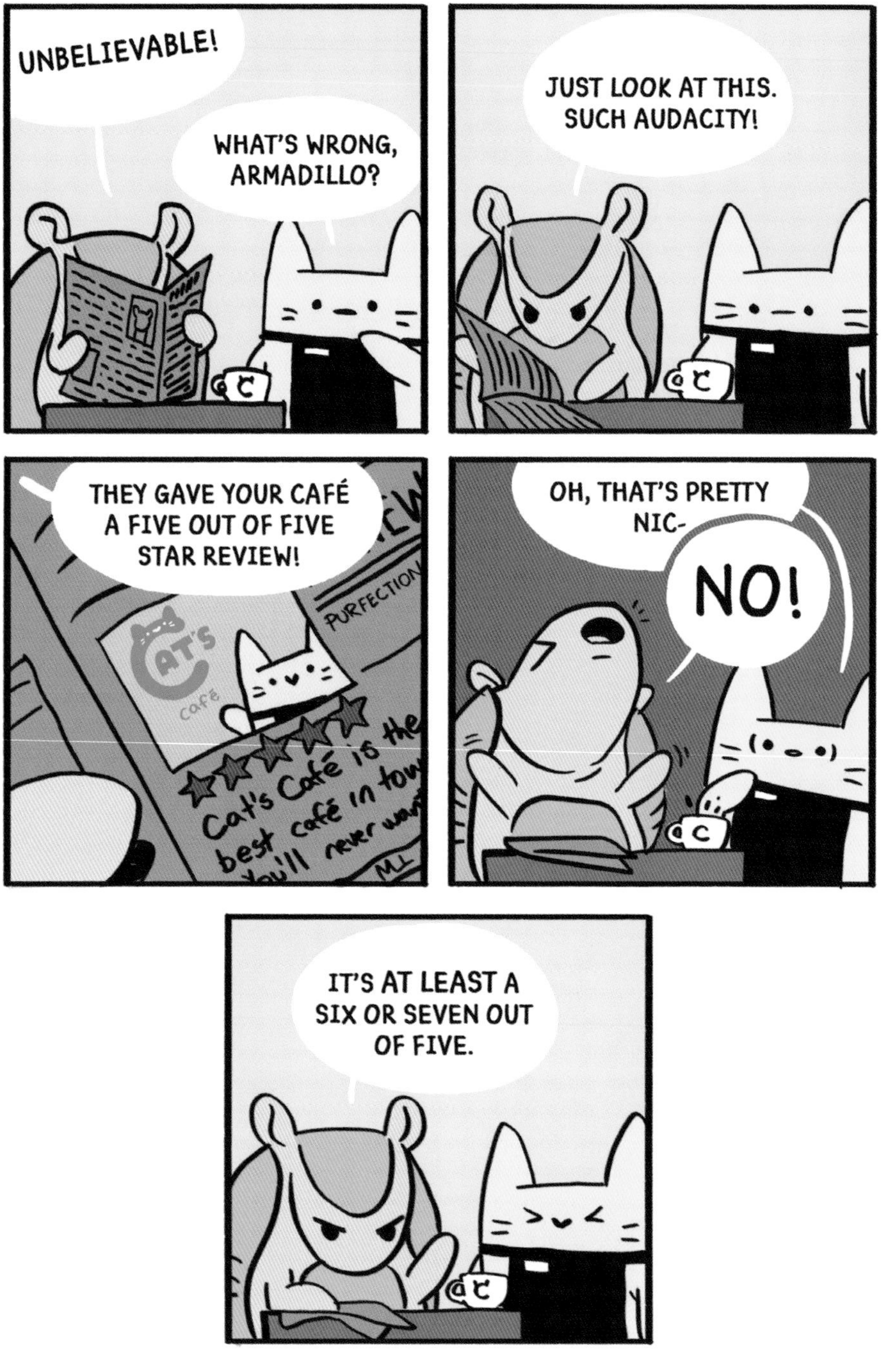
UNBELIEVABLE!
WHAT'S WRONG, ARMADILLO?
JUST LOOK AT THIS. SUCH AUDACITY!
THEY GAVE YOUR CAFÉ A FIVE OUT OF FIVE STAR REVIEW!
PURFECTION
CAT'S café
Cat's Café is the best café in tow
OH, THAT'S PRETTY NIC-
NO!
IT'S AT LEAST A SIX OR SEVEN OUT OF FIVE.

I WOULD LOVE ONE OF EVERYTHING, PLEASE!
SURE THING!
SIP
SIP
SIP
SIP
SIP
SIP
HMM?
SOB
YOU ARE SO LUCKY.

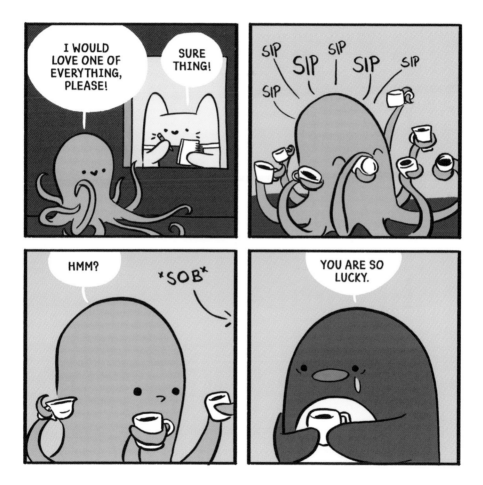

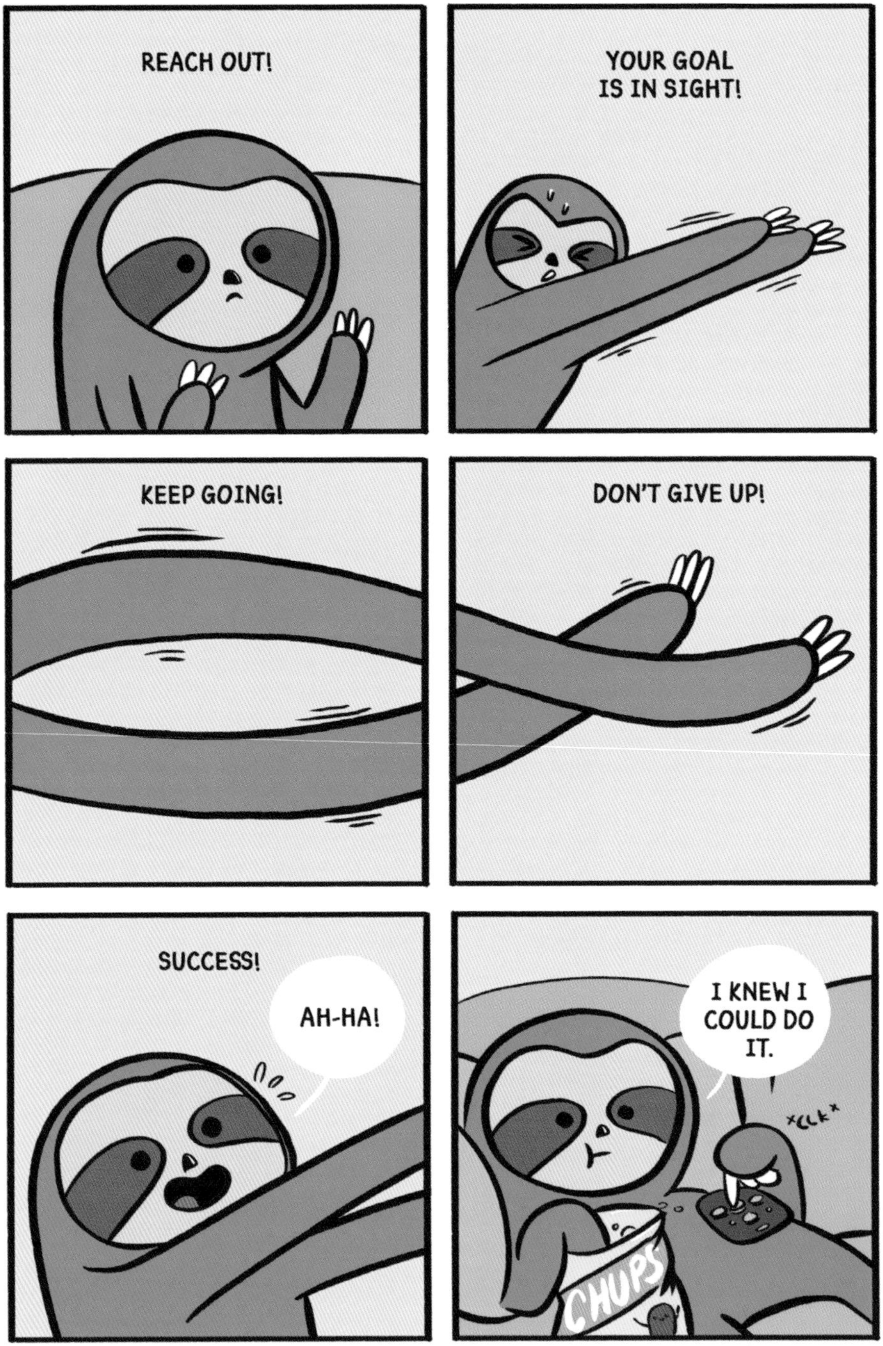
REACH OUT!
YOUR GOAL IS IN SIGHT!
KEEP GOING!
DON'T GIVE UP!
SUCCESS!
AH-HA!
I KNEW I COULD DO IT.
CHUPS

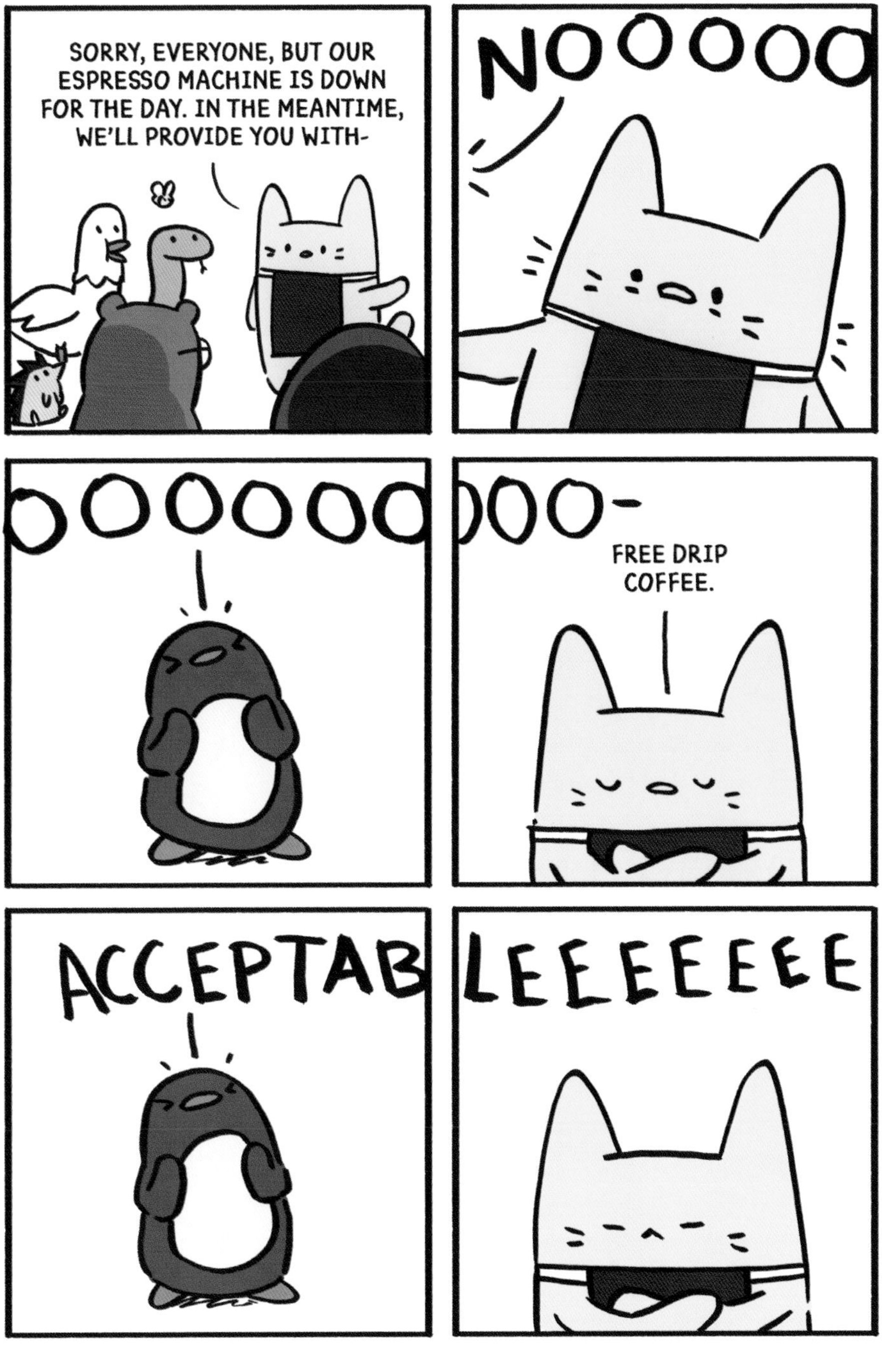
SORRY, EVERYONE, BUT OUR ESPRESSO MACHINE IS DOWN FOR THE DAY. IN THE MEANTIME, WE'LL PROVIDE YOU WITH-
NOOOOO
OOOOOOOOO-
FREE DRIP COFFEE.
ACCEPTABLEEEEEEE

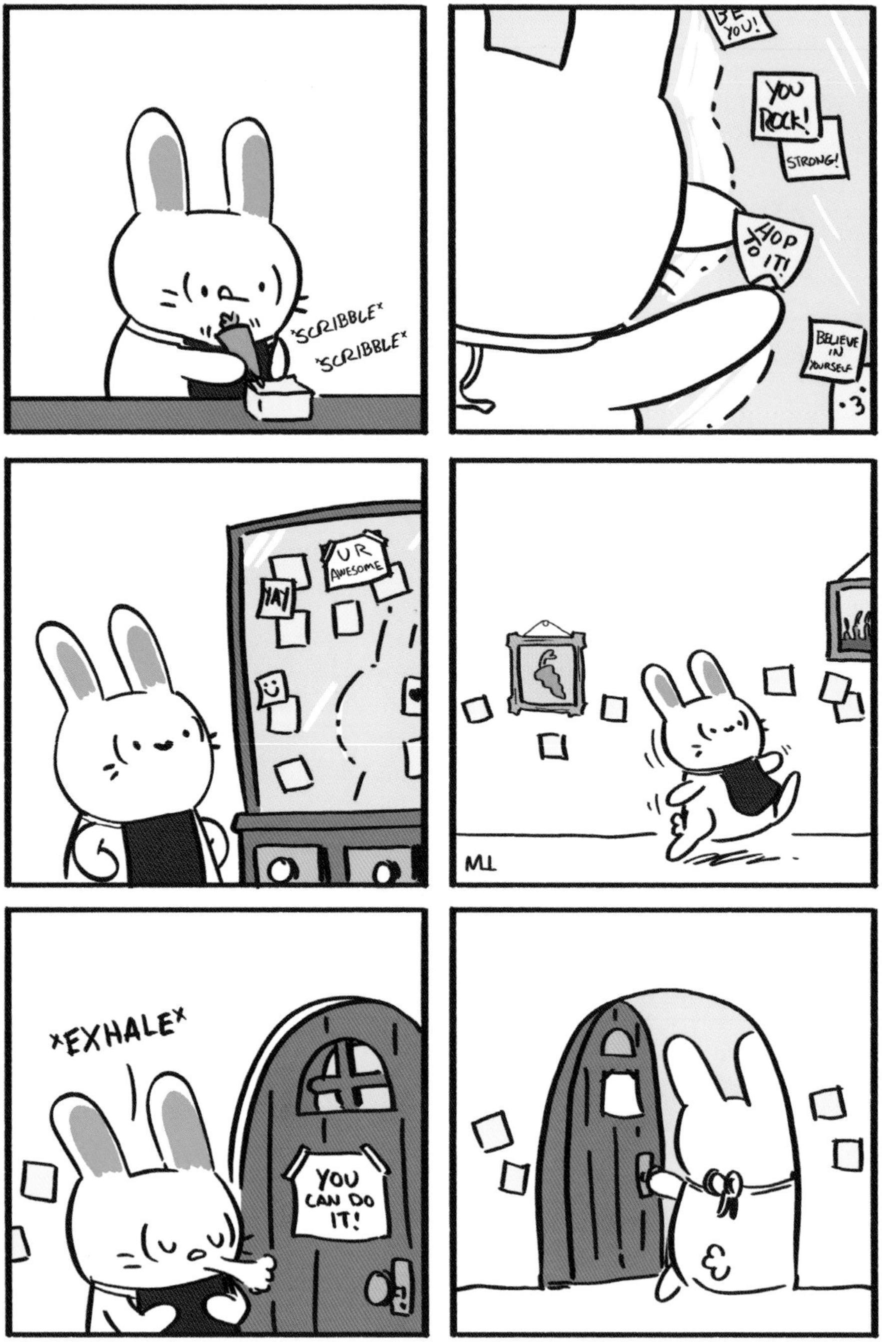
SCRIBBLE
SCRIBBLE
BE YOU!
YOU ROCK!
STRONG!
HOP TO IT!
BELIEVE IN YOURSELF
UR AWESOME
YAY
ML
EXHALE
YOU CAN DO IT!

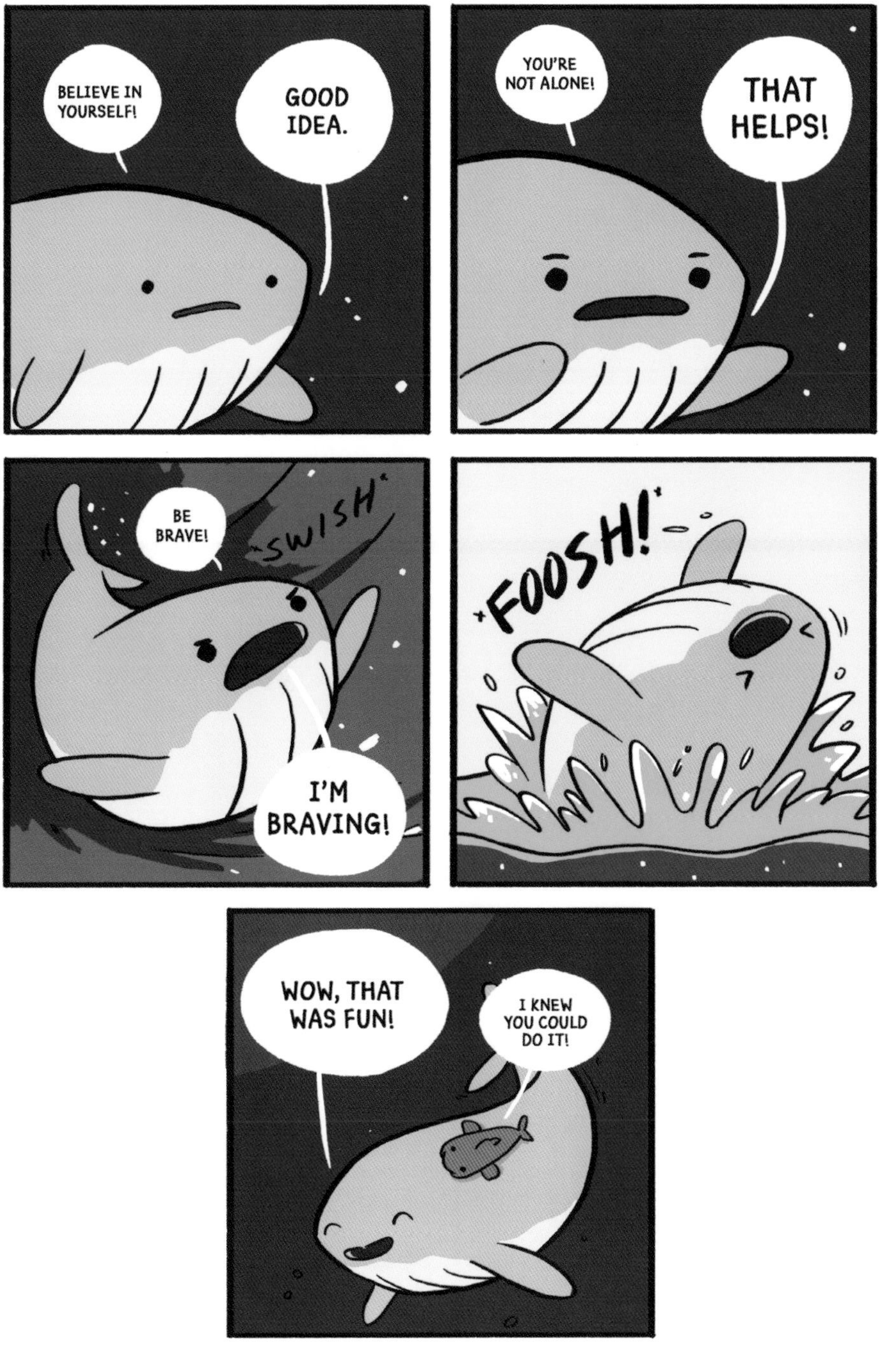
BELIEVE IN YOURSELF!
GOOD IDEA.
YOU'RE NOT ALONE!
THAT HELPS!
BE BRAVE!
SWISH
I'M BRAVING!
FOOSH!
WOW, THAT WAS FUN!
I KNEW YOU COULD DO IT!

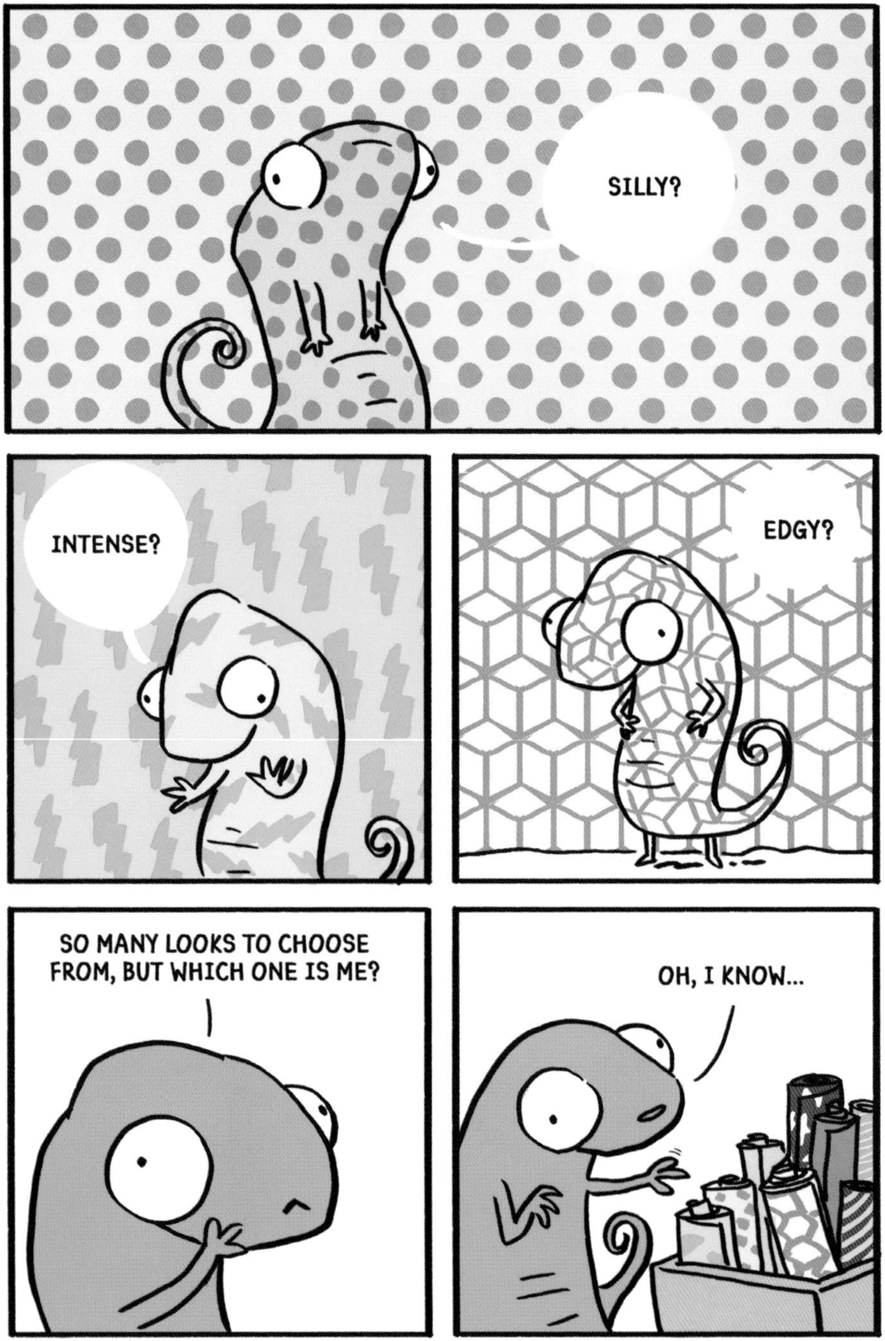
SILLY?
INTENSE?
EDGY?
SO MANY LOOKS TO CHOOSE FROM, BUT WHICH ONE IS ME?
OH, I KNOW...

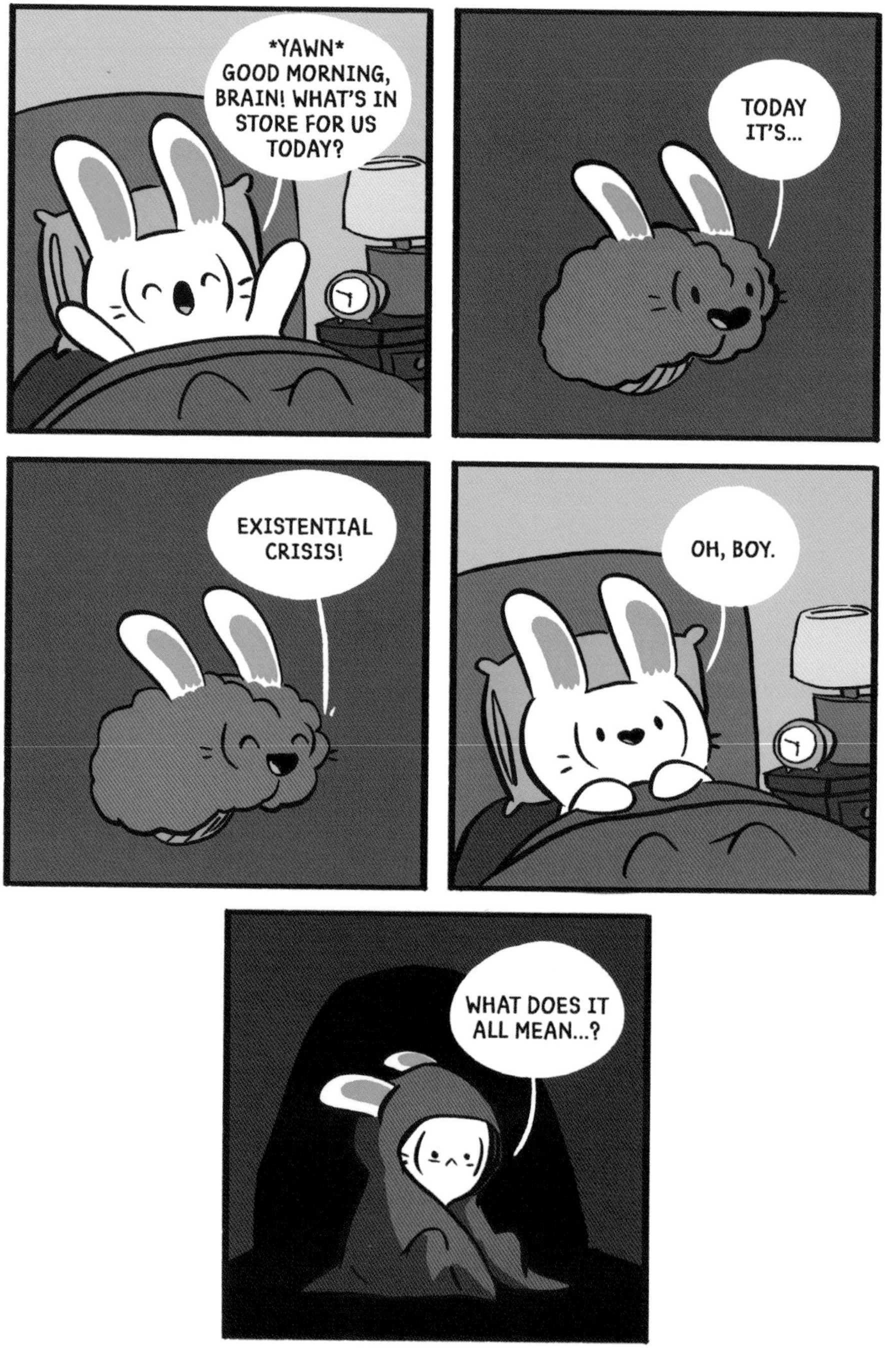
YAWN GOOD MORNING, BRAIN! WHAT'S IN STORE FOR US TODAY?
TODAY IT'S...
EXISTENTIAL CRISIS!
OH, BOY.
WHAT DOES IT ALL MEAN...?

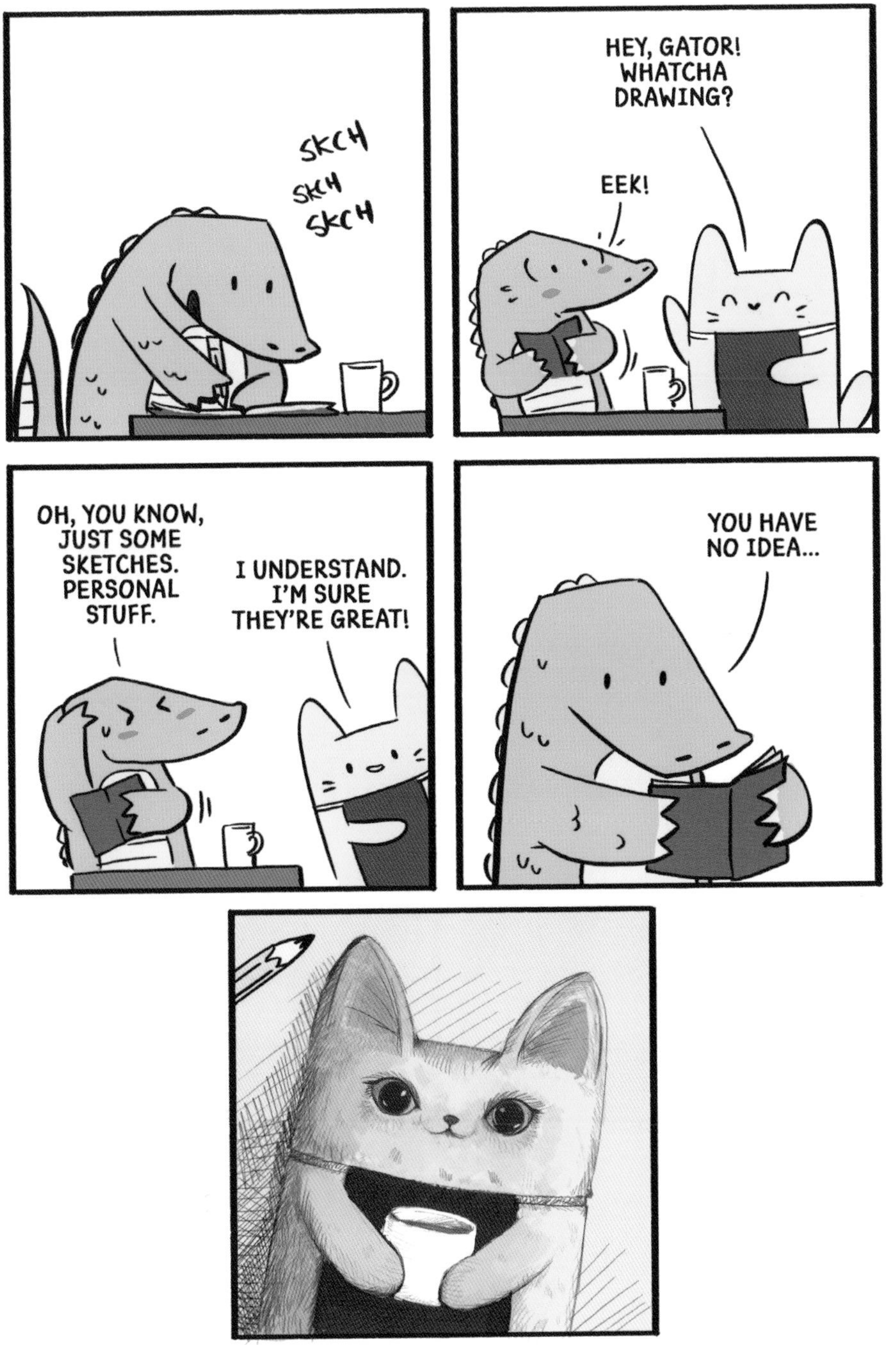
SKCH
SKCH
SKCH
HEY, GATOR! WHATCHA DRAWING?
EEK!
OH, YOU KNOW, JUST SOME SKETCHES. PERSONAL STUFF.
I UNDERSTAND. I'M SURE THEY'RE GREAT!
YOU HAVE NO IDEA...

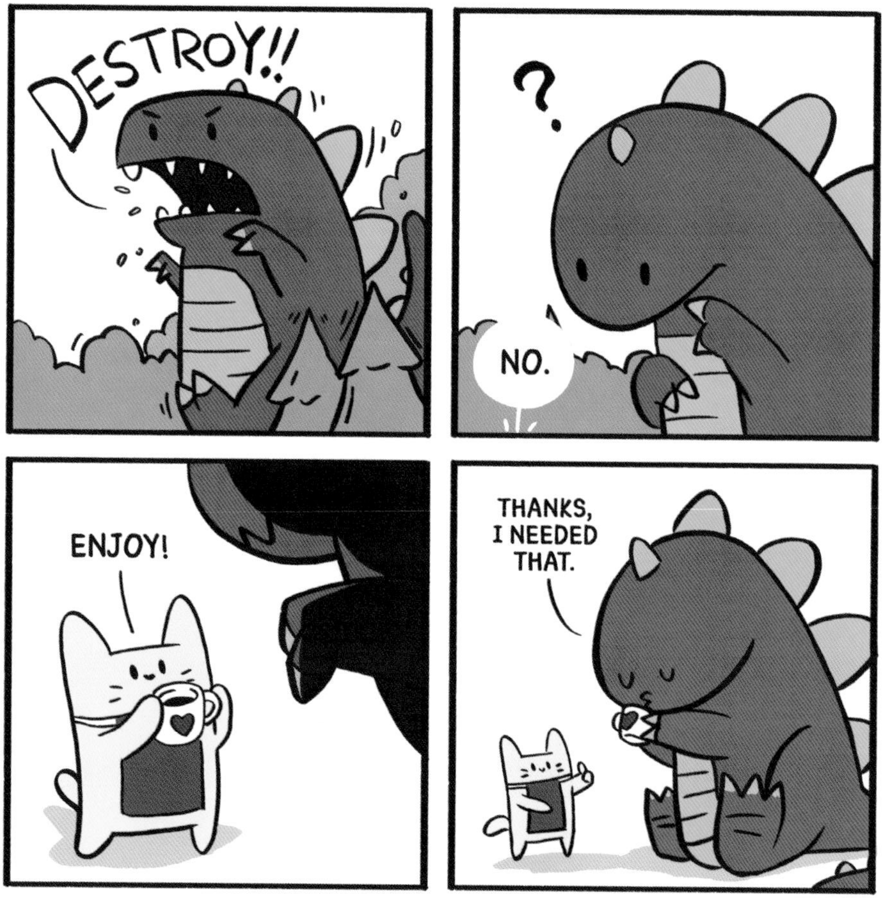

DESTROY!!
?
NO.
ENJOY!
THANKS, I NEEDED THAT.

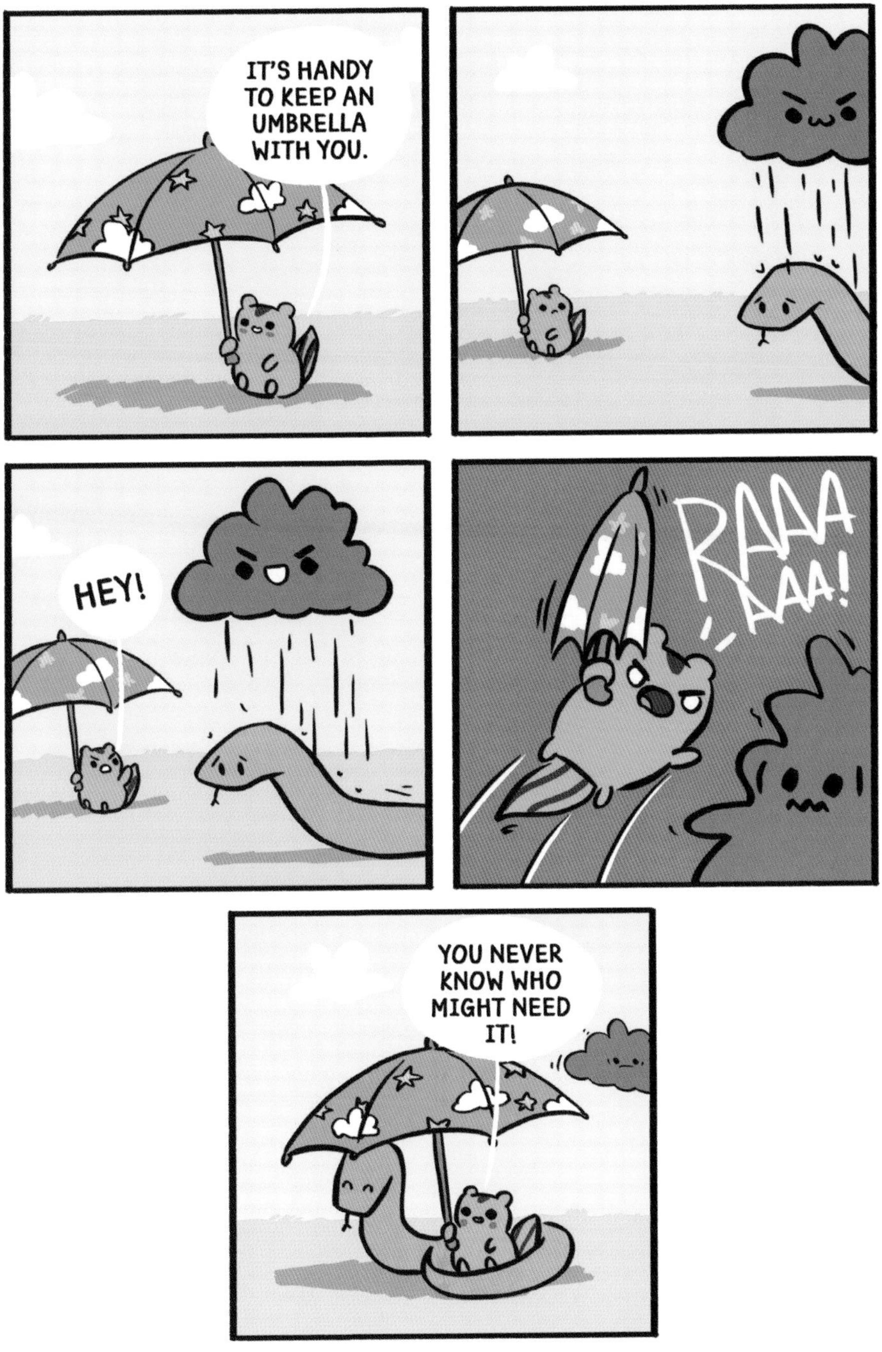
IT'S HANDY TO KEEP AN UMBRELLA WITH YOU.
HEY!
RAAA AAA!
YOU NEVER KNOW WHO MIGHT NEED IT!

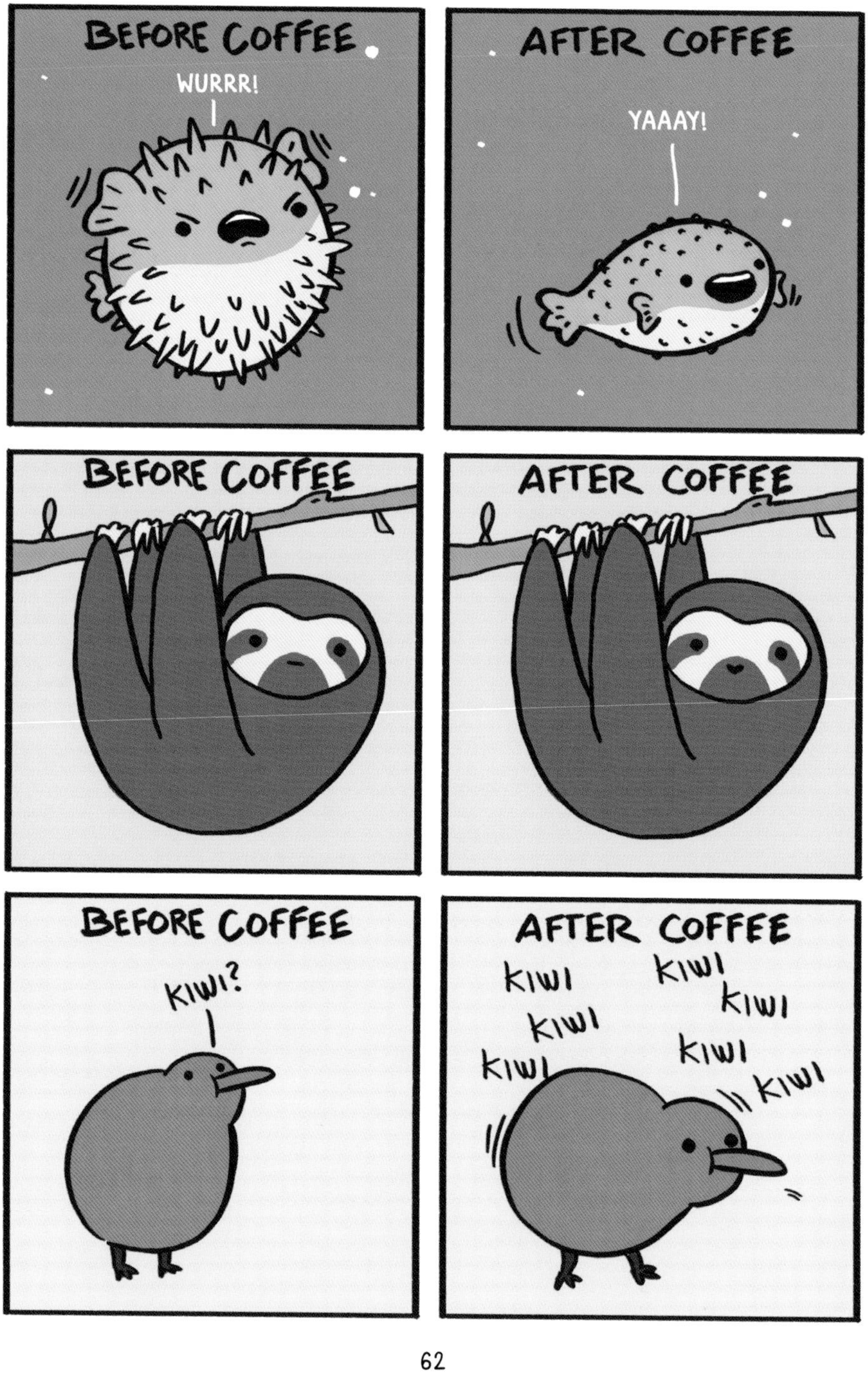
BEFORE COFFEE
WURRR!
AFTER COFFEE
YAAAY!
BEFORE COFFEE
AFTER COFFEE
BEFORE COFFEE
KIWI?
AFTER COFFEE
KIWI
KIWI
KIWI
KIWI
KIWI
KIWI
KIWI

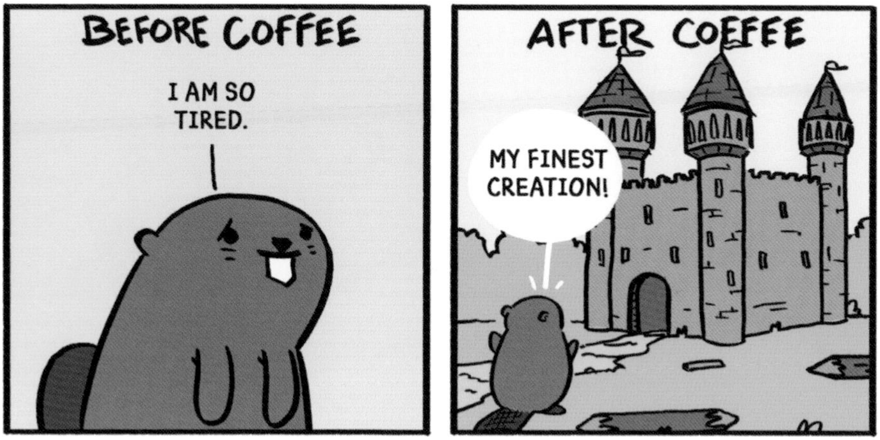
BEFORE COFFEE
I AM SO TIRED.
AFTER COFFEE
MY FINEST CREATION!

SPOT THE DIFFERENCE: WHO IS ON A DEADLINE??

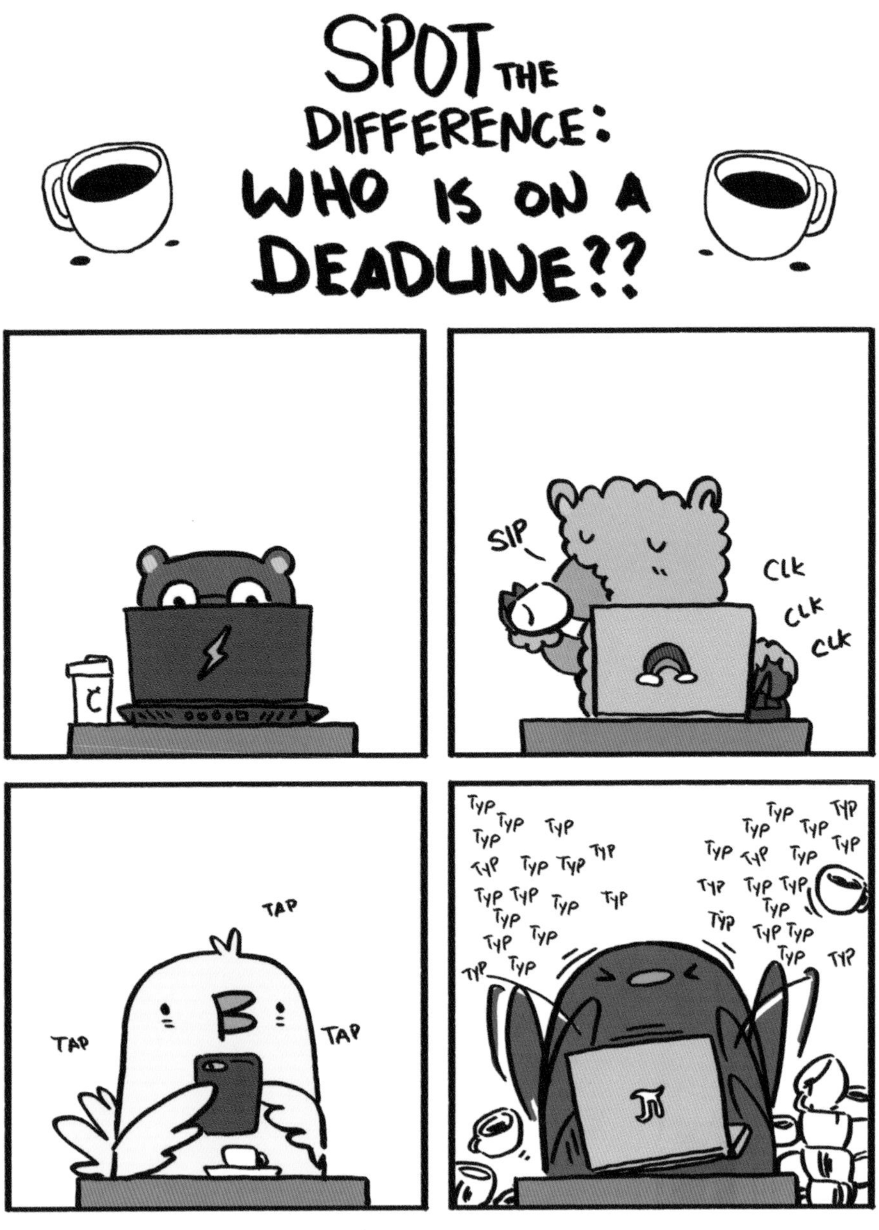
SIP
CLK CLK CLK
TAP
TAP
TAP
TYP TYP TYP TYP TYP TYP TYP TYP TYP TYP TYP TYP TYP TYP TYP TYP TYP
TYP TYP TYP TYP TYP TYP TYP TYP TYP TYP TYP TYP TYP TYP TYP TYP TYP

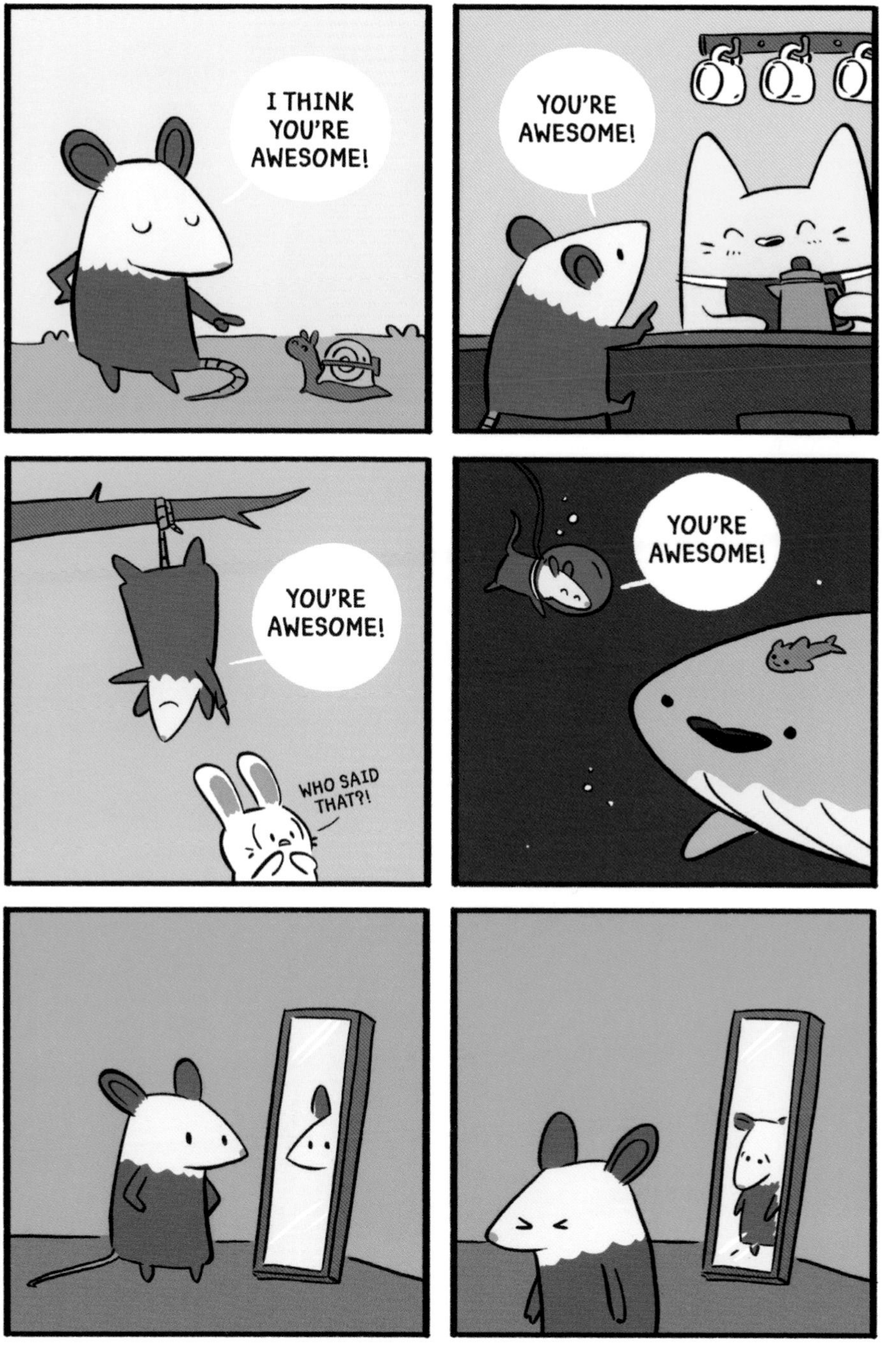
I THINK YOU'RE AWESOME!
YOU'RE AWESOME!
YOU'RE AWESOME!
WHO SAID THAT?!
YOU'RE AWESOME!

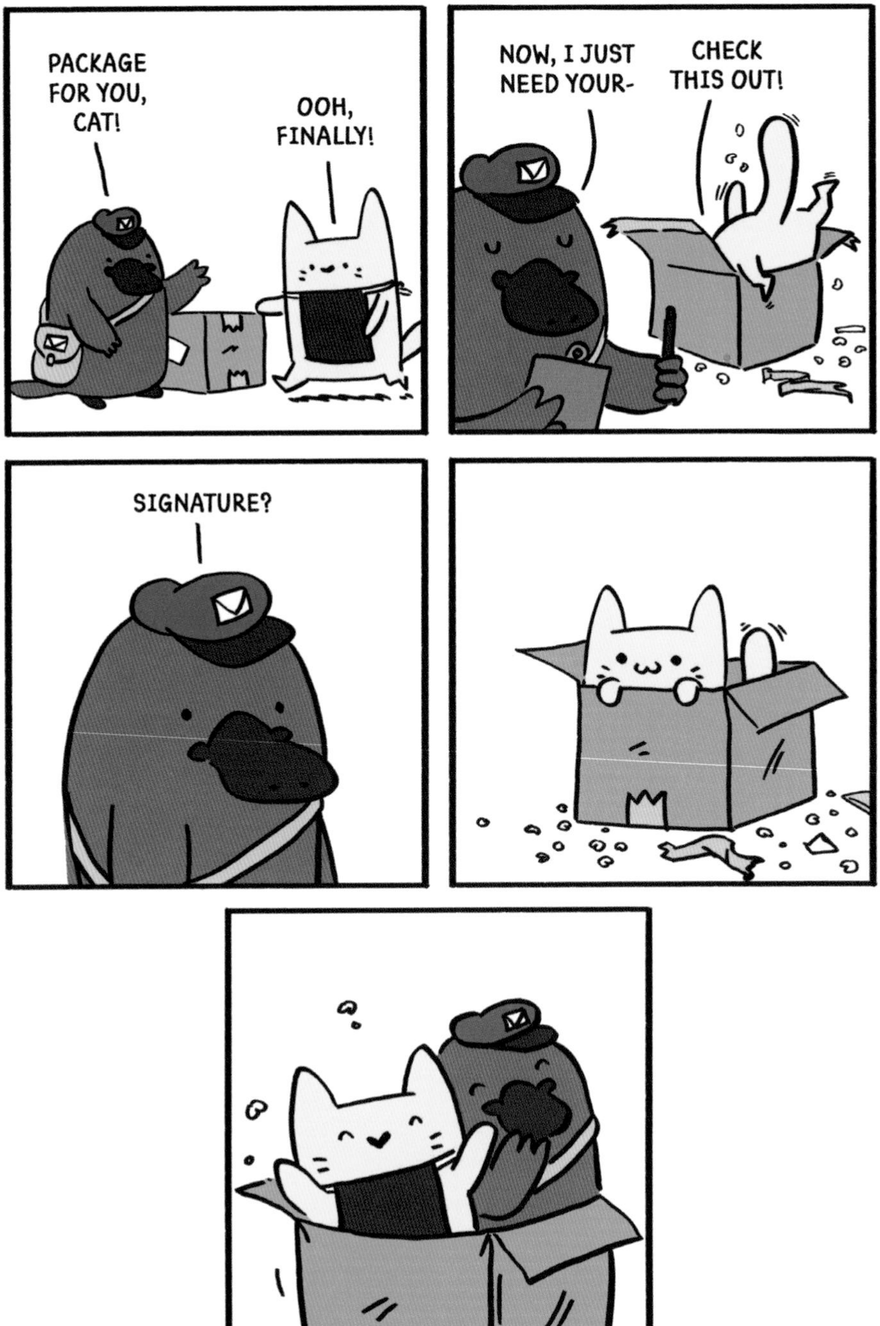
PACKAGE FOR YOU, CAT!
OOH, FINALLY!
NOW, I JUST NEED YOUR-
CHECK THIS OUT!
SIGNATURE?

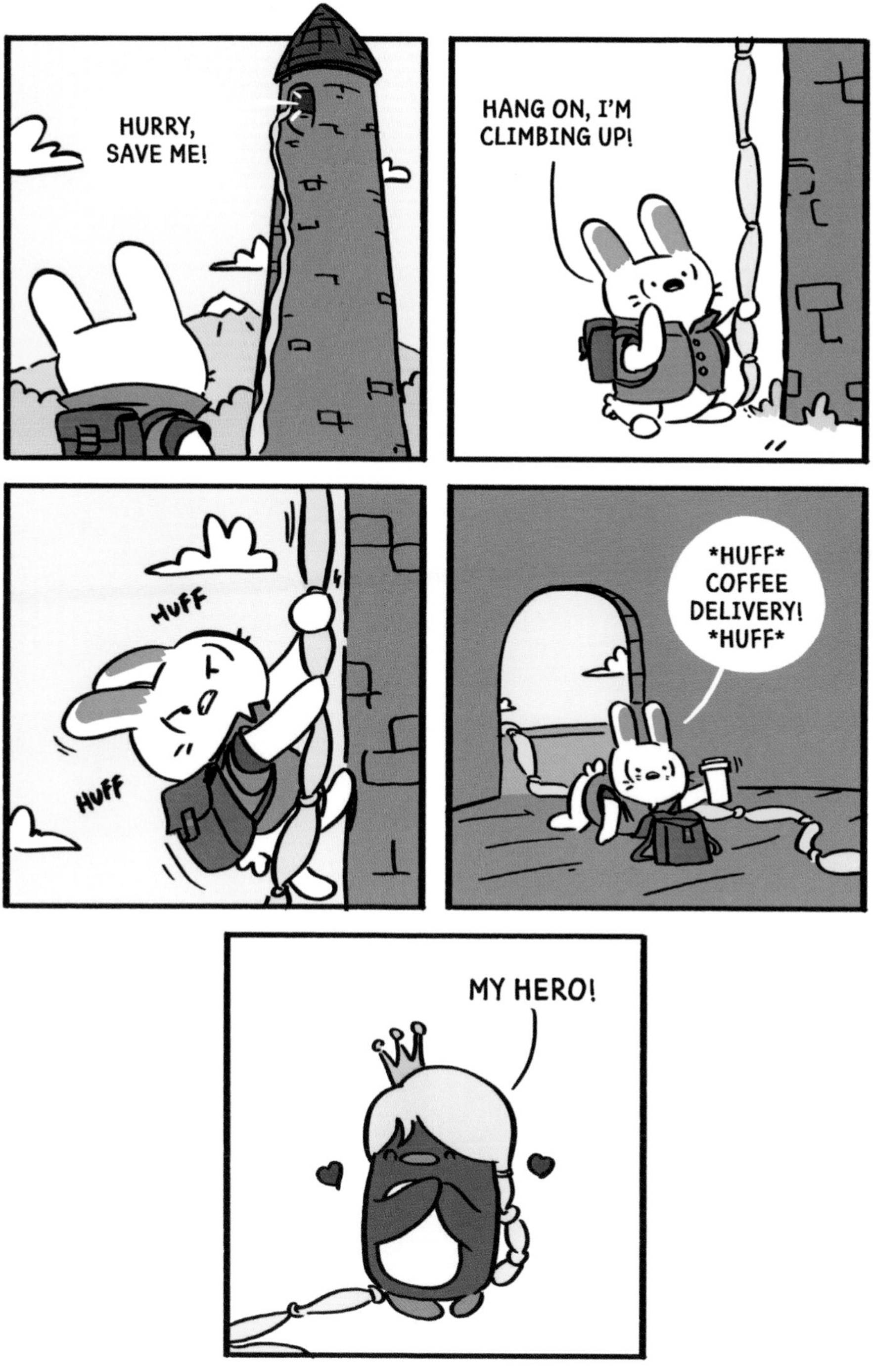
HURRY, SAVE ME!
HANG ON, I'M CLIMBING UP!
HUFF
HUFF
HUFF COFFEE DELIVERY! *HUFF*
MY HERO!

DUCK, ARE YOU OKAY!?
YEAH, I'LL BE FINE...
JUST GOT A LITTLE WAKE-UP CALL.
EARLIER...
THUNK

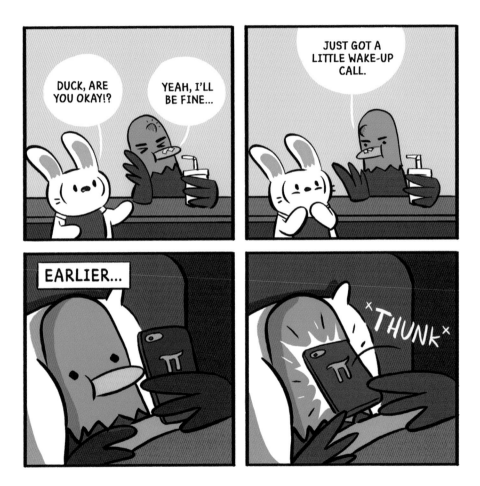

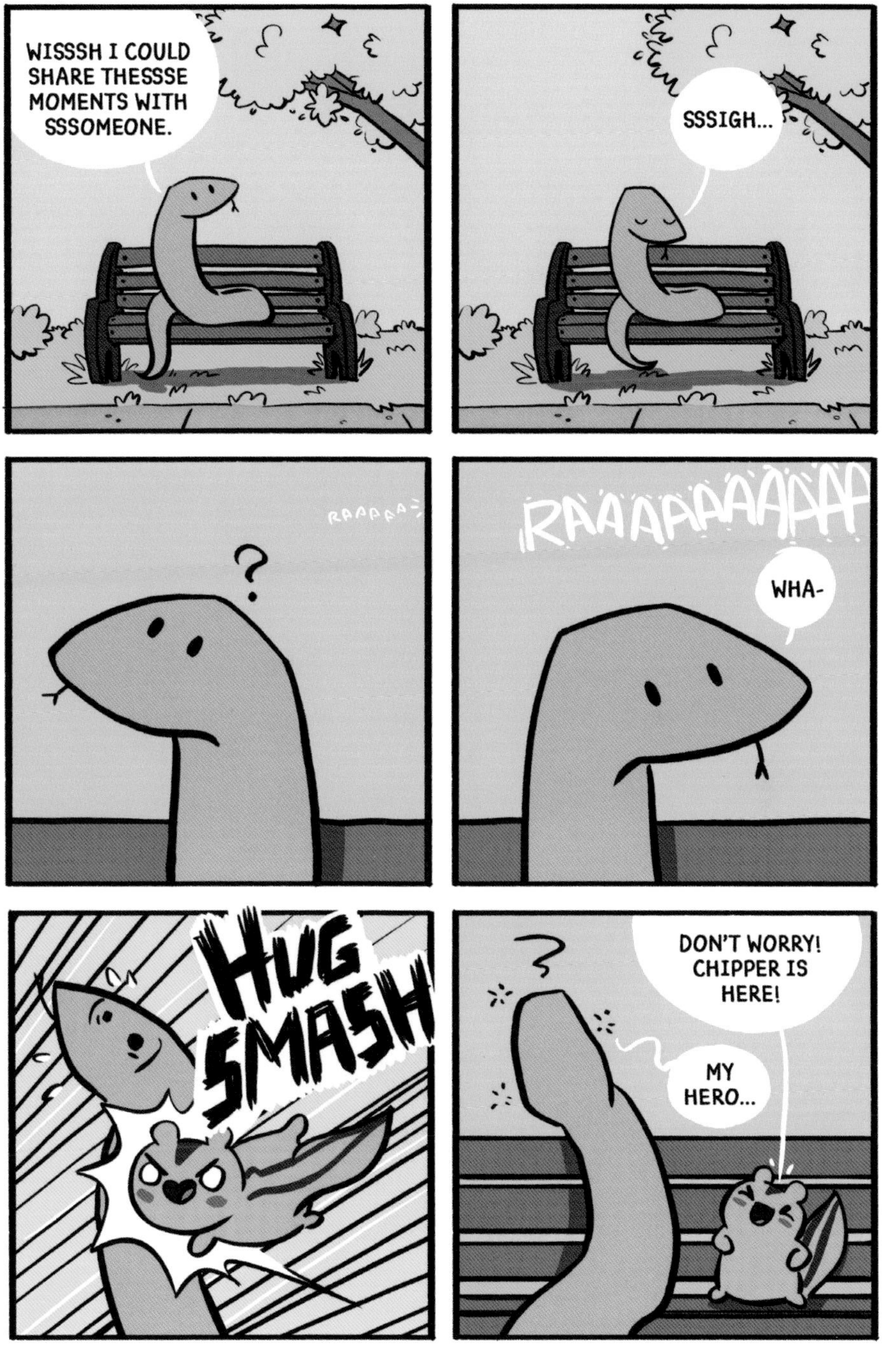
WISSSH I COULD SHARE THESSSE MOMENTS WITH SSSOMEONE.
SSSIGH...
RAAAAA
RAAAAAAAAAA
WHA-
HUG SMASH
DON'T WORRY! CHIPPER IS HERE!
MY HERO...

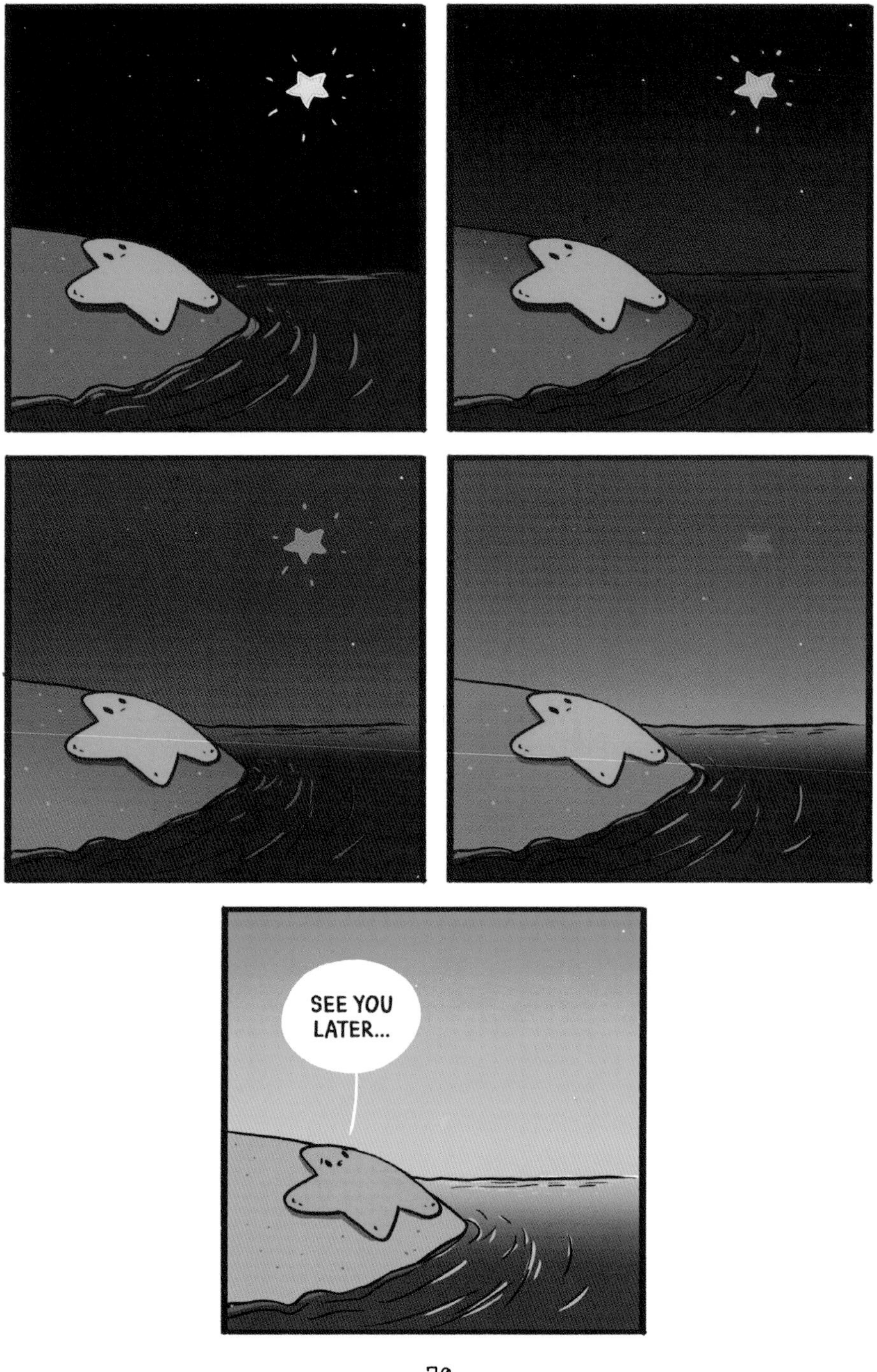
SEE YOU LATER...

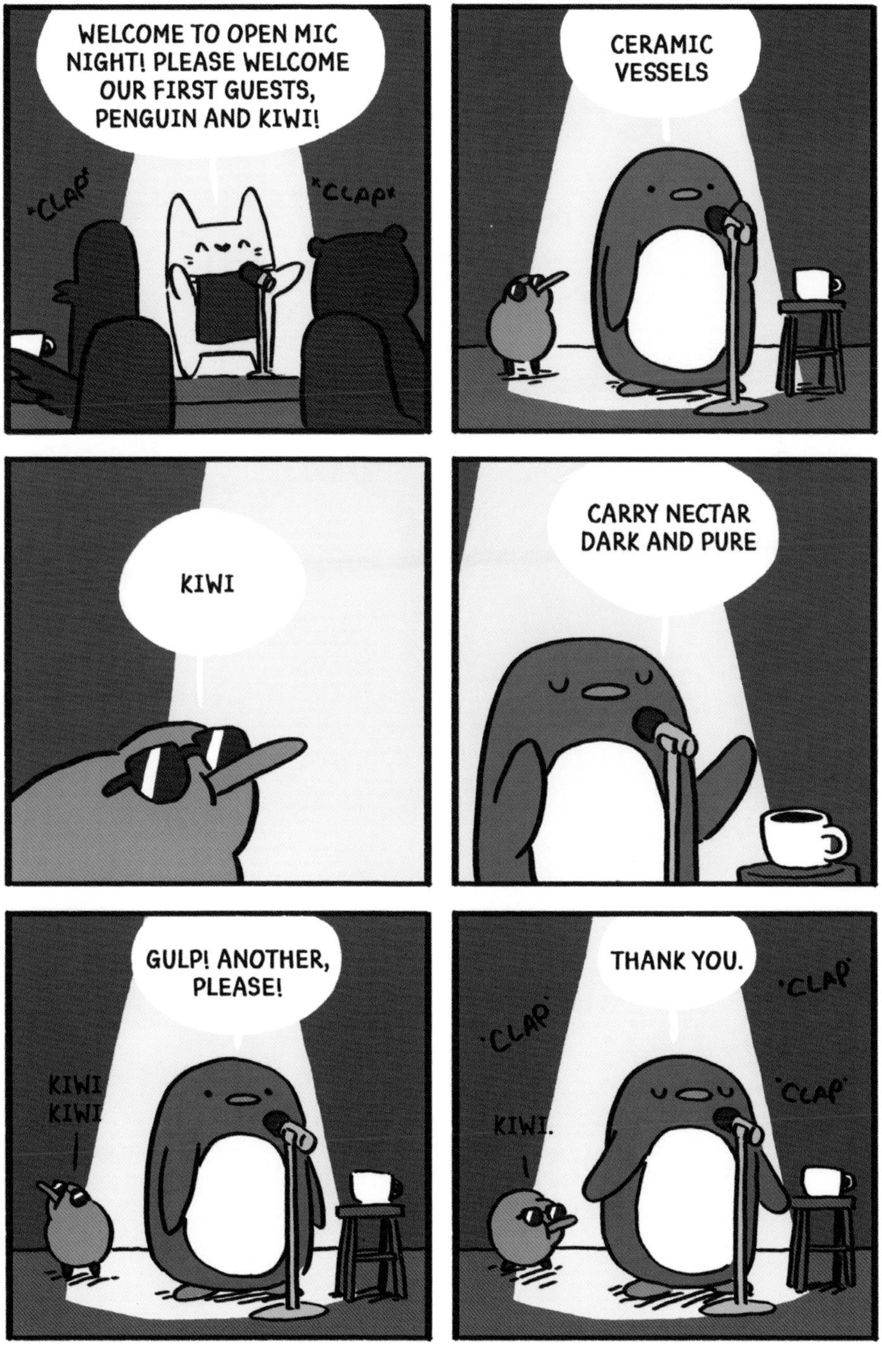
WELCOME TO OPEN MIC NIGHT! PLEASE WELCOME OUR FIRST GUESTS, PENGUIN AND KIWI!
CLAP
CLAP
CERAMIC VESSELS
KIWI
CARRY NECTAR DARK AND PURE
GULP! ANOTHER, PLEASE!
KIWI KIWI
THANK YOU.
CLAP
CLAP
CLAP
KIWI.

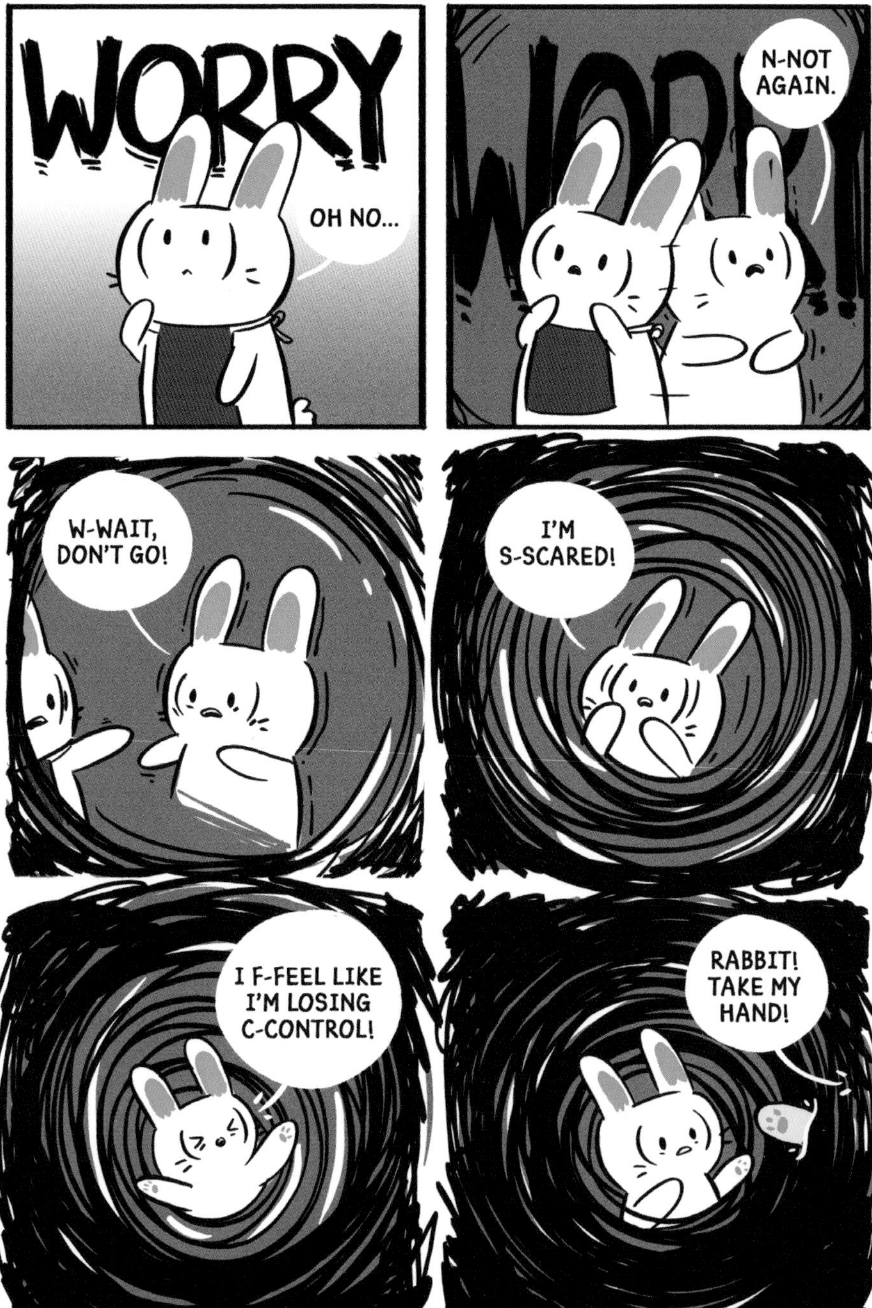
WORRY
OH NO...
N-NOT AGAIN.
W-WAIT, DON'T GO!
I'M S-SCARED!
I F-FEEL LIKE I'M LOSING C-CONTROL!
RABBIT! TAKE MY HAND!

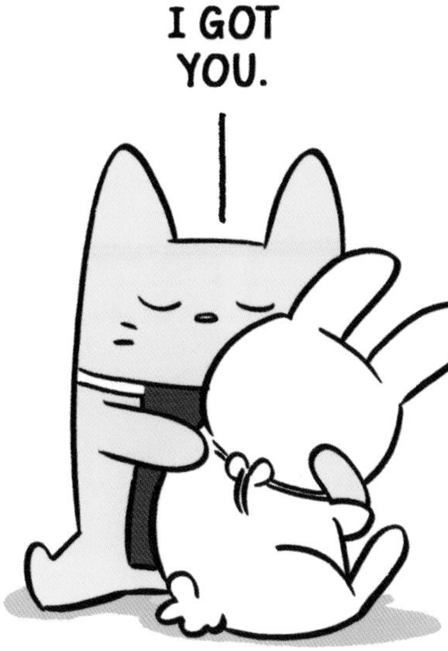
I GOT
YOU.

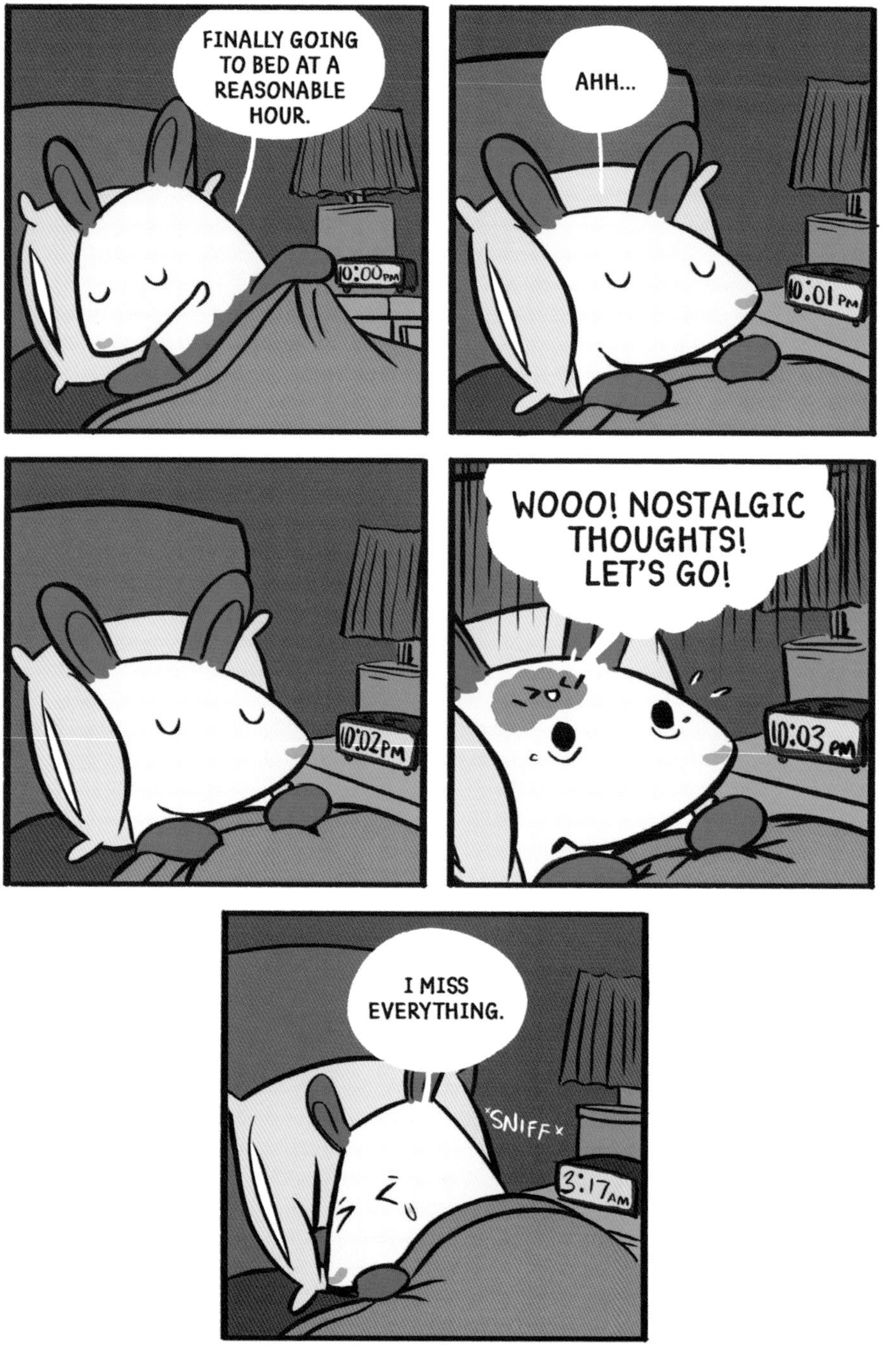
FINALLY GOING TO BED AT A REASONABLE HOUR.
10:00PM
AHH...
10:01PM
10:02PM
WOOO! NOSTALGIC THOUGHTS! LET'S GO!
10:03PM
I MISS EVERYTHING.
SNIFF
3:17AM

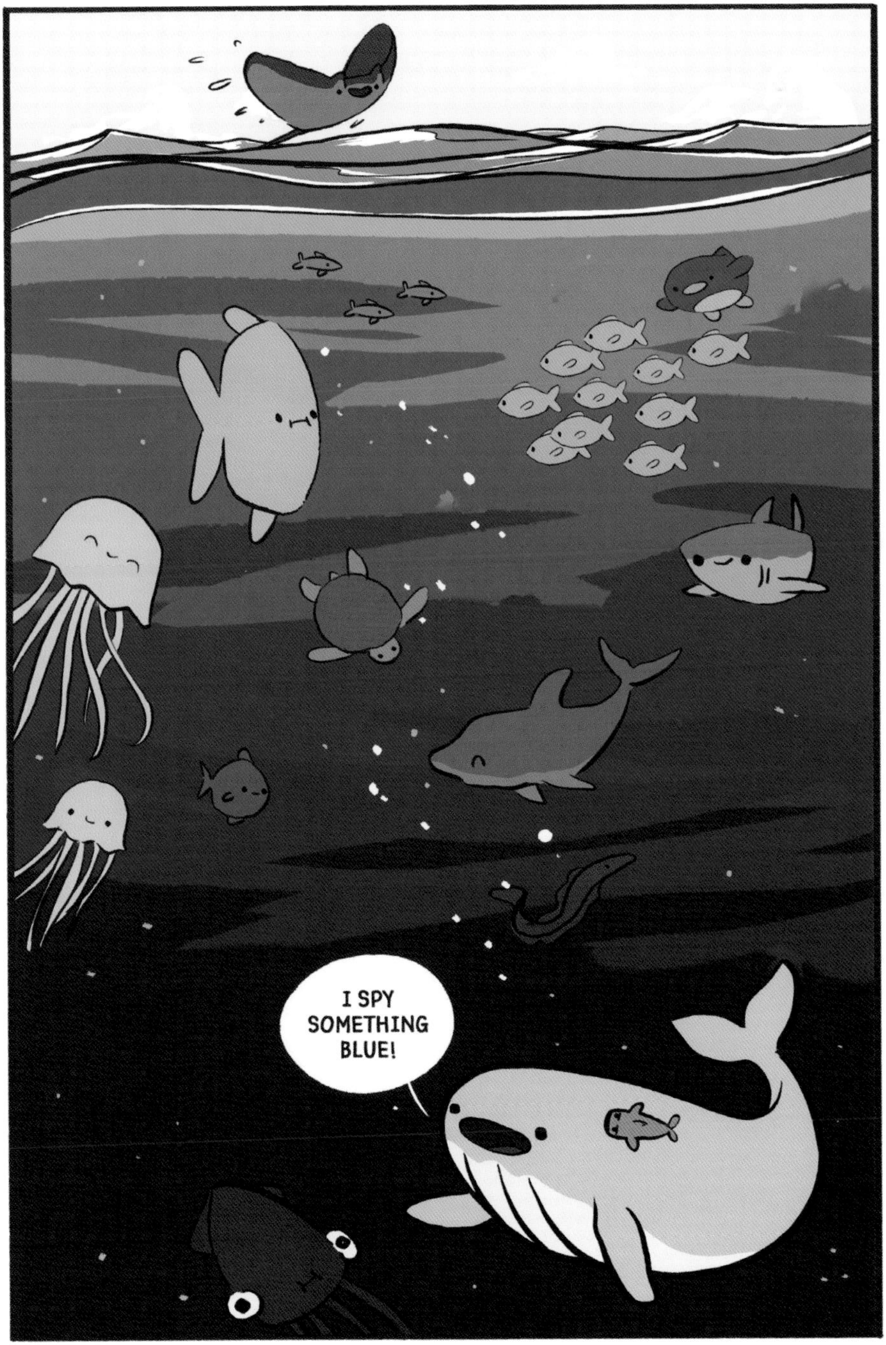
I SPY SOMETHING BLUE!

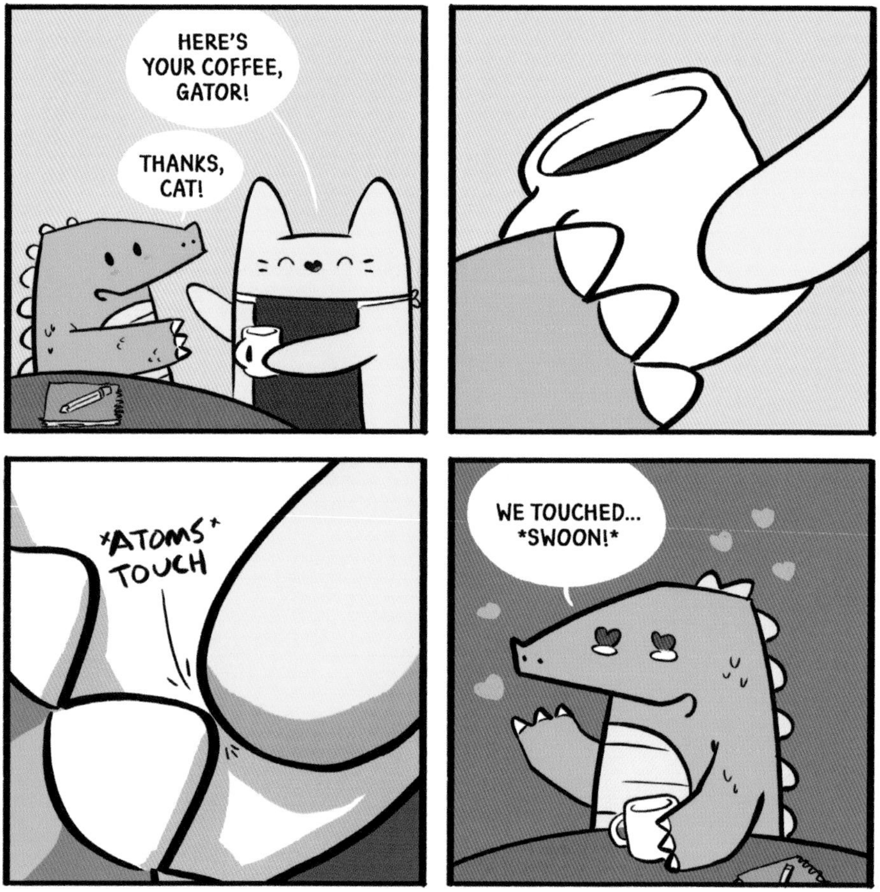
HERE'S YOUR COFFEE, GATOR!
THANKS, CAT!
ATOMS TOUCH
WE TOUCHED... *SWOON!*

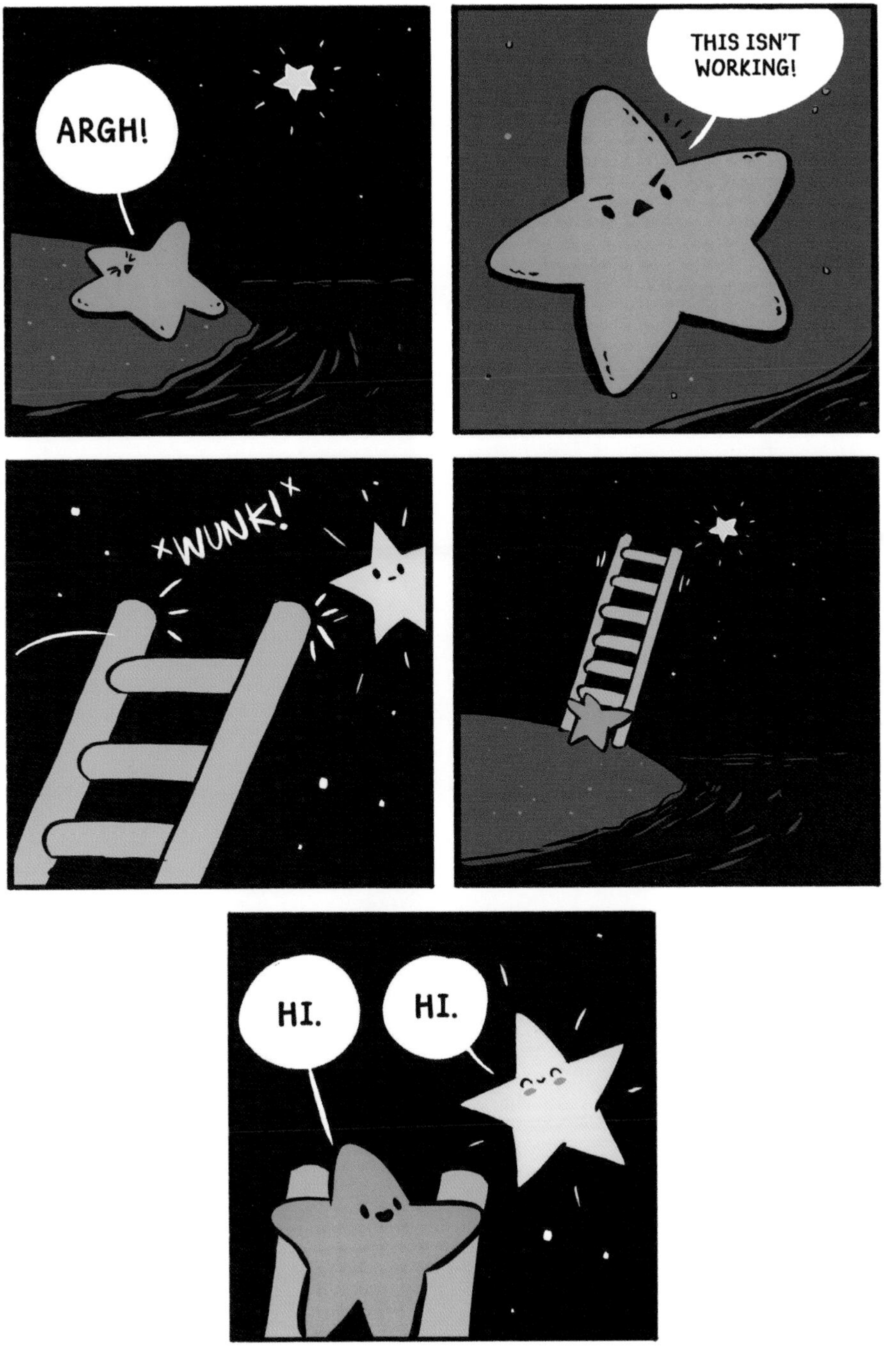
ARGH!
THIS ISN'T WORKING!
WUNK!
HI.
HI.

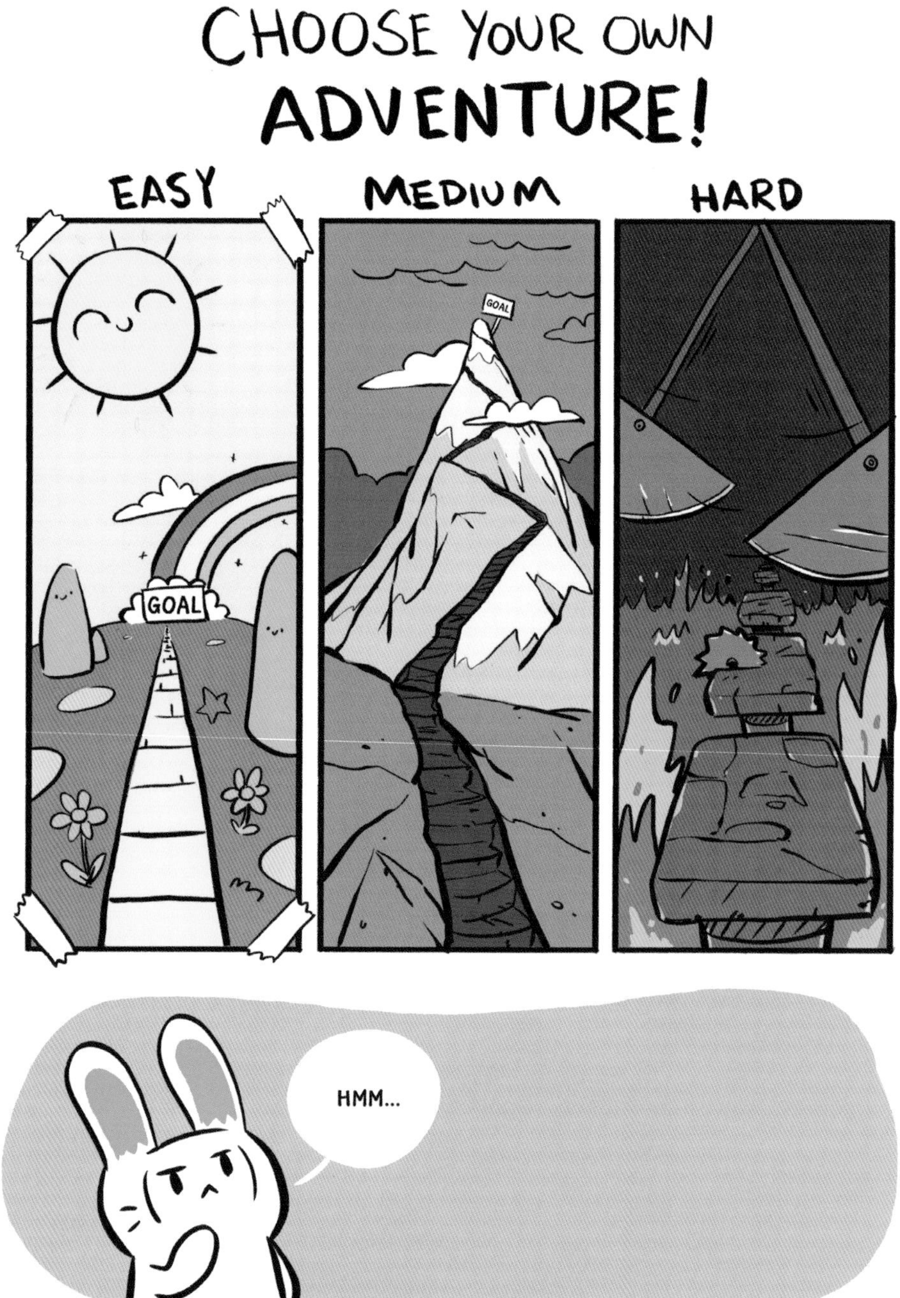
CHOOSE YOUR OWN
ADVENTURE!
EASY
MEDIUM
HARD
GOAL
GOAL
HMM...

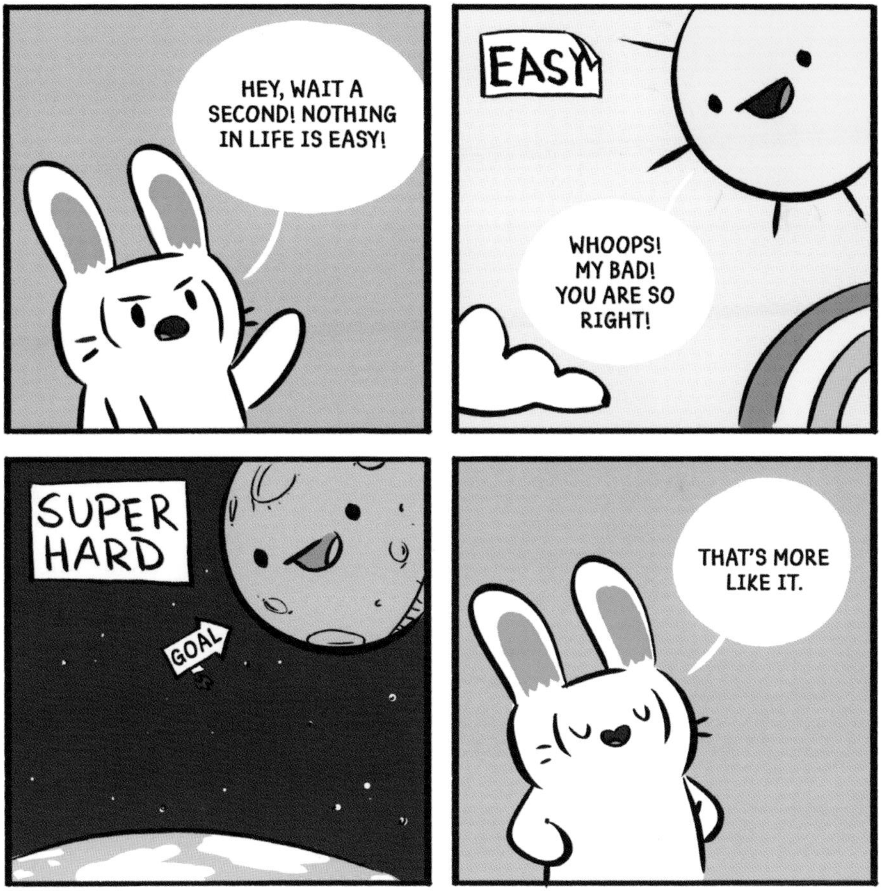
HEY, WAIT A SECOND! NOTHING IN LIFE IS EASY!
EASY
WHOOPS! MY BAD! YOU ARE SO RIGHT!
SUPER HARD
GOAL
THAT'S MORE LIKE IT.

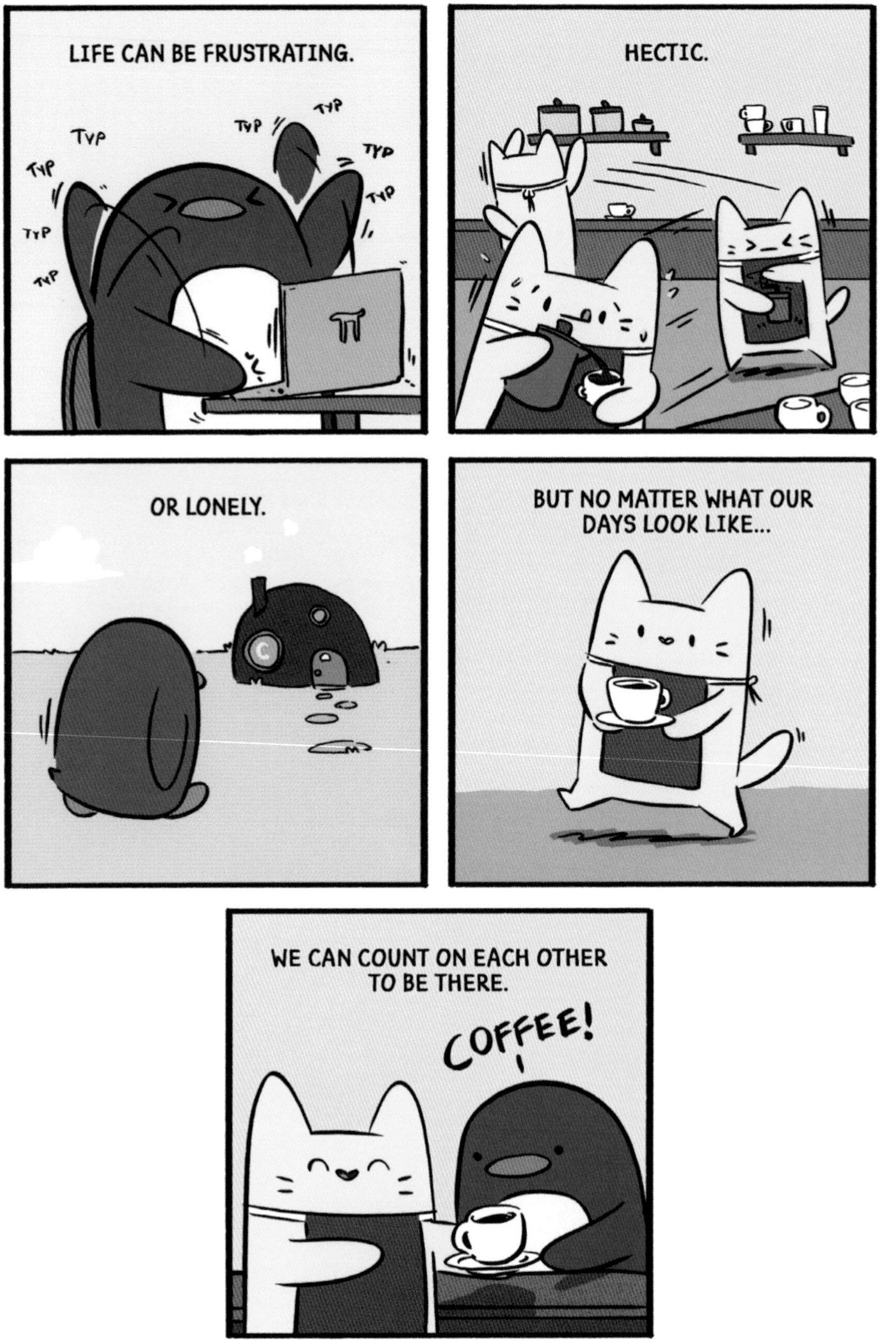
LIFE CAN BE FRUSTRATING.
TYP TYP TYP TYP TYP TYP TYP TYP
HECTIC.
OR LONELY.
BUT NO MATTER WHAT OUR DAYS LOOK LIKE...
WE CAN COUNT ON EACH OTHER TO BE THERE.
COFFEE!

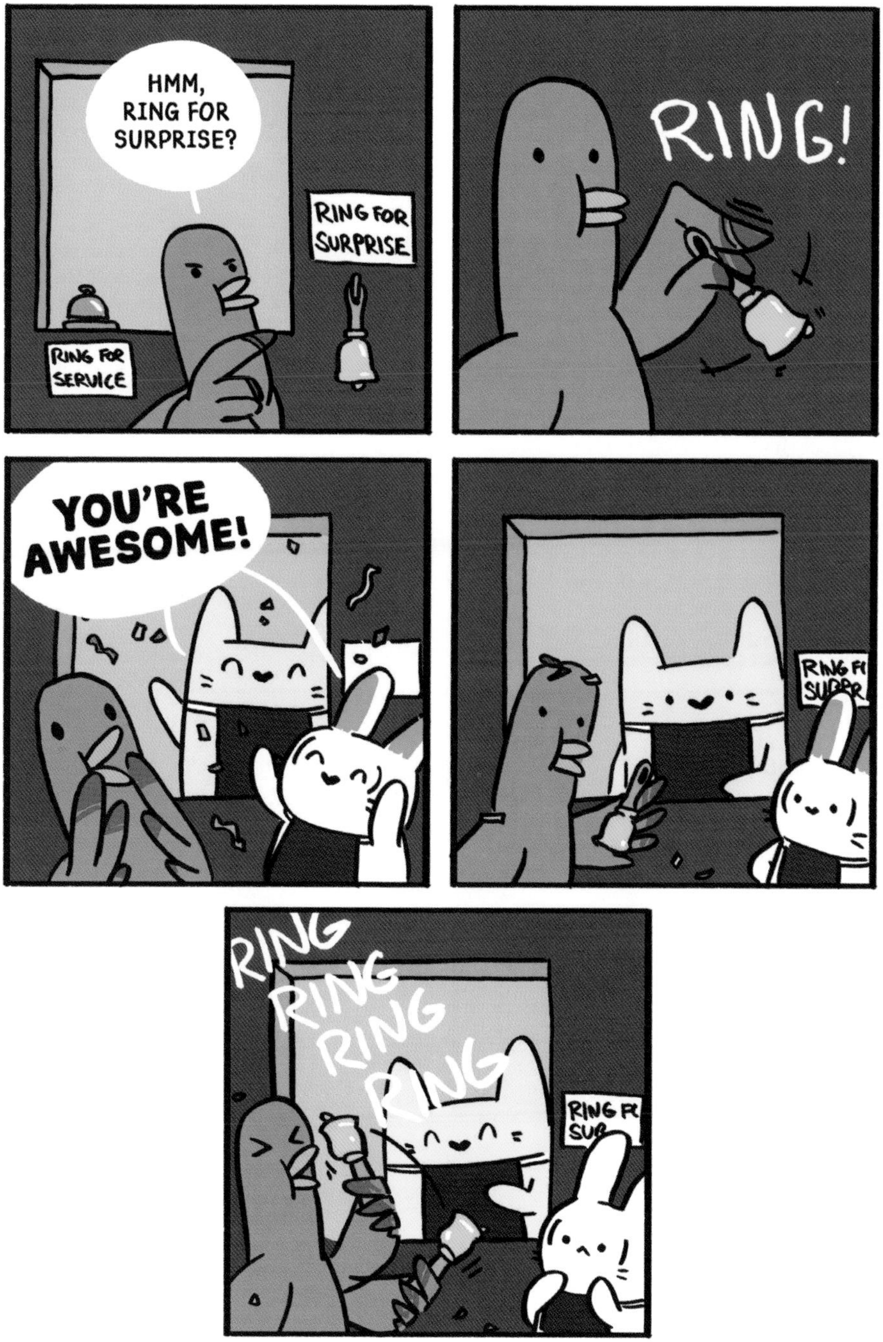
HMM, RING FOR SURPRISE?
RING FOR SURPRISE
RING FOR SERVICE
RING!
YOU'RE AWESOME!
RING RING RING RING

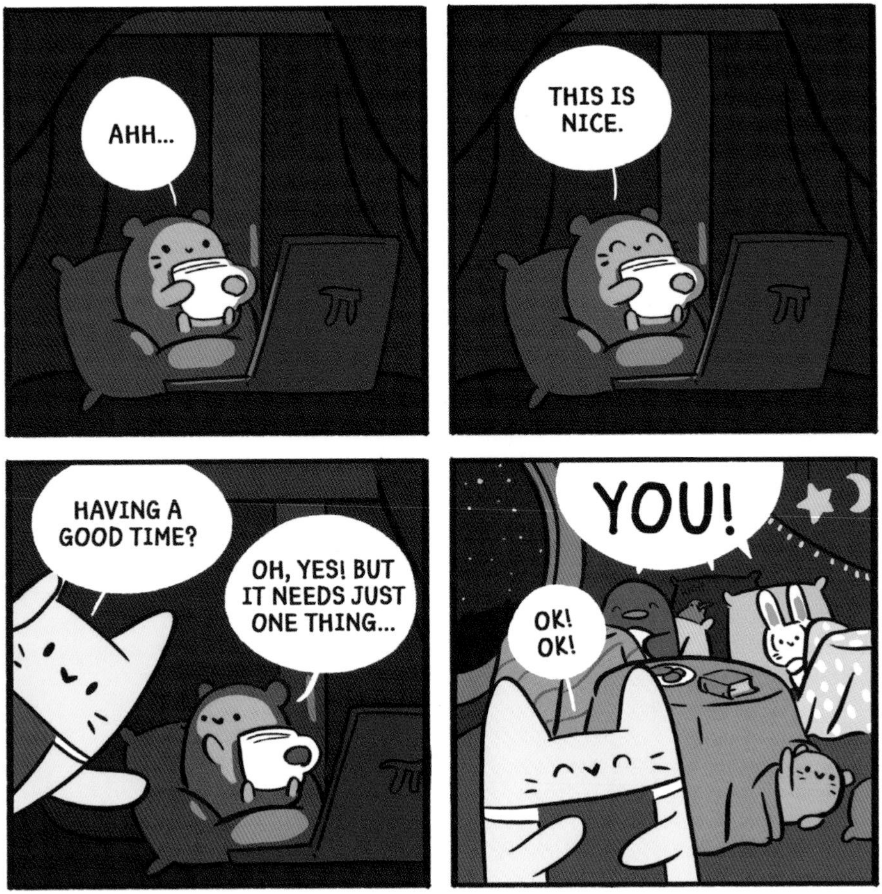
AHH...
THIS IS NICE.
HAVING A GOOD TIME?
OH, YES! BUT IT NEEDS JUST ONE THING...
YOU!
OK! OK!

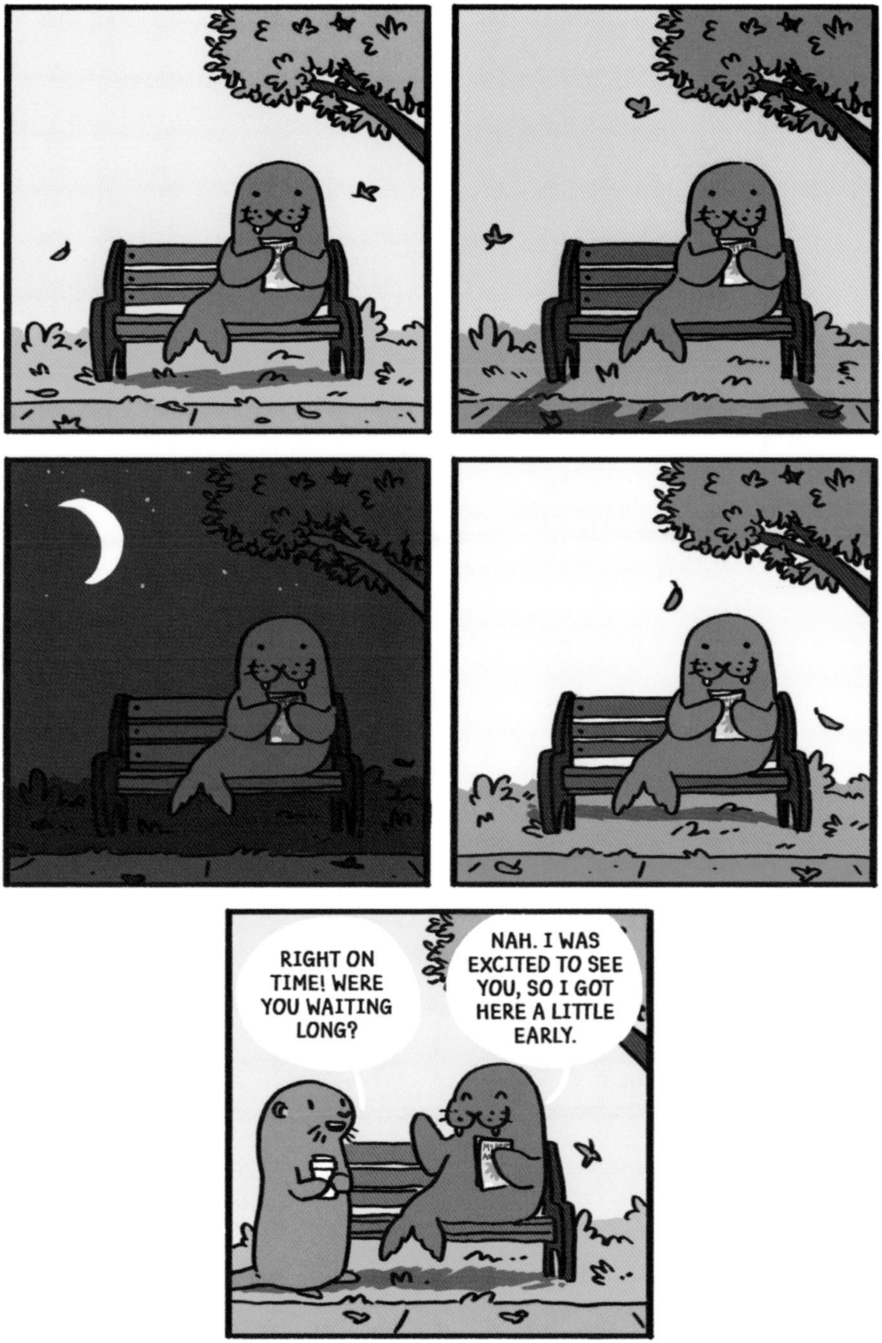
RIGHT ON TIME! WERE YOU WAITING LONG?
NAH. I WAS EXCITED TO SEE YOU, SO I GOT HERE A LITTLE EARLY.

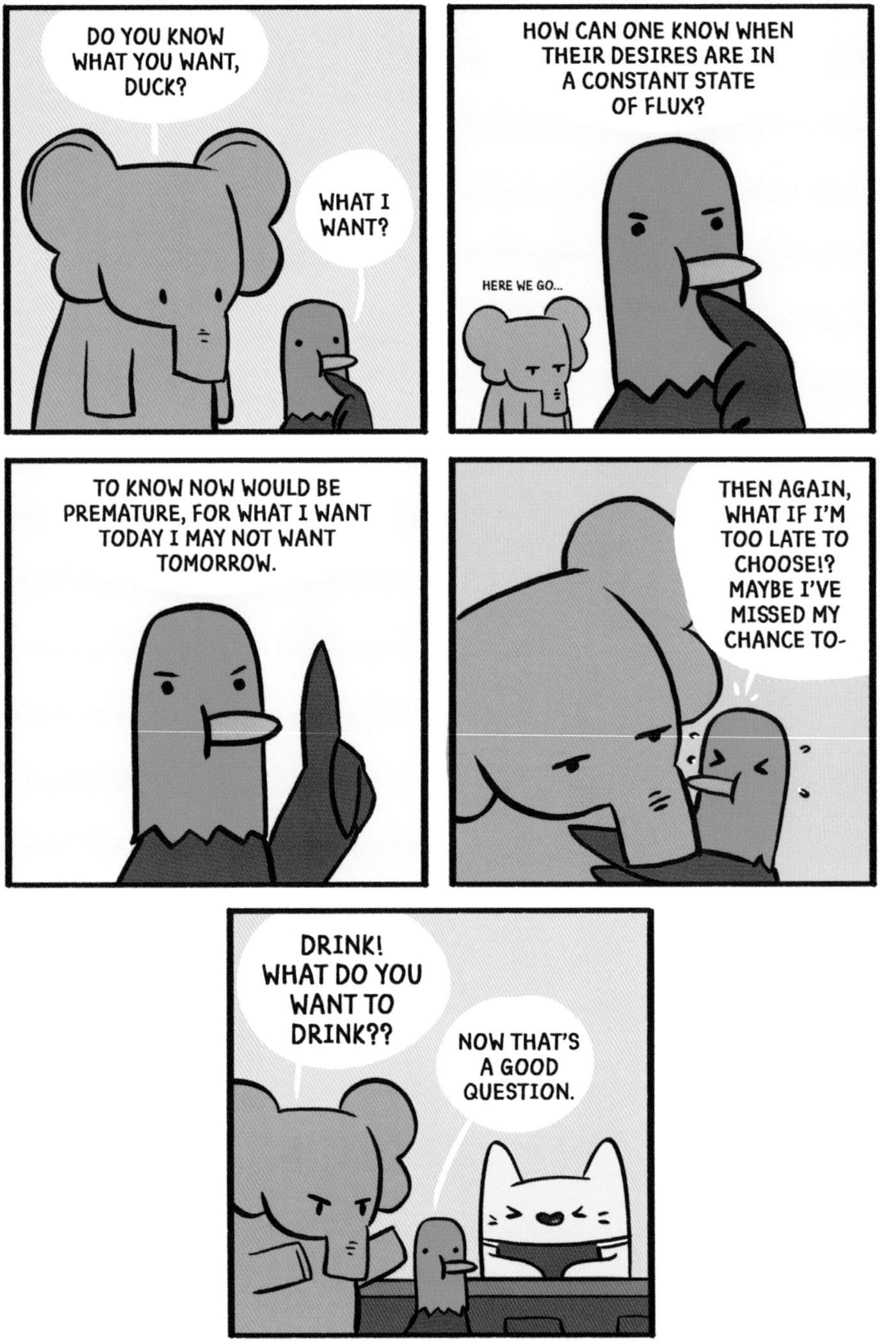
DO YOU KNOW WHAT YOU WANT, DUCK?
WHAT I WANT?
HOW CAN ONE KNOW WHEN THEIR DESIRES ARE IN A CONSTANT STATE OF FLUX?
HERE WE GO...
TO KNOW NOW WOULD BE PREMATURE, FOR WHAT I WANT TODAY I MAY NOT WANT TOMORROW.
THEN AGAIN, WHAT IF I'M TOO LATE TO CHOOSE!? MAYBE I'VE MISSED MY CHANCE TO-
DRINK! WHAT DO YOU WANT TO DRINK??
NOW THAT'S A GOOD QUESTION.

FALL LOOKS

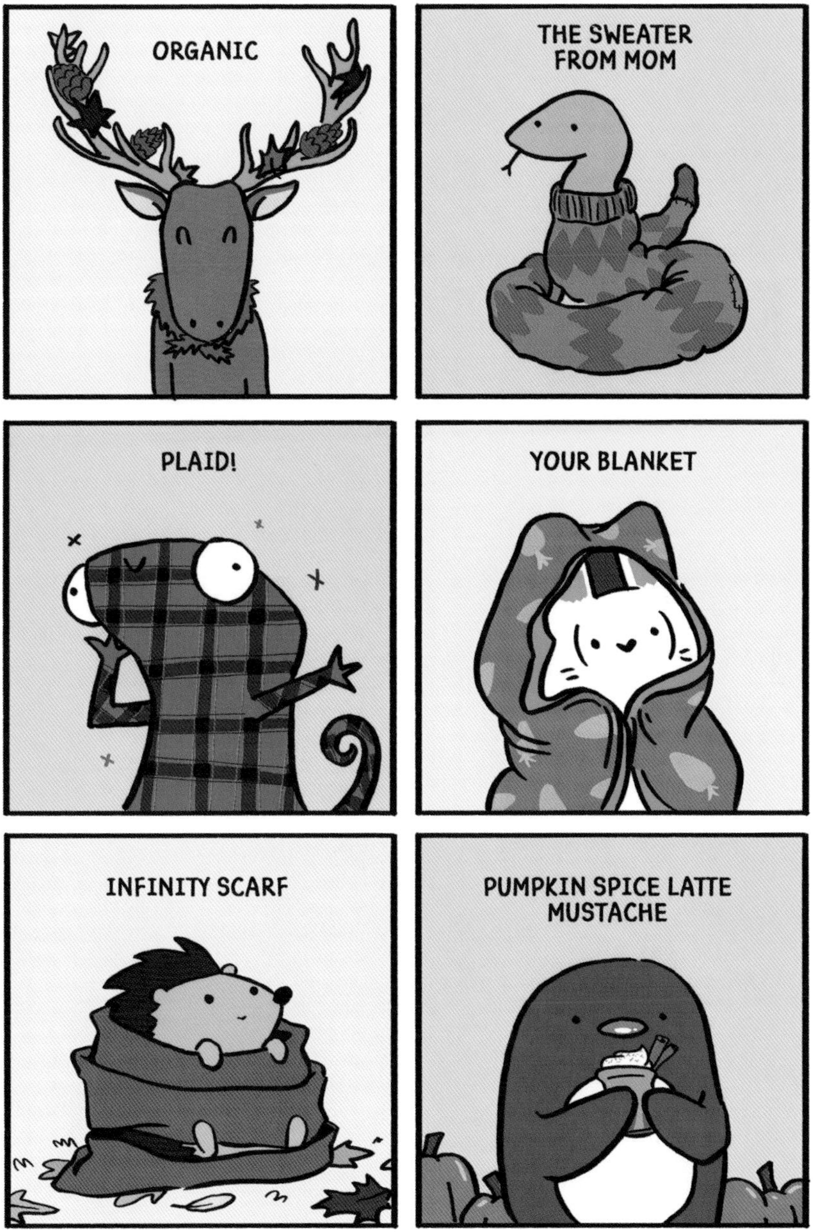
ORGANIC
THE SWEATER FROM MOM
PLAID!
YOUR BLANKET
INFINITY SCARF
PUMPKIN SPICE LATTE MUSTACHE

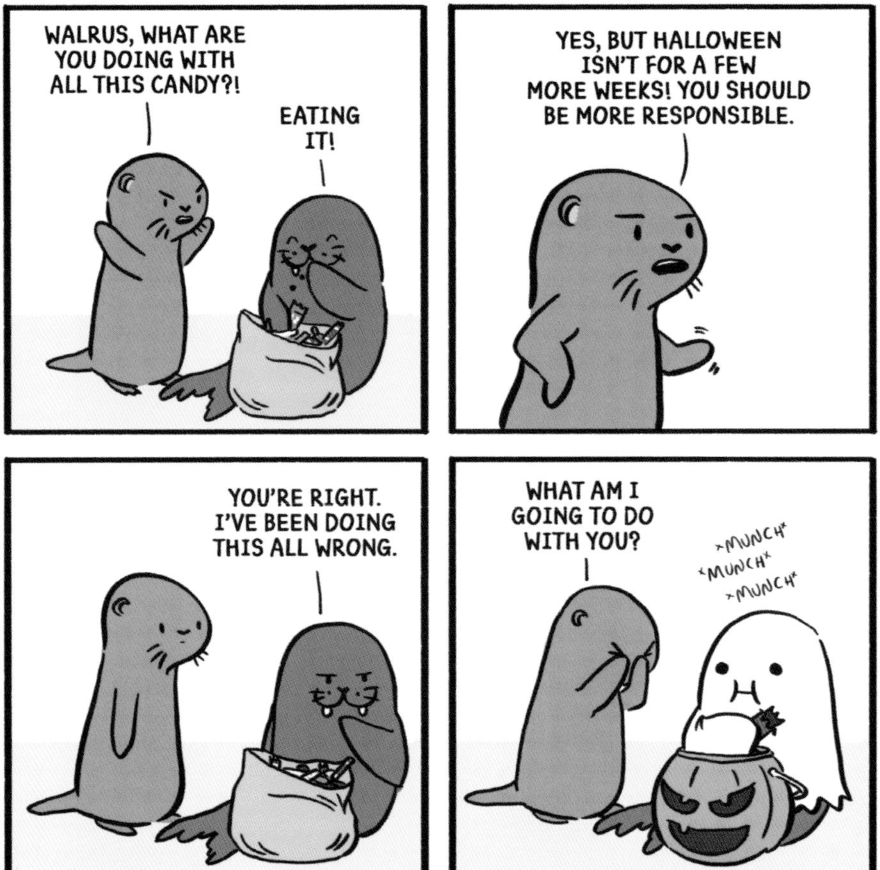
WALRUS, WHAT ARE YOU DOING WITH ALL THIS CANDY?!
EATING IT!
YES, BUT HALLOWEEN ISN'T FOR A FEW MORE WEEKS! YOU SHOULD BE MORE RESPONSIBLE.
YOU'RE RIGHT. I'VE BEEN DOING THIS ALL WRONG.
WHAT AM I GOING TO DO WITH YOU?
MUNCH
MUNCH
MUNCH

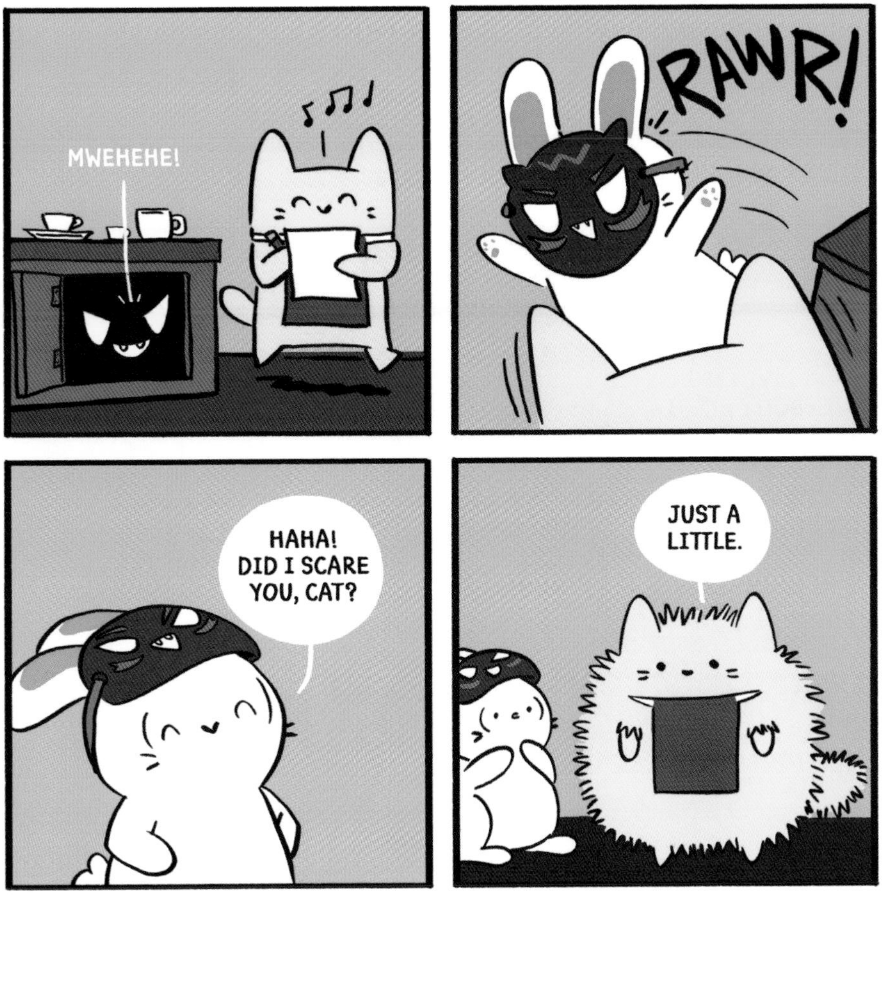
MWEHEHE!
RAWR!
HAHA! DID I SCARE YOU, CAT?
JUST A LITTLE.

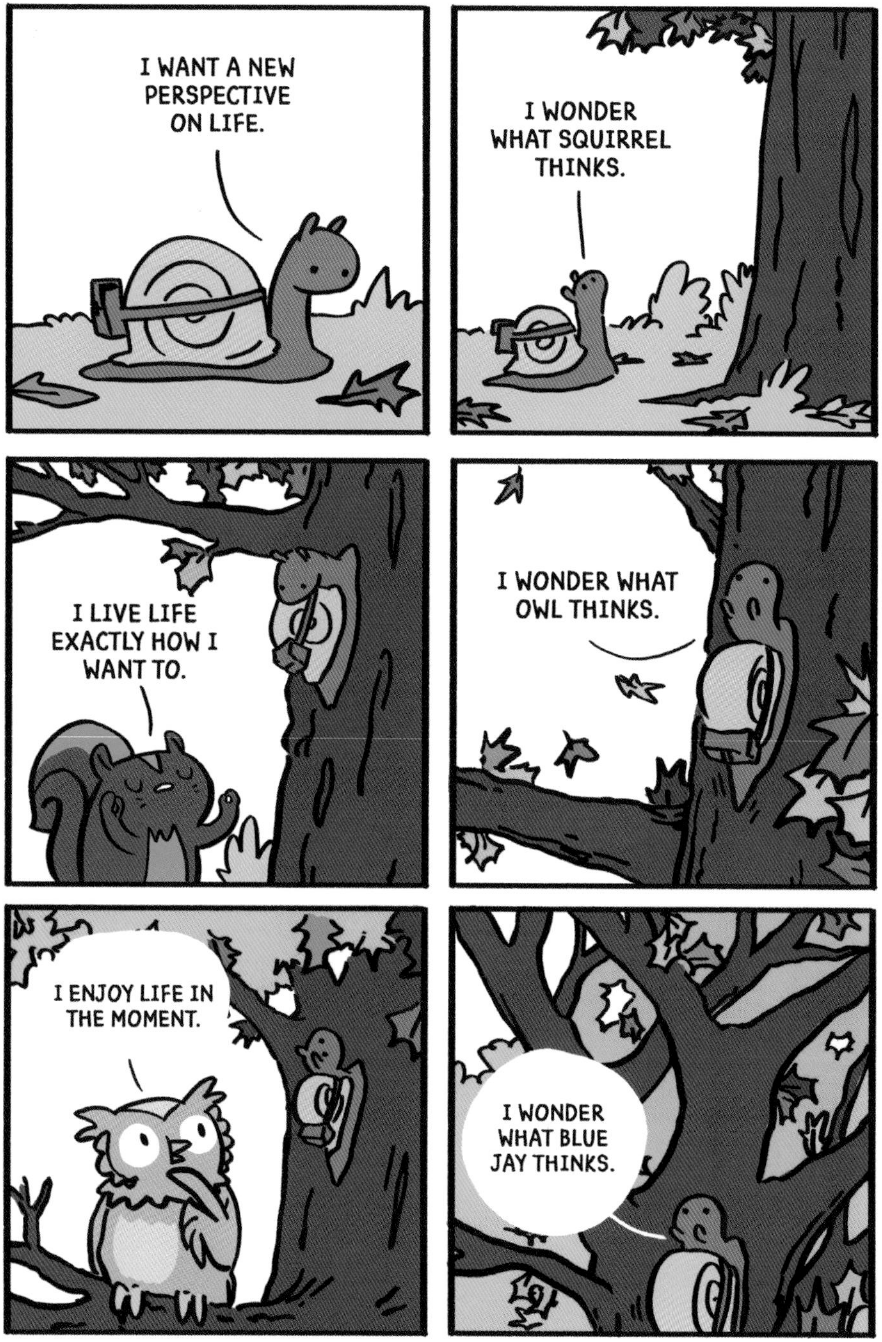
I WANT A NEW PERSPECTIVE ON LIFE.
I WONDER WHAT SQUIRREL THINKS.
I LIVE LIFE EXACTLY HOW I WANT TO.
I WONDER WHAT OWL THINKS.
I ENJOY LIFE IN THE MOMENT.
I WONDER WHAT BLUE JAY THINKS.

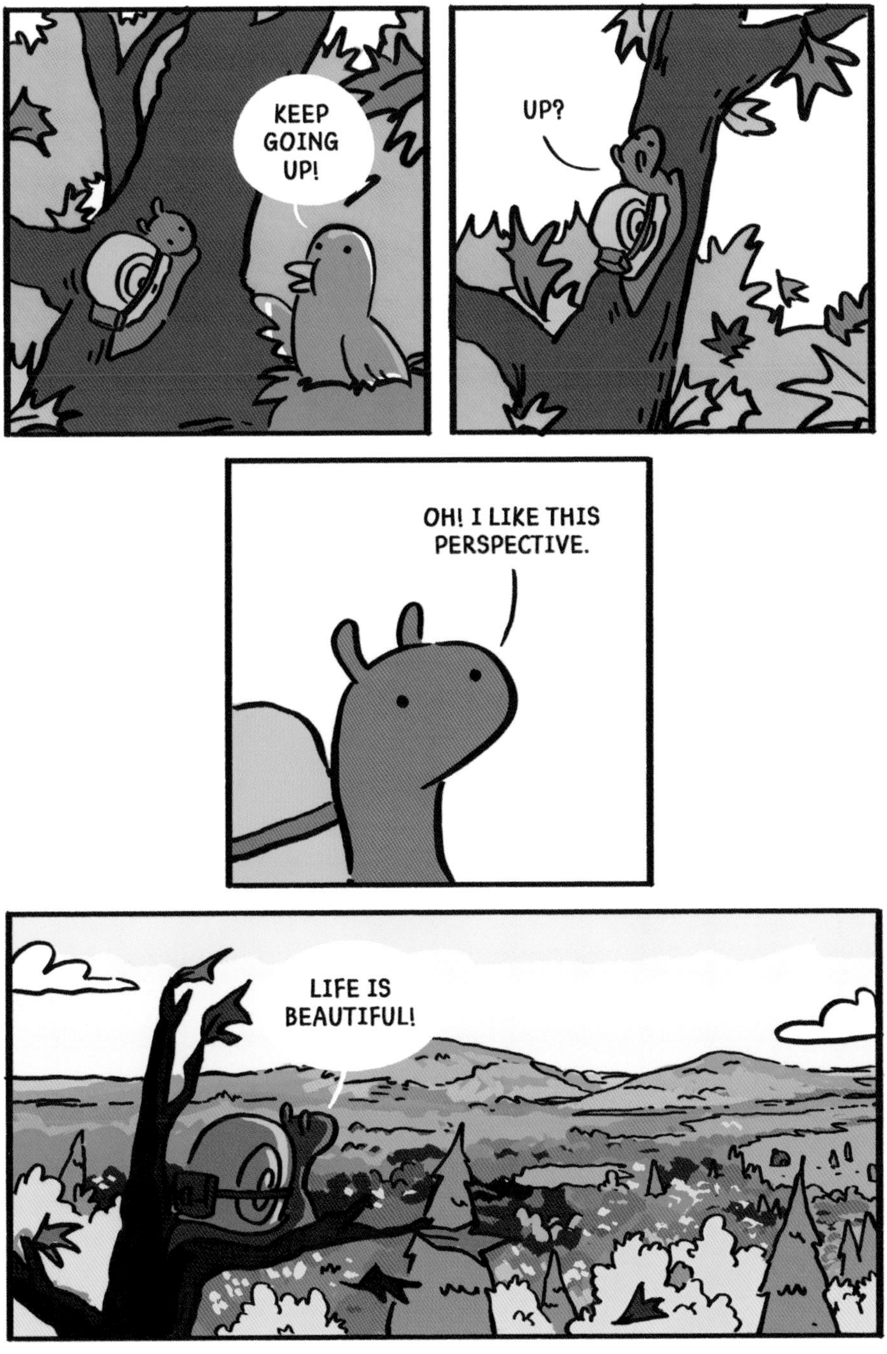

KEEP GOING UP!
UP?
OH! I LIKE THIS PERSPECTIVE.
LIFE IS BEAUTIFUL!

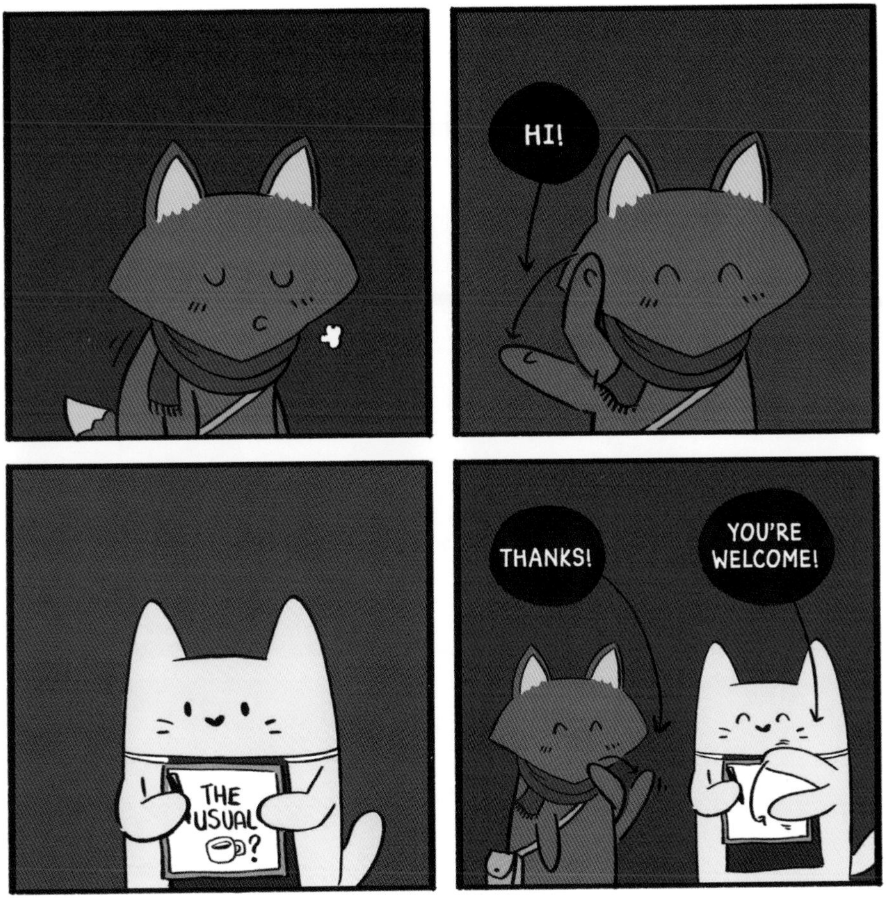
HI!
THE USUAL ☕?
THANKS!
YOU'RE WELCOME!

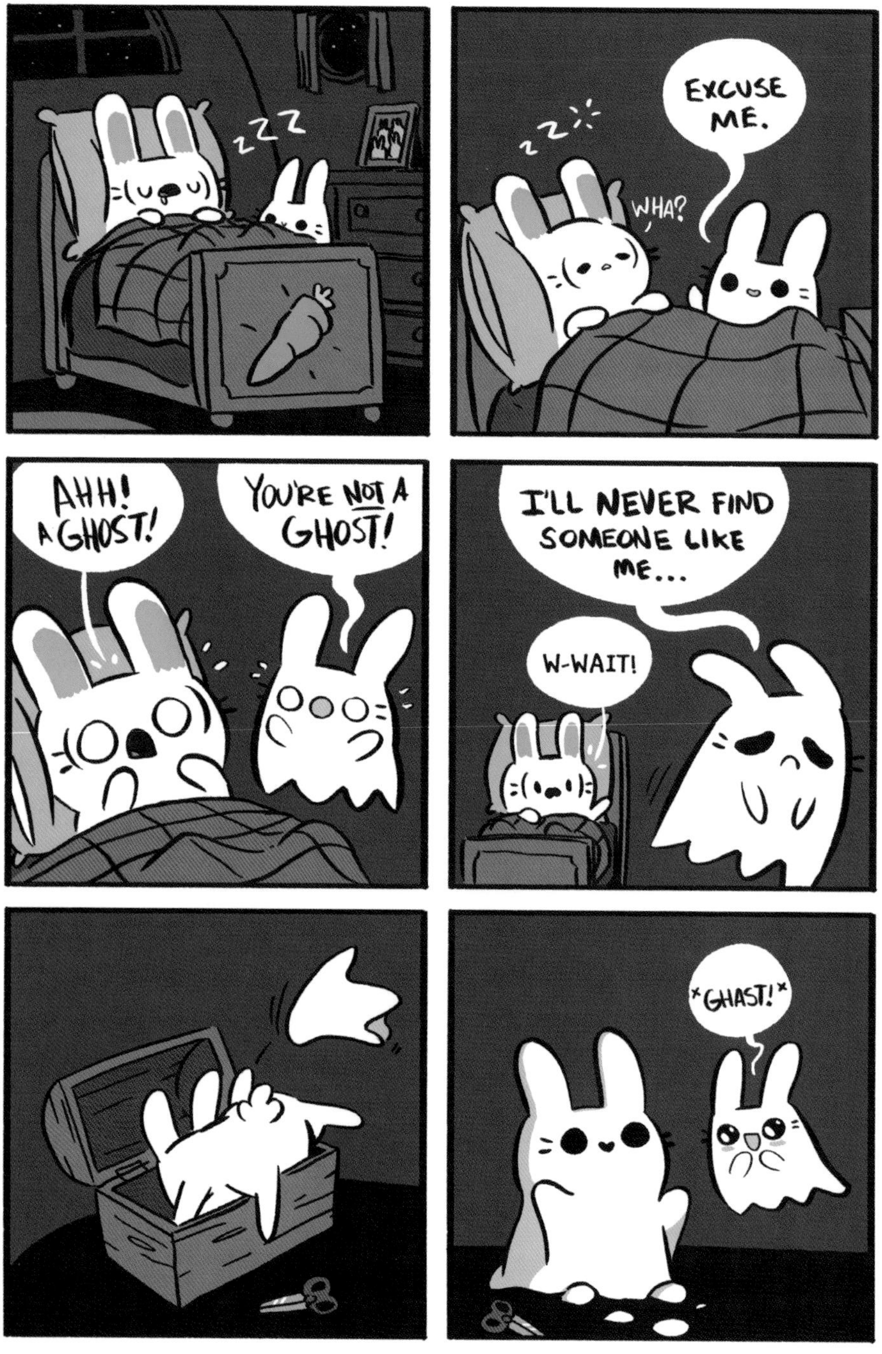

Z Z Z
Z Z
EXCUSE ME.
WHA?
AHH! A GHOST!
YOU'RE NOT A GHOST!
I'LL NEVER FIND SOMEONE LIKE ME...
W-WAIT!
GHAST!

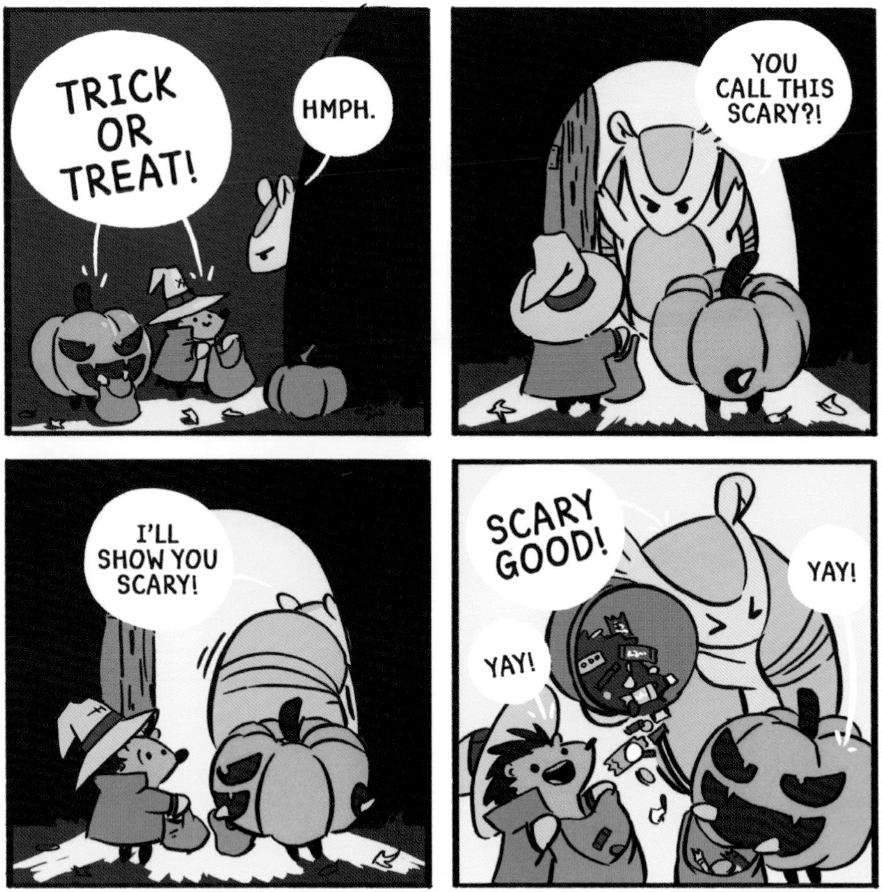
TRICK OR TREAT!
HMPH.
YOU CALL THIS SCARY?!
I'LL SHOW YOU SCARY!
SCARY GOOD!
YAY!
YAY!

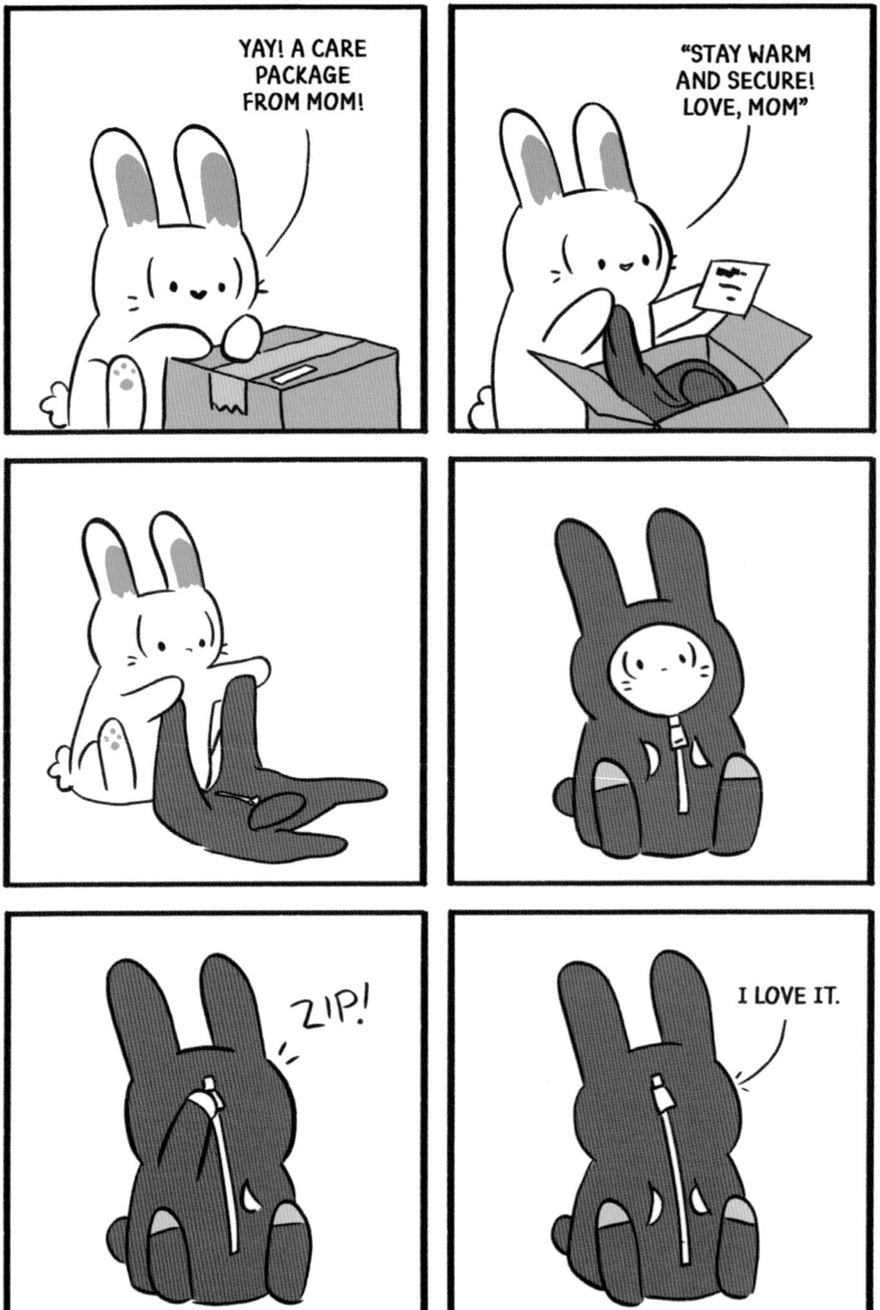
YAY! A CARE PACKAGE FROM MOM!
"STAY WARM AND SECURE! LOVE, MOM"
ZIP!
I LOVE IT.

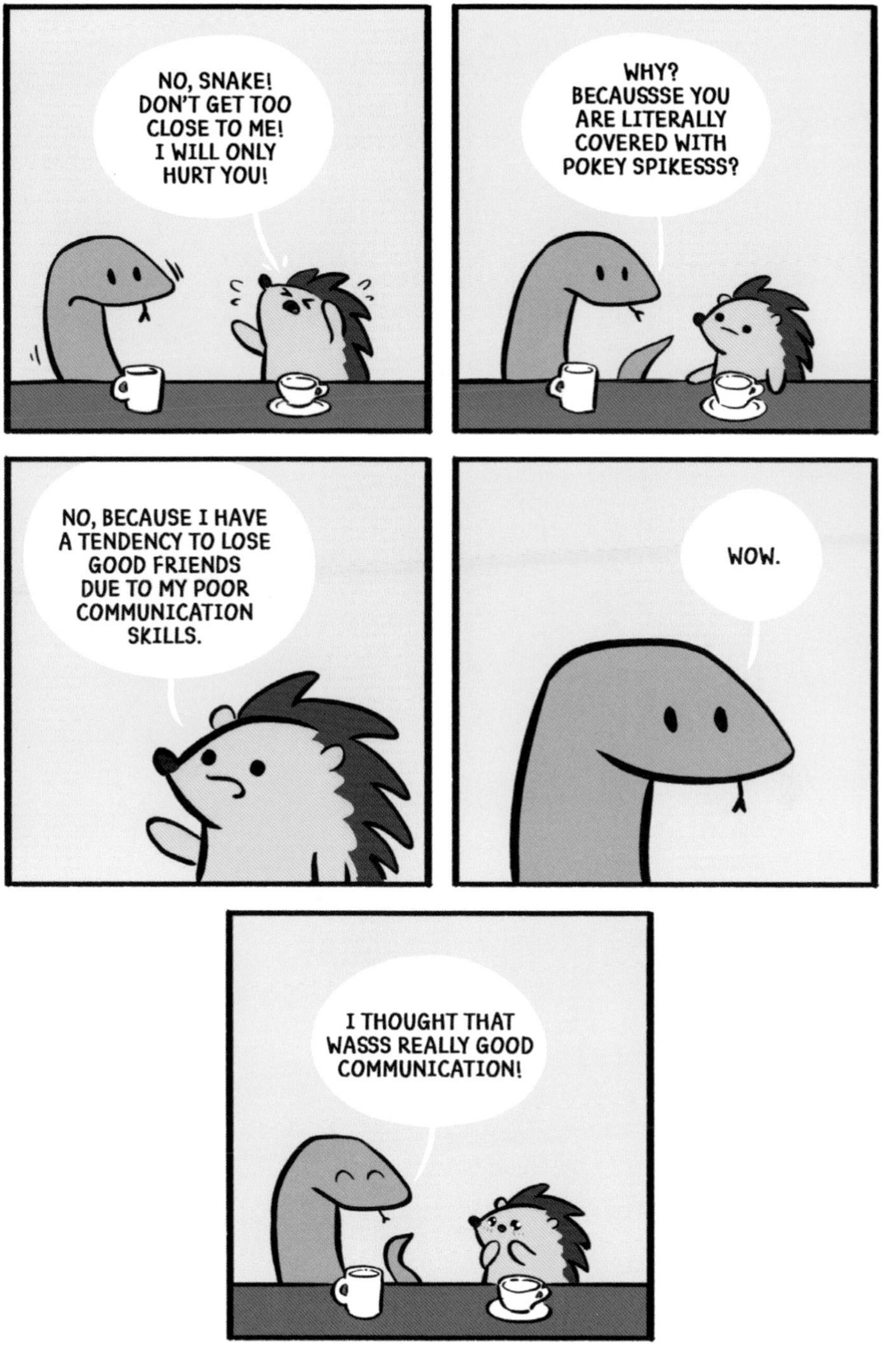
NO, SNAKE! DON'T GET TOO CLOSE TO ME! I WILL ONLY HURT YOU!
WHY? BECAUSSSE YOU ARE LITERALLY COVERED WITH POKEY SPIKESSS?
NO, BECAUSE I HAVE A TENDENCY TO LOSE GOOD FRIENDS DUE TO MY POOR COMMUNICATION SKILLS.
WOW.
I THOUGHT THAT WASSS REALLY GOOD COMMUNICATION!

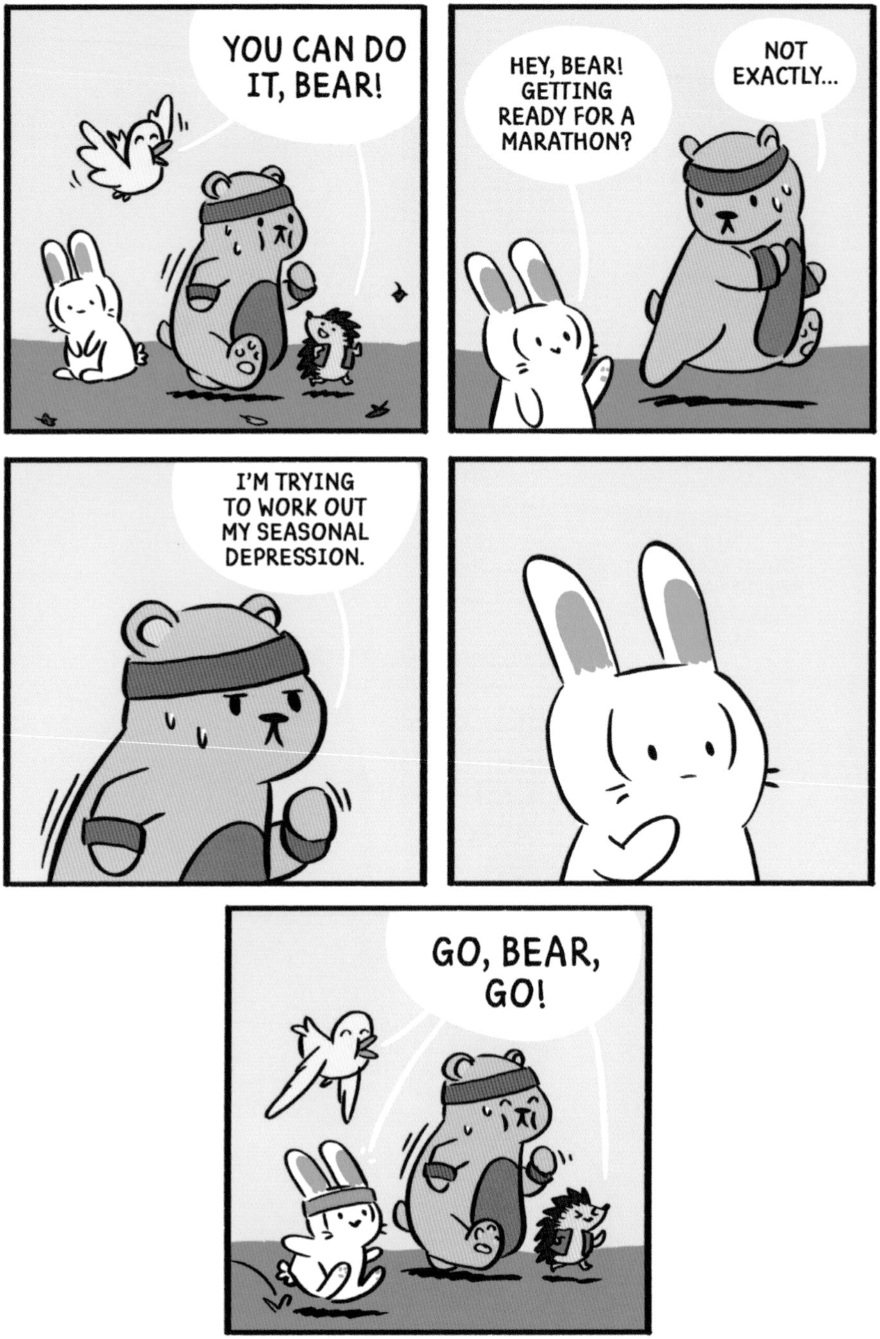
YOU CAN DO IT, BEAR!
HEY, BEAR! GETTING READY FOR A MARATHON?
NOT EXACTLY...
I'M TRYING TO WORK OUT MY SEASONAL DEPRESSION.
GO, BEAR, GO!

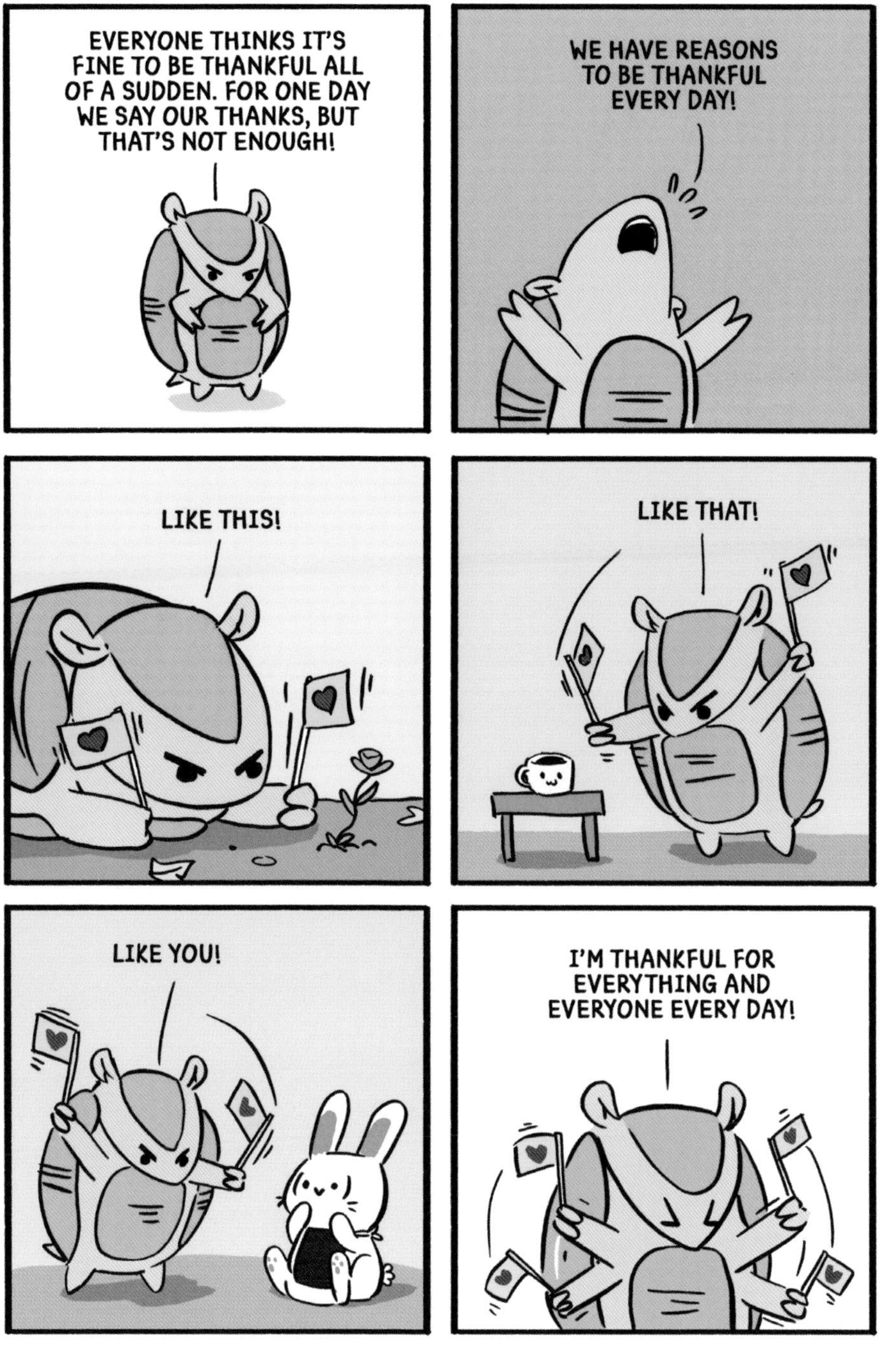
EVERYONE THINKS IT'S FINE TO BE THANKFUL ALL OF A SUDDEN. FOR ONE DAY WE SAY OUR THANKS, BUT THAT'S NOT ENOUGH!
WE HAVE REASONS TO BE THANKFUL EVERY DAY!
LIKE THIS!
LIKE THAT!
LIKE YOU!
I'M THANKFUL FOR EVERYTHING AND EVERYONE EVERY DAY!

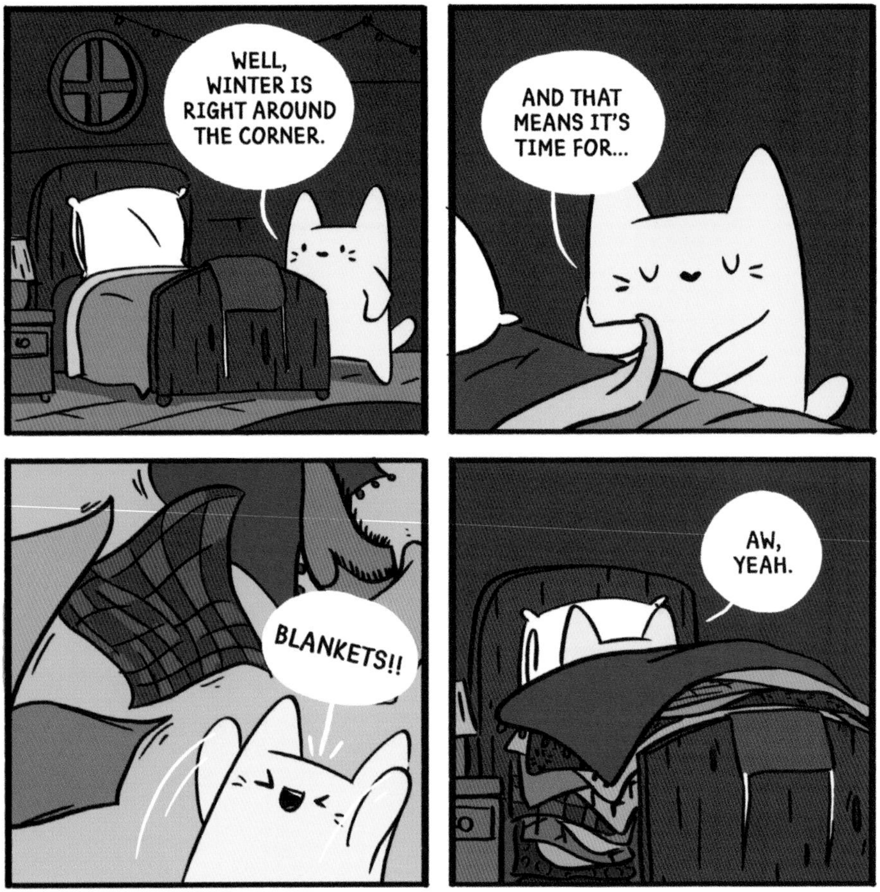
WELL, WINTER IS RIGHT AROUND THE CORNER.
AND THAT MEANS IT'S TIME FOR...
BLANKETS!!
AW, YEAH.

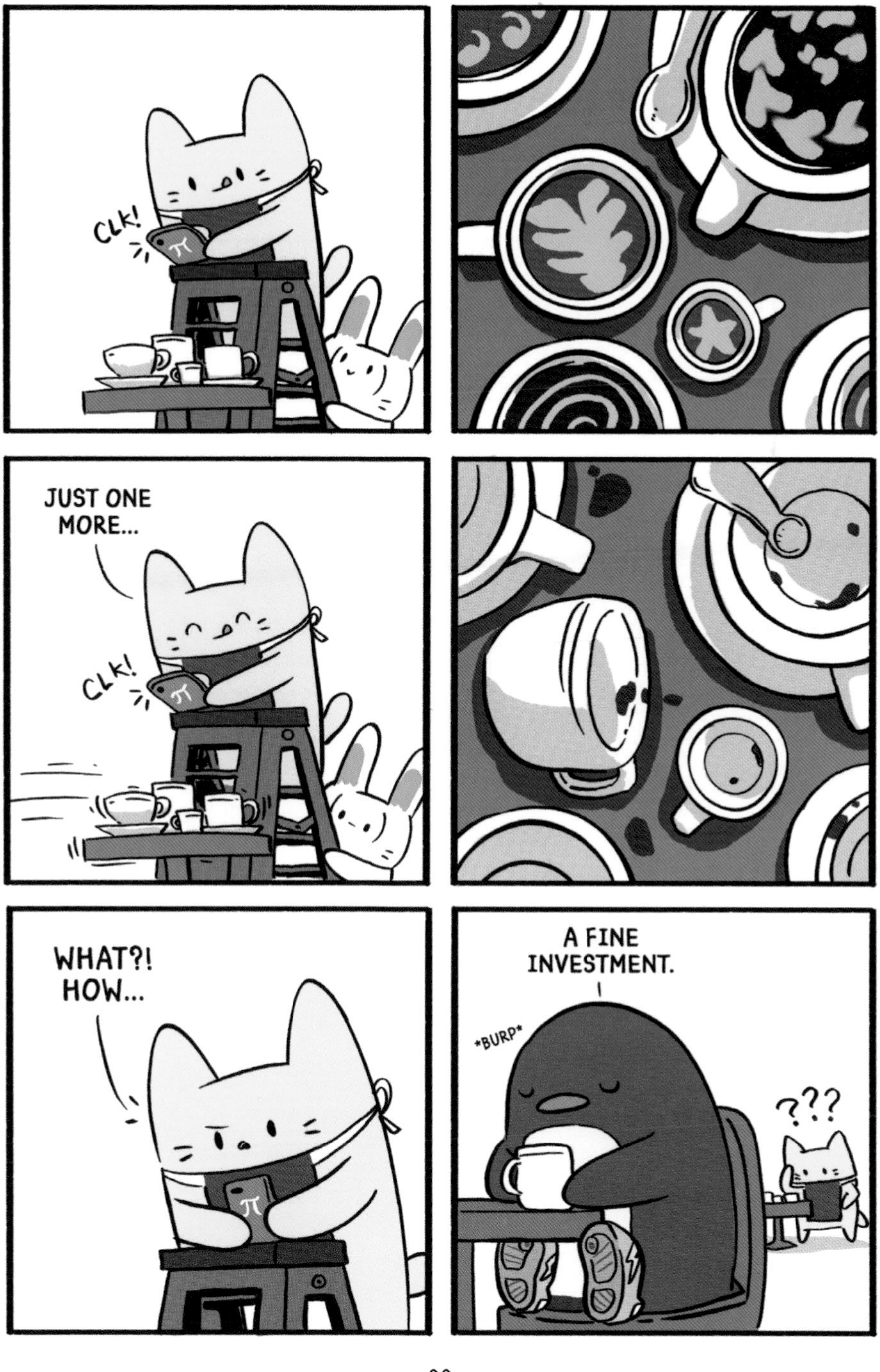
CLK!
JUST ONE MORE...
CLK!
WHAT?! HOW...
A FINE INVESTMENT.
BURP
???

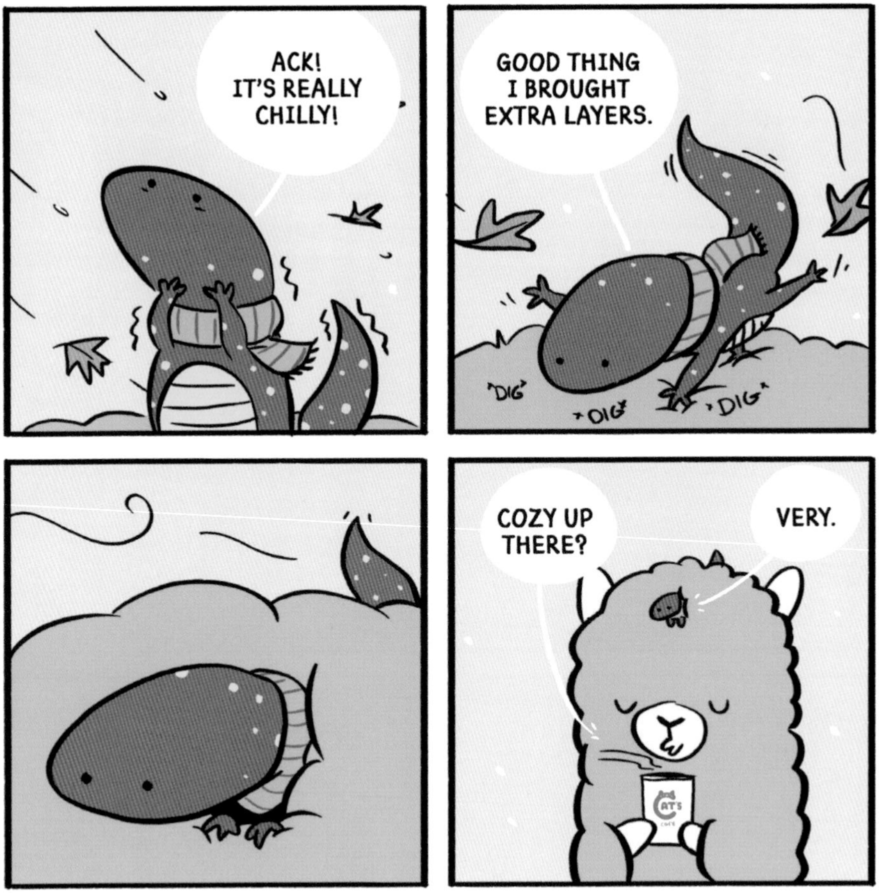
ACK! IT'S REALLY CHILLY!
GOOD THING I BROUGHT EXTRA LAYERS.
DIG
DIG
DIG
COZY UP THERE?
VERY.

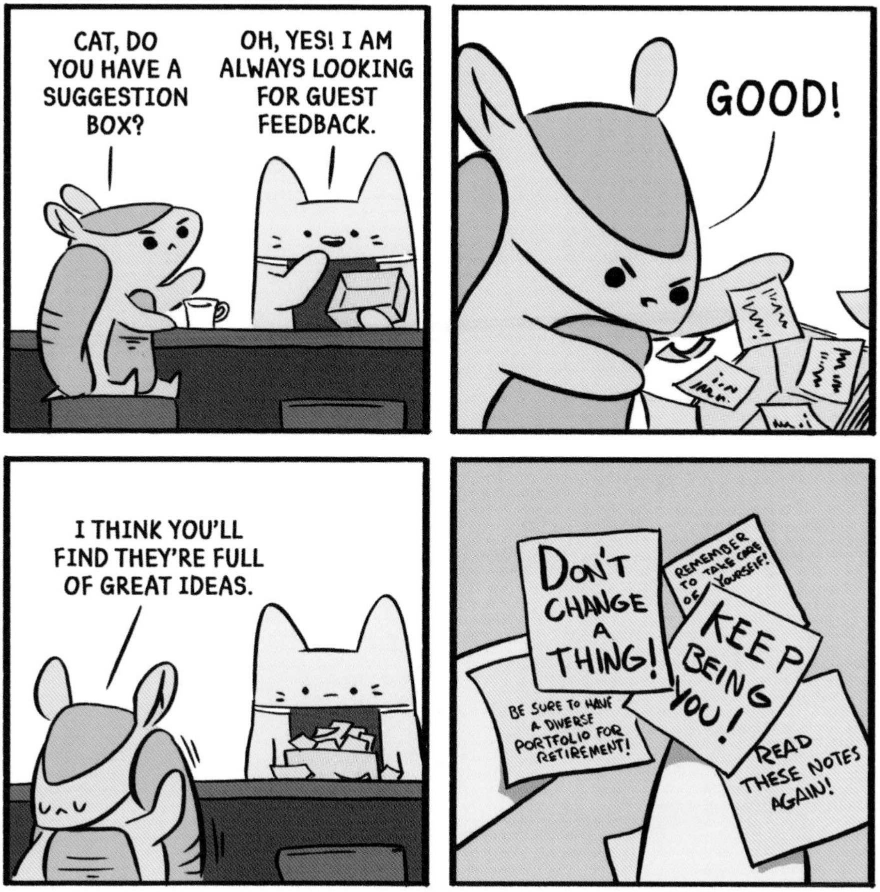
CAT, DO YOU HAVE A SUGGESTION BOX?
OH, YES! I AM ALWAYS LOOKING FOR GUEST FEEDBACK.
GOOD!
I THINK YOU'LL FIND THEY'RE FULL OF GREAT IDEAS.
DON'T CHANGE A THING!
REMEMBER TO TAKE CARE OF YOURSELF!
KEEP BEING YOU!
BE SURE TO HAVE A DIVERSE PORTFOLIO FOR RETIREMENT!
READ THESE NOTES AGAIN!

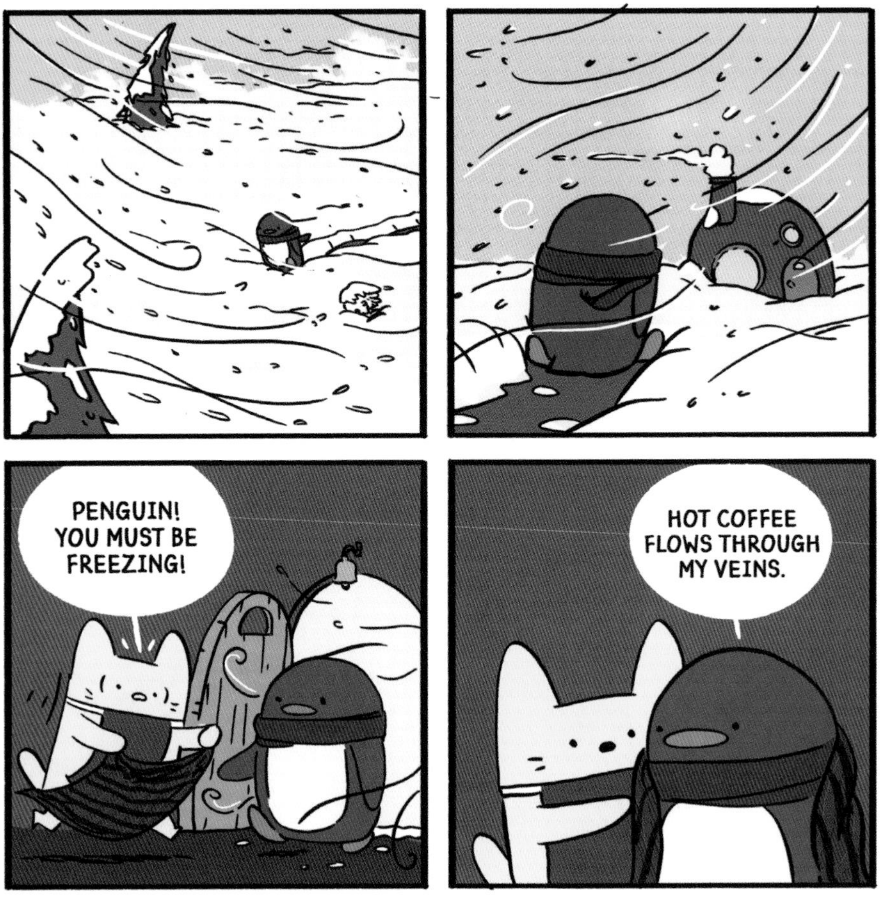
PENGUIN! YOU MUST BE FREEZING!
HOT COFFEE FLOWS THROUGH MY VEINS.

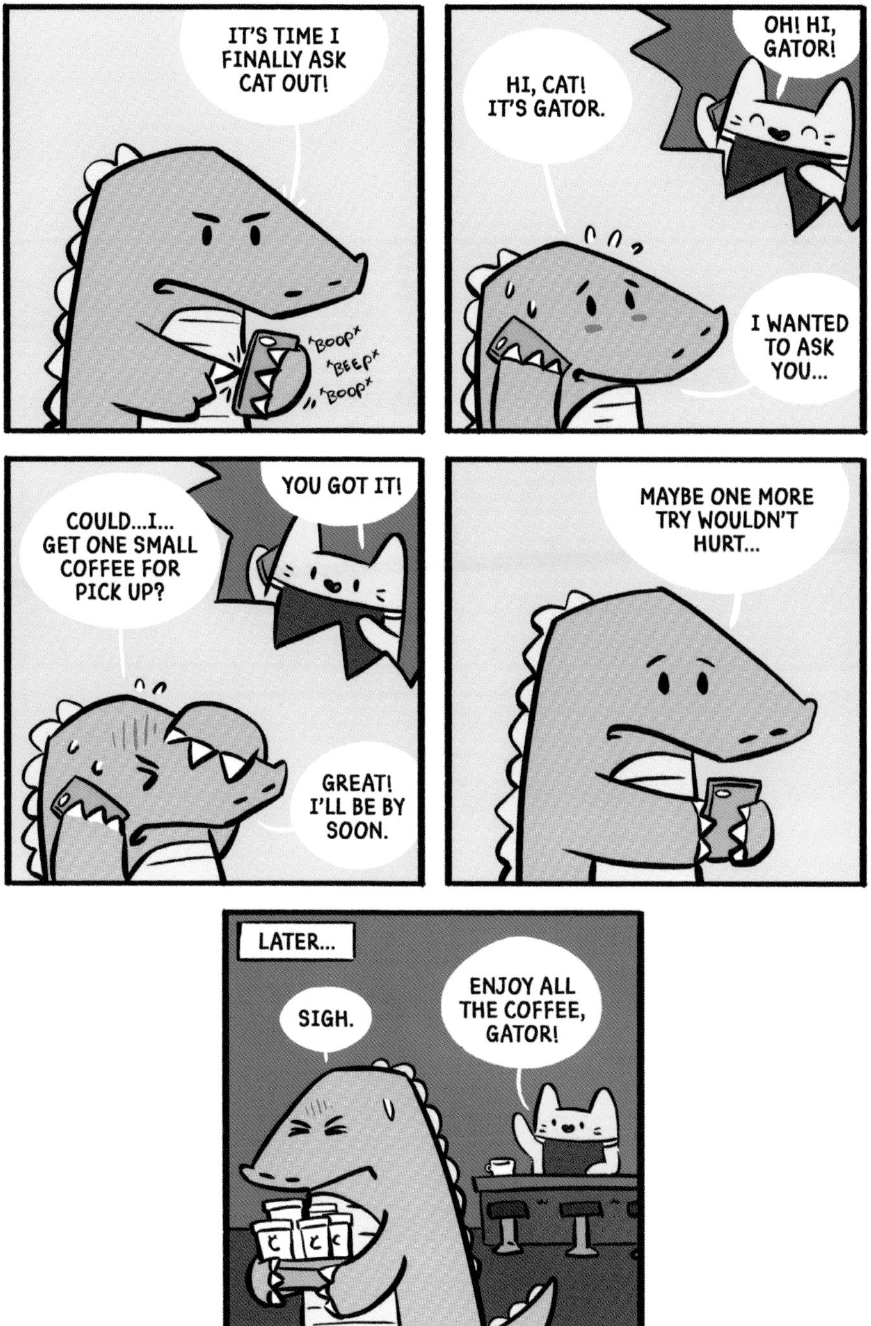
IT'S TIME I FINALLY ASK CAT OUT!
BOOP *BEEP* *BOOP*
HI, CAT! IT'S GATOR.
OH! HI, GATOR!
I WANTED TO ASK YOU...
COULD...I... GET ONE SMALL COFFEE FOR PICK UP?
YOU GOT IT!
GREAT! I'LL BE BY SOON.
MAYBE ONE MORE TRY WOULDN'T HURT...
LATER...
SIGH.
ENJOY ALL THE COFFEE, GATOR!

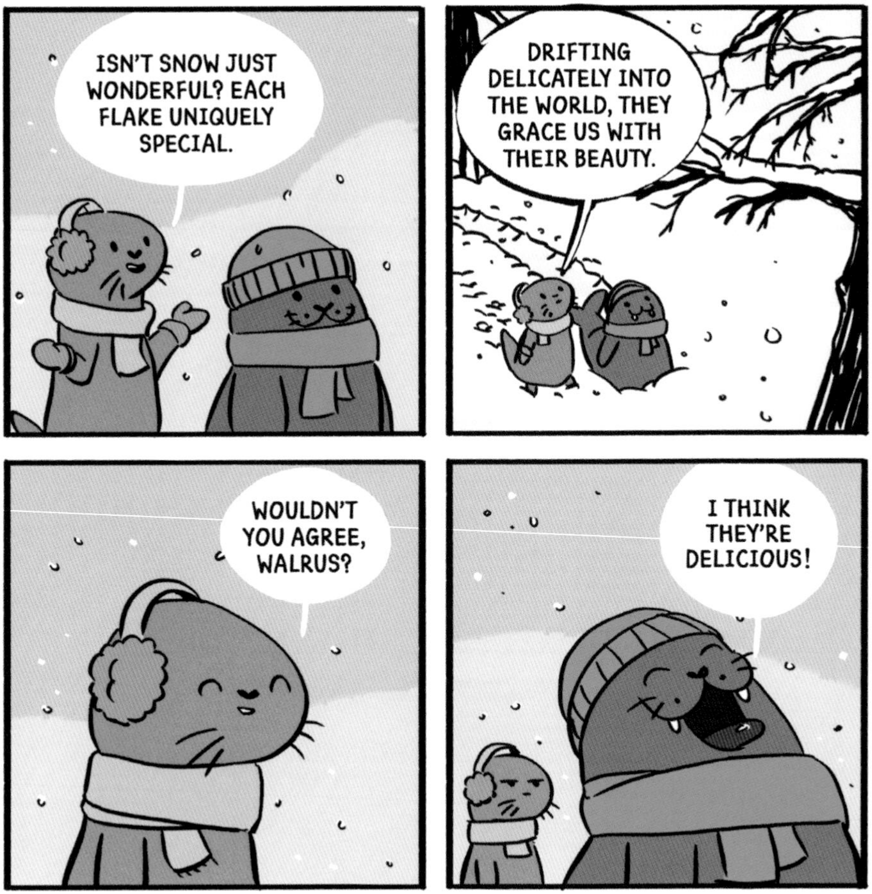
ISN'T SNOW JUST WONDERFUL? EACH FLAKE UNIQUELY SPECIAL.
DRIFTING DELICATELY INTO THE WORLD, THEY GRACE US WITH THEIR BEAUTY.
WOULDN'T YOU AGREE, WALRUS?
I THINK THEY'RE DELICIOUS!

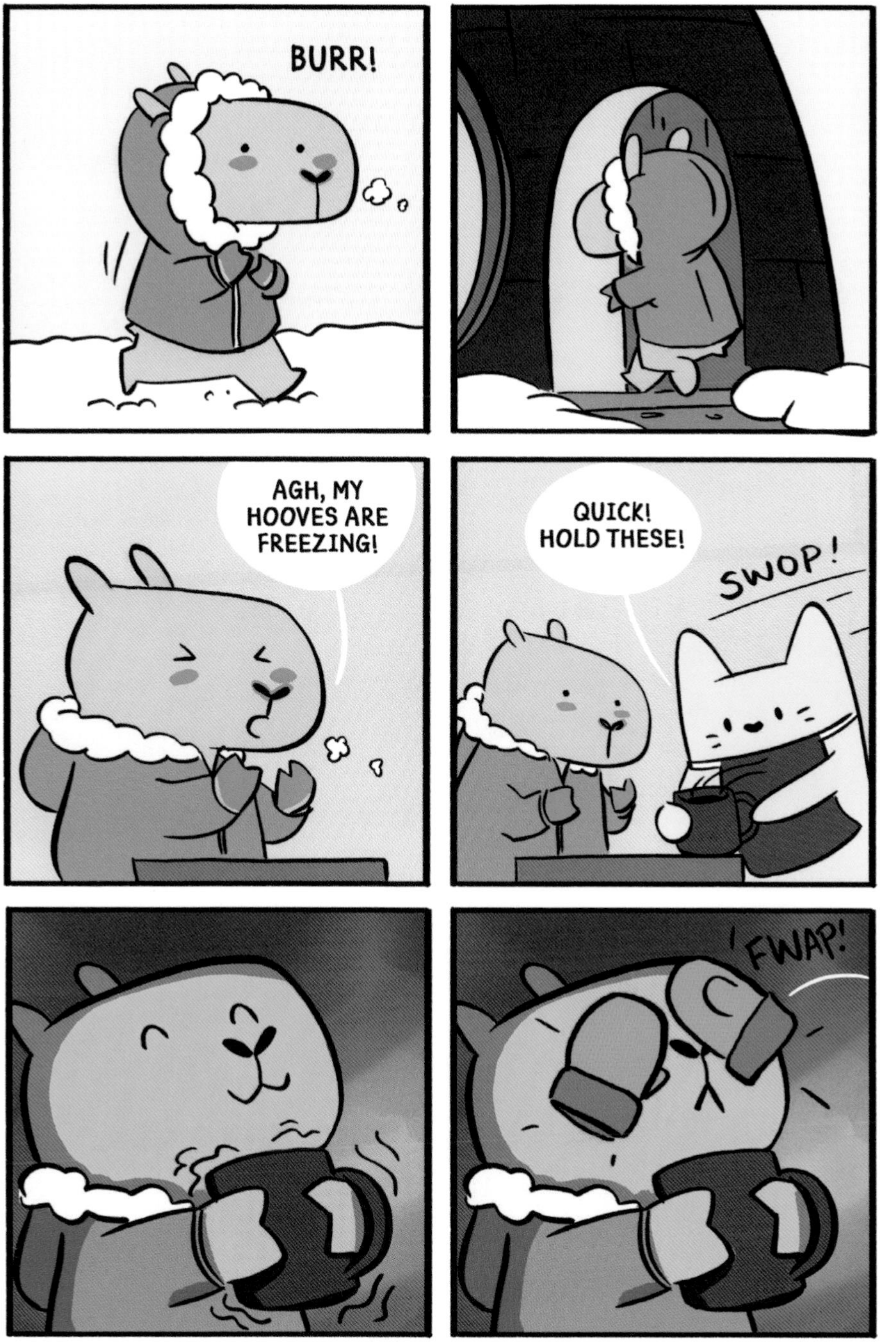
BURR!
AGH, MY HOOVES ARE FREEZING!
QUICK! HOLD THESE!
SWOP!
FWAP!

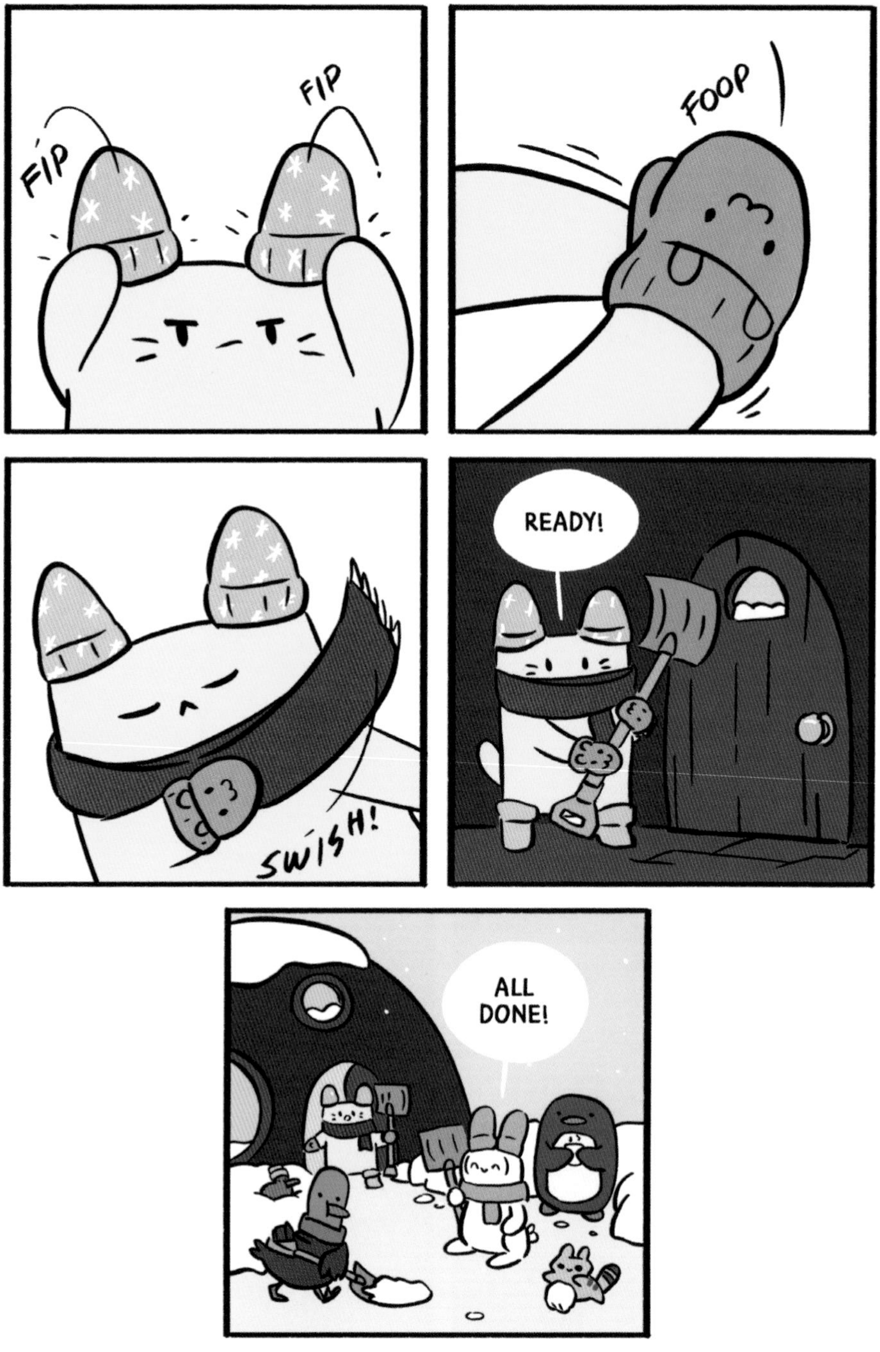
FIP
FIP
FOOP
SWISH!
READY!
ALL DONE!

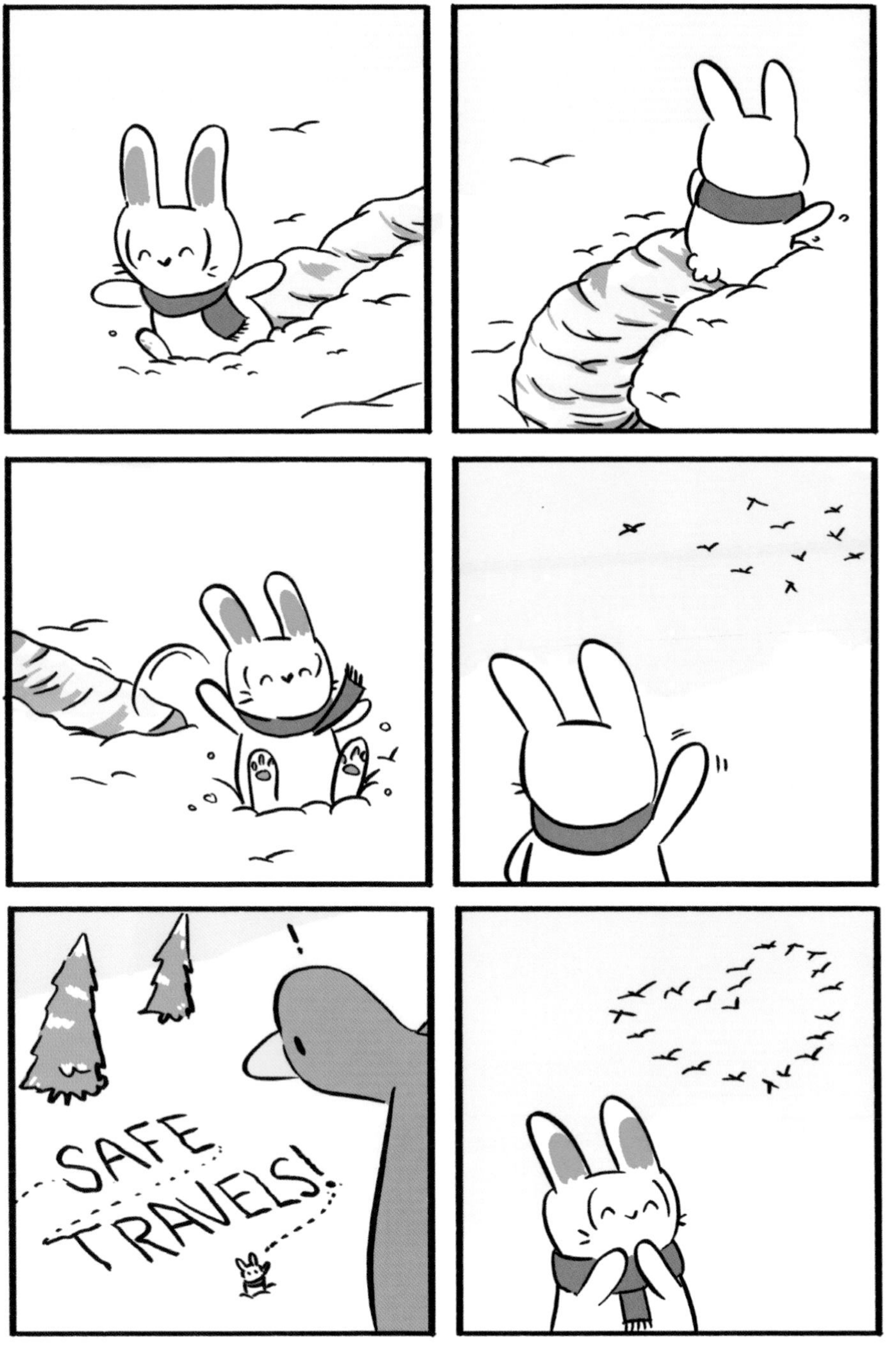
!
SAFE TRAVELS!

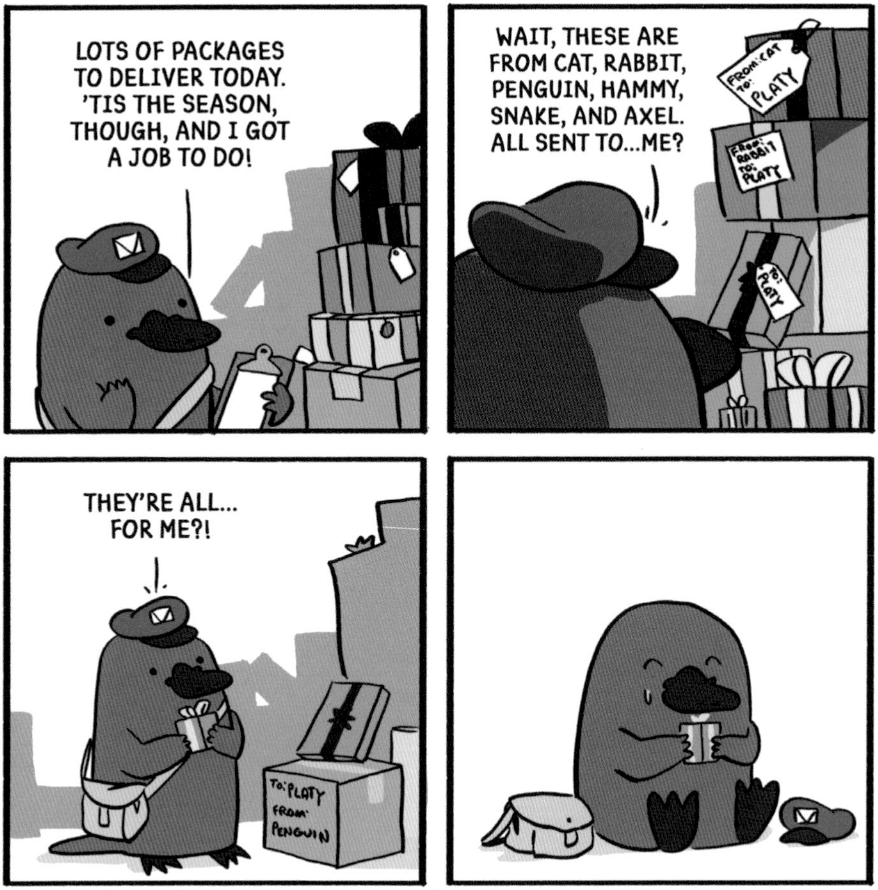
LOTS OF PACKAGES TO DELIVER TODAY. 'TIS THE SEASON, THOUGH, AND I GOT A JOB TO DO!
WAIT, THESE ARE FROM CAT, RABBIT, PENGUIN, HAMMY, SNAKE, AND AXEL. ALL SENT TO...ME?
FROM: CAT TO: PLATY
FROM: RABBIT TO: PLATY
TO: PLATY
THEY'RE ALL... FOR ME?!
TO: PLATY FROM: PENGUIN

HI! NICE TO MEET YOU!
NEW YEAR RESSSOLUTIONSSS
MAKE A NEW FRIEND
WORK OUT

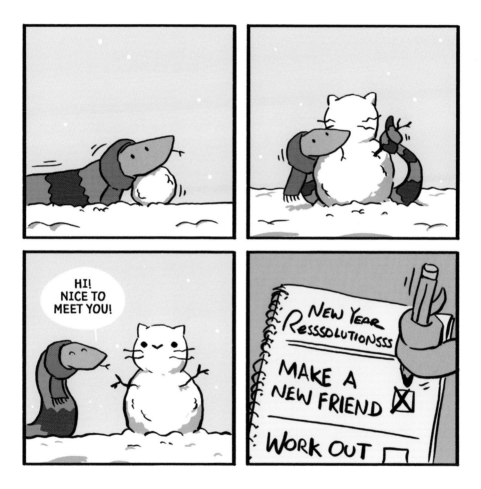

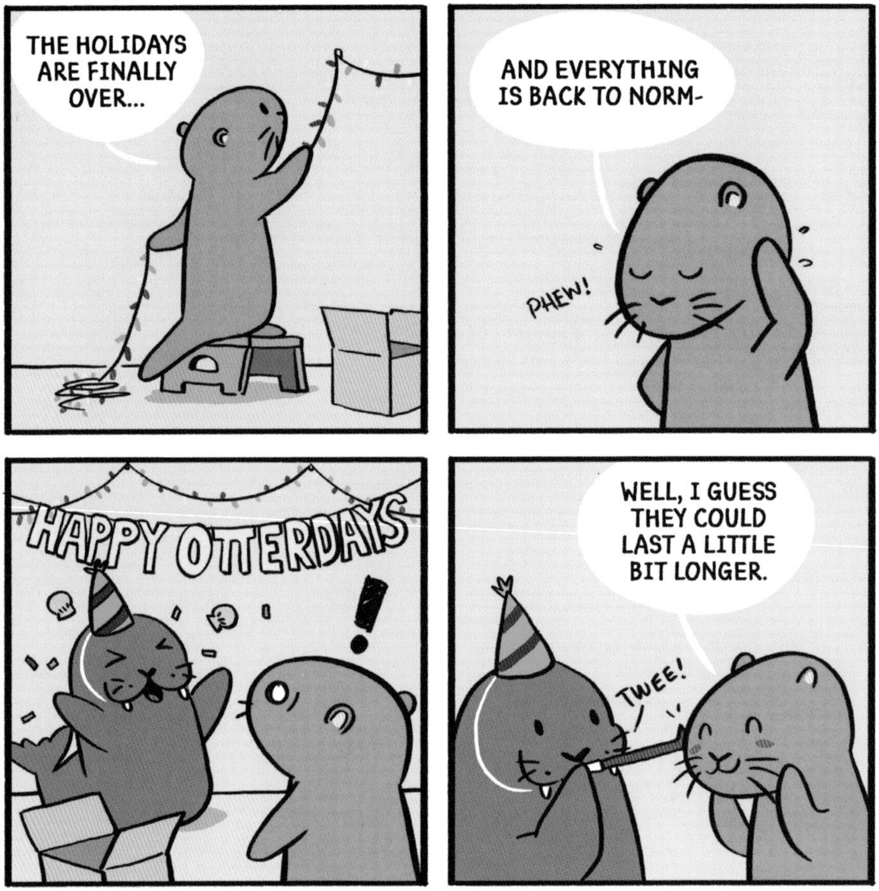
THE HOLIDAYS ARE FINALLY OVER...
AND EVERYTHING IS BACK TO NORM-
PHEW!
HAPPY OTTERDAYS
!
WELL, I GUESS THEY COULD LAST A LITTLE BIT LONGER.
TWEE!

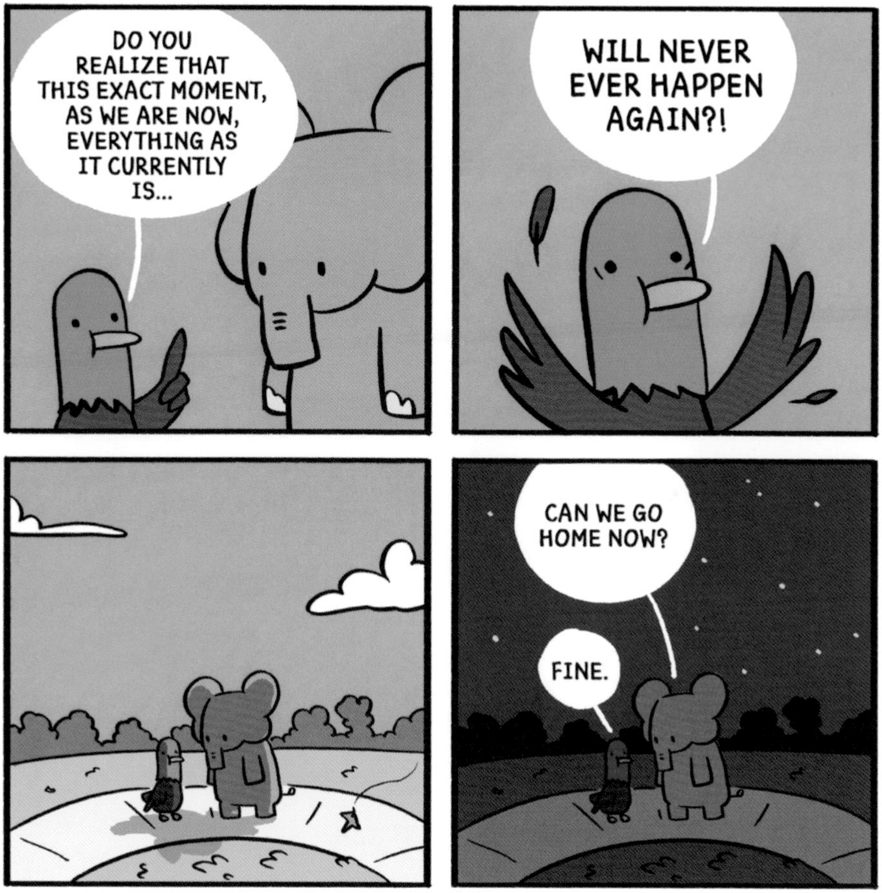
DO YOU REALIZE THAT THIS EXACT MOMENT, AS WE ARE NOW, EVERYTHING AS IT CURRENTLY IS...
WILL NEVER EVER HAPPEN AGAIN?!
CAN WE GO HOME NOW?
FINE.

PENGUIN'S COFFEE FLOWCHART

HAVE COFFEE?
YES!
NO...
DRINK IT!
SIP!
MORE!
ALL OF IT!
EMPTY?
YES
NO
WHAT?!
GET COFFEE!
HAVE COFFEE NOW??
YES
NO

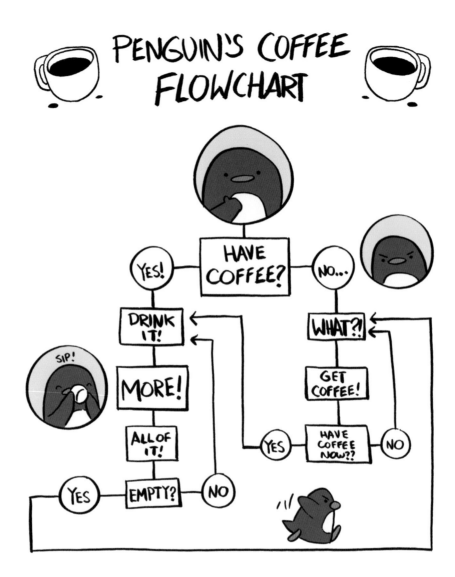

RABBIT'S FLOWCHART

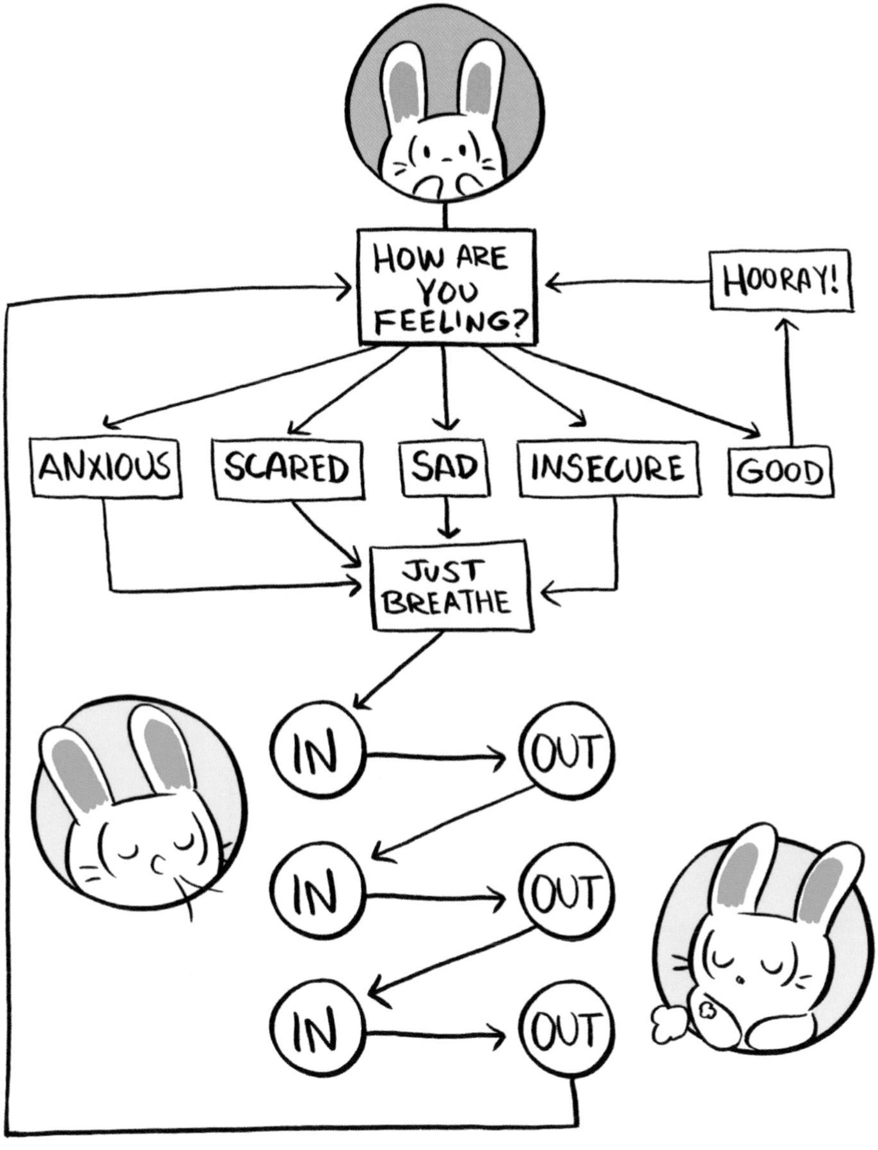

HOW ARE YOU FEELING?
HOORAY!
ANXIOUS
SCARED
SAD
INSECURE
GOOD
JUST BREATHE
IN
OUT
IN
OUT
IN
OUT

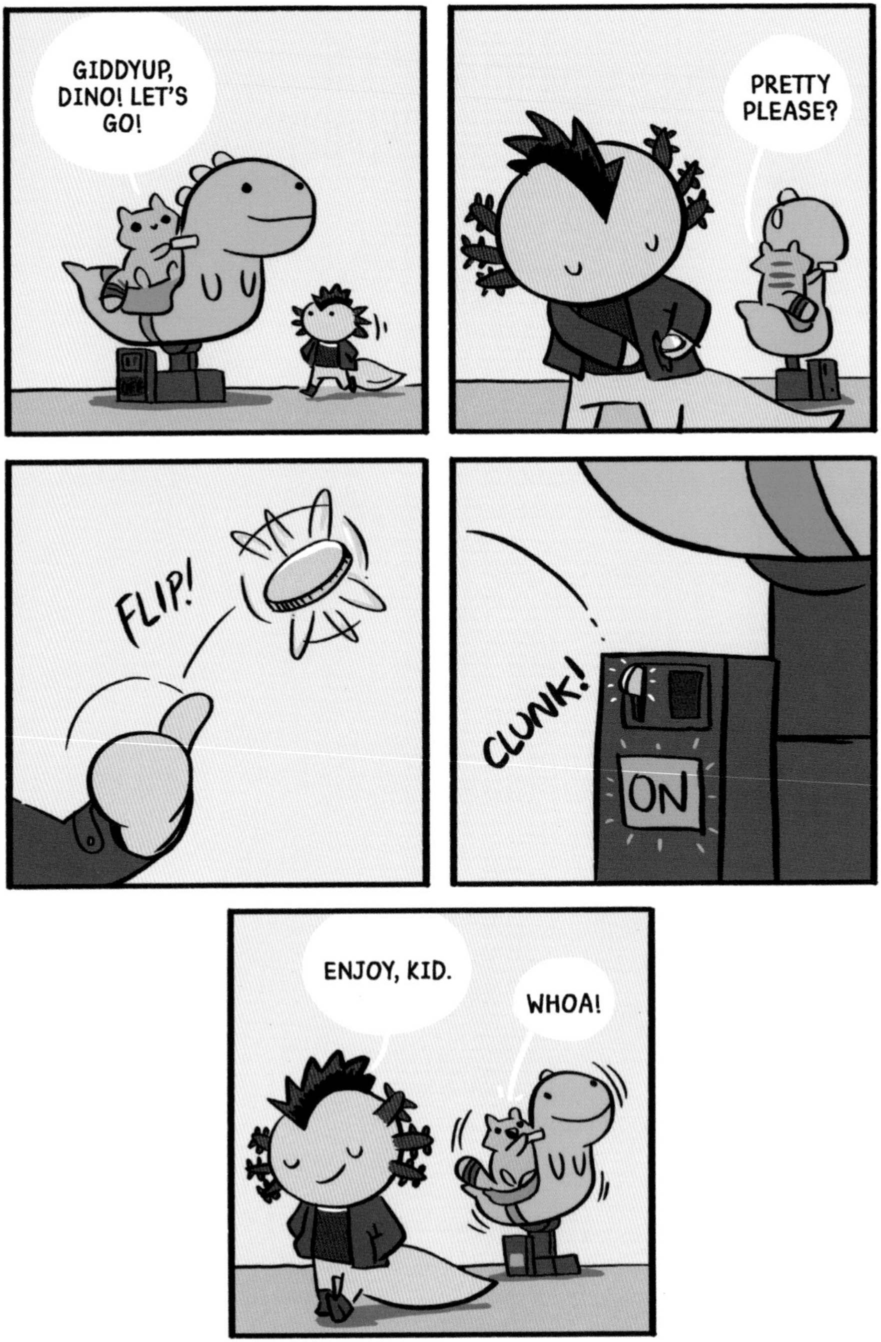
GIDDYUP, DINO! LET'S GO!
PRETTY PLEASE?
FLIP!
CLUNK!
ON
ENJOY, KID.
WHOA!

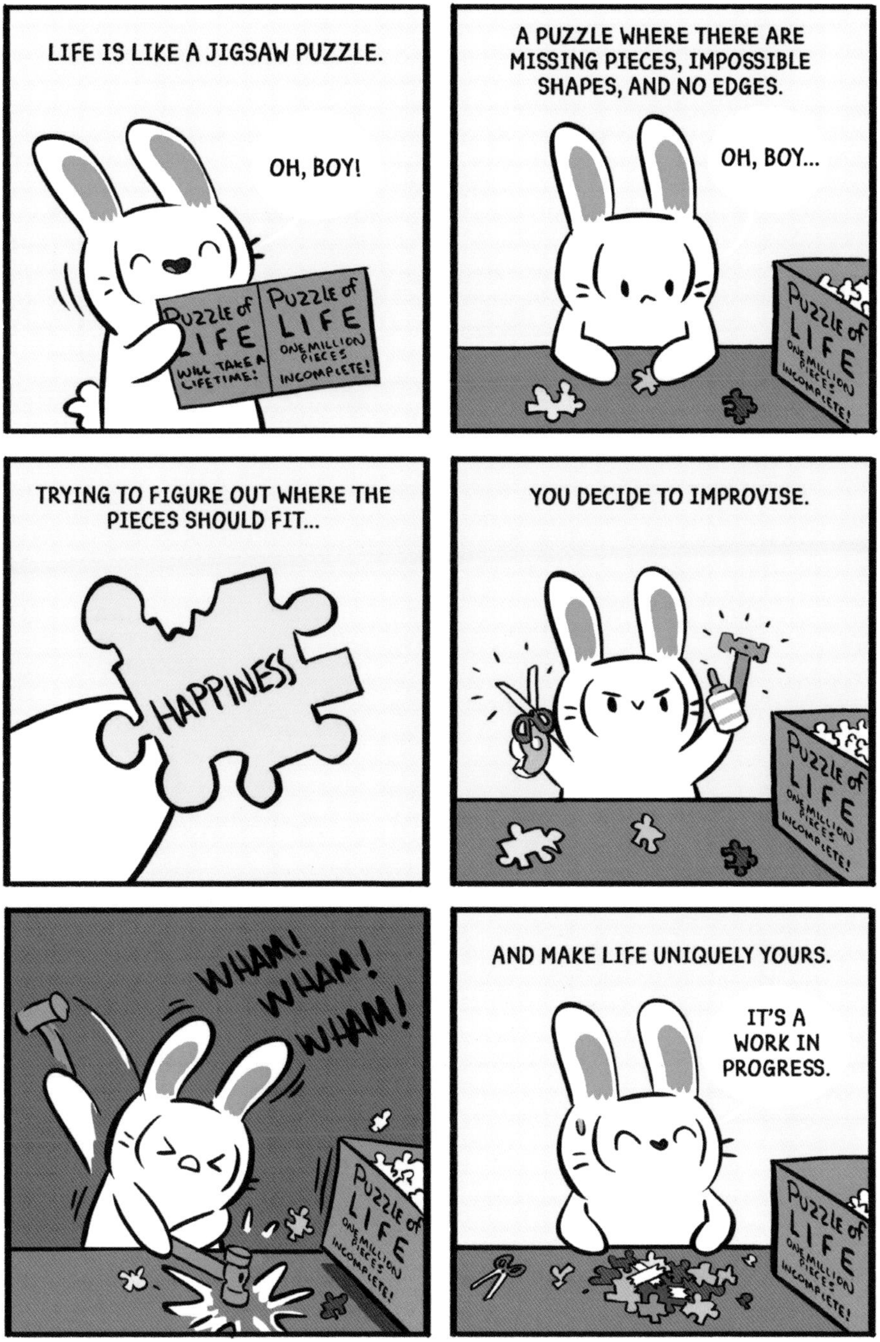

LIFE IS LIKE A JIGSAW PUZZLE.
OH, BOY!
WILL TAKE A LIFETIME!
Puzzle of LIFE ONE MILLION PIECES INCOMPLETE!
A PUZZLE WHERE THERE ARE MISSING PIECES, IMPOSSIBLE SHAPES, AND NO EDGES.
OH, BOY...
Puzzle of LIFE ONE MILLION PIECES INCOMPLETE!
TRYING TO FIGURE OUT WHERE THE PIECES SHOULD FIT...
HAPPINESS
YOU DECIDE TO IMPROVISE.
Puzzle of LIFE ONE MILLION PIECES INCOMPLETE!
WHAM! WHAM! WHAM!
Puzzle of LIFE ONE MILLION PIECES INCOMPLETE!
AND MAKE LIFE UNIQUELY YOURS.
IT'S A WORK IN PROGRESS.
Puzzle of LIFE ONE MILLION PIECES INCOMPLETE!

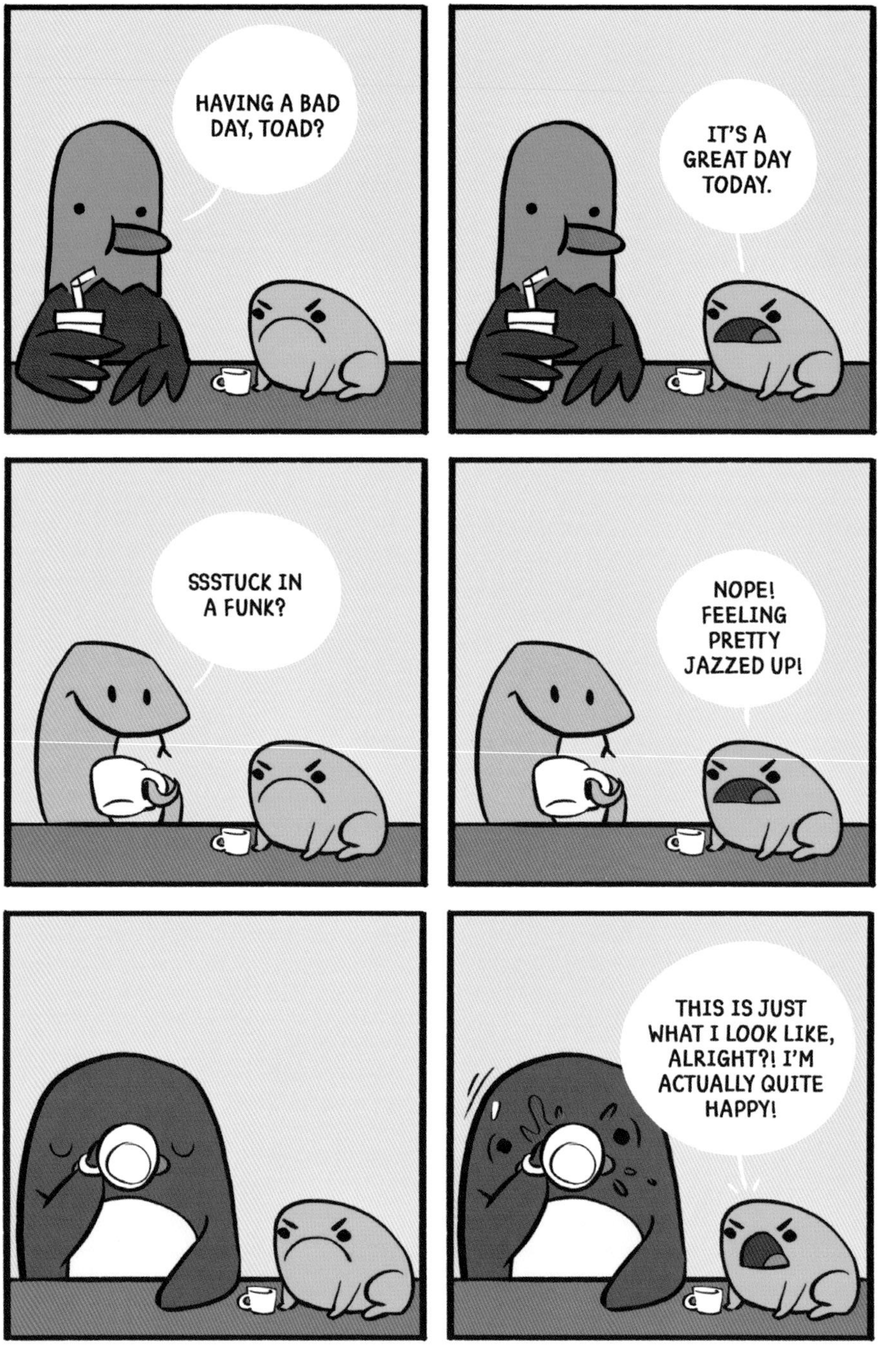
HAVING A BAD DAY, TOAD?
IT'S A GREAT DAY TODAY.
SSSTUCK IN A FUNK?
NOPE! FEELING PRETTY JAZZED UP!
THIS IS JUST WHAT I LOOK LIKE, ALRIGHT?! I'M ACTUALLY QUITE HAPPY!

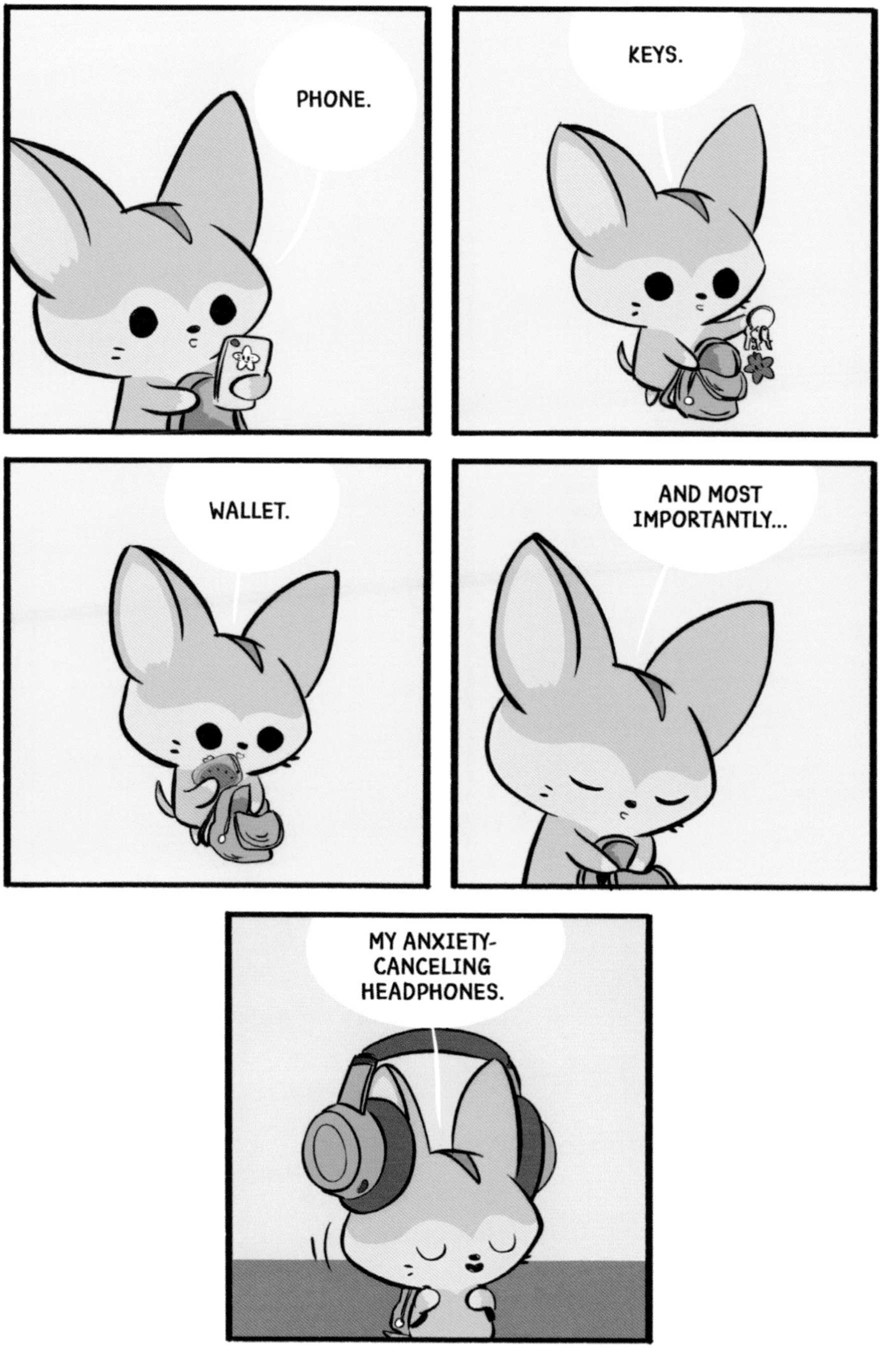
PHONE.
KEYS.
WALLET.
AND MOST IMPORTANTLY...
MY ANXIETY-CANCELING HEADPHONES.

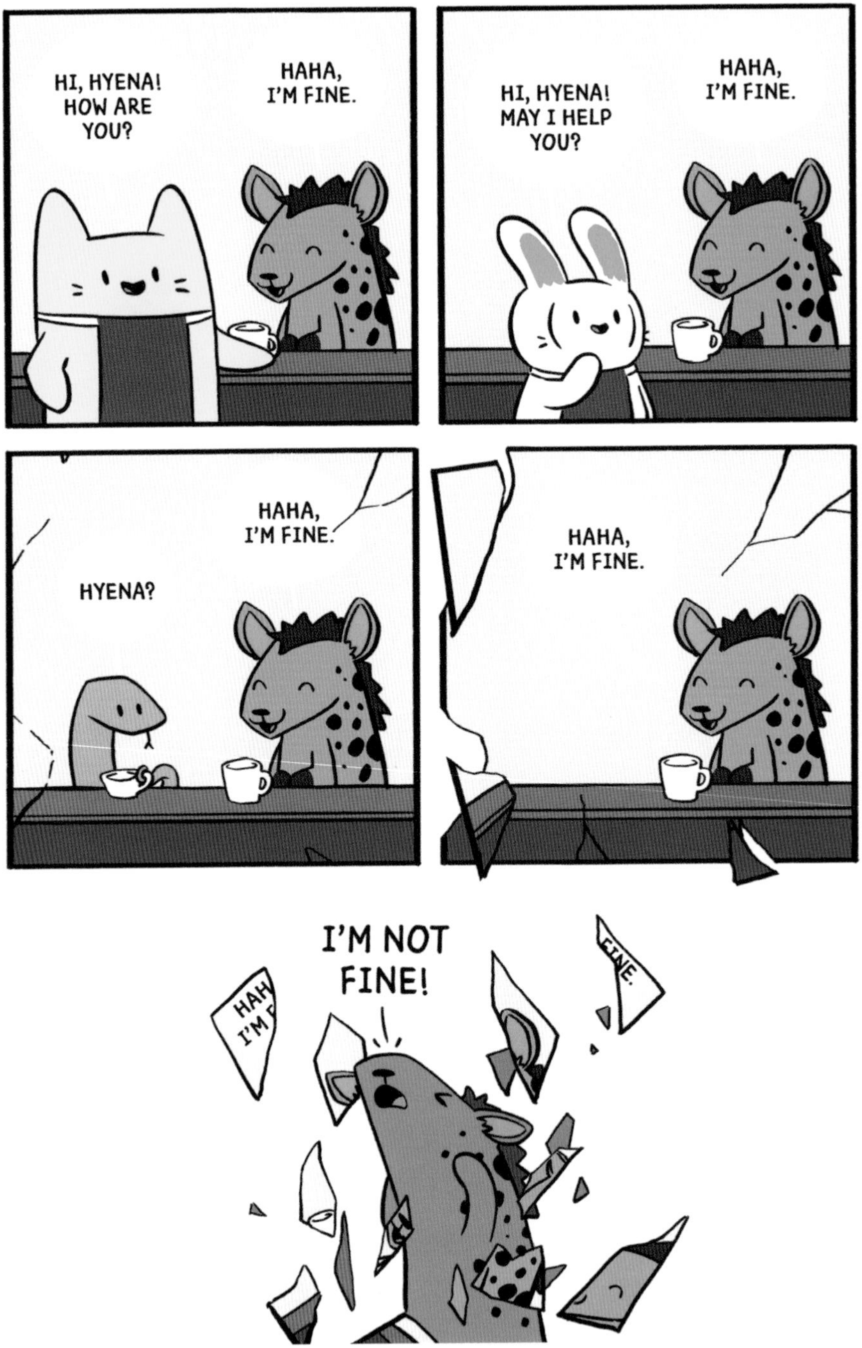
HI, HYENA! HOW ARE YOU?
HAHA, I'M FINE.
HI, HYENA! MAY I HELP YOU?
HAHA, I'M FINE.
HYENA?
HAHA, I'M FINE.
HAHA, I'M FINE.
I'M NOT FINE!

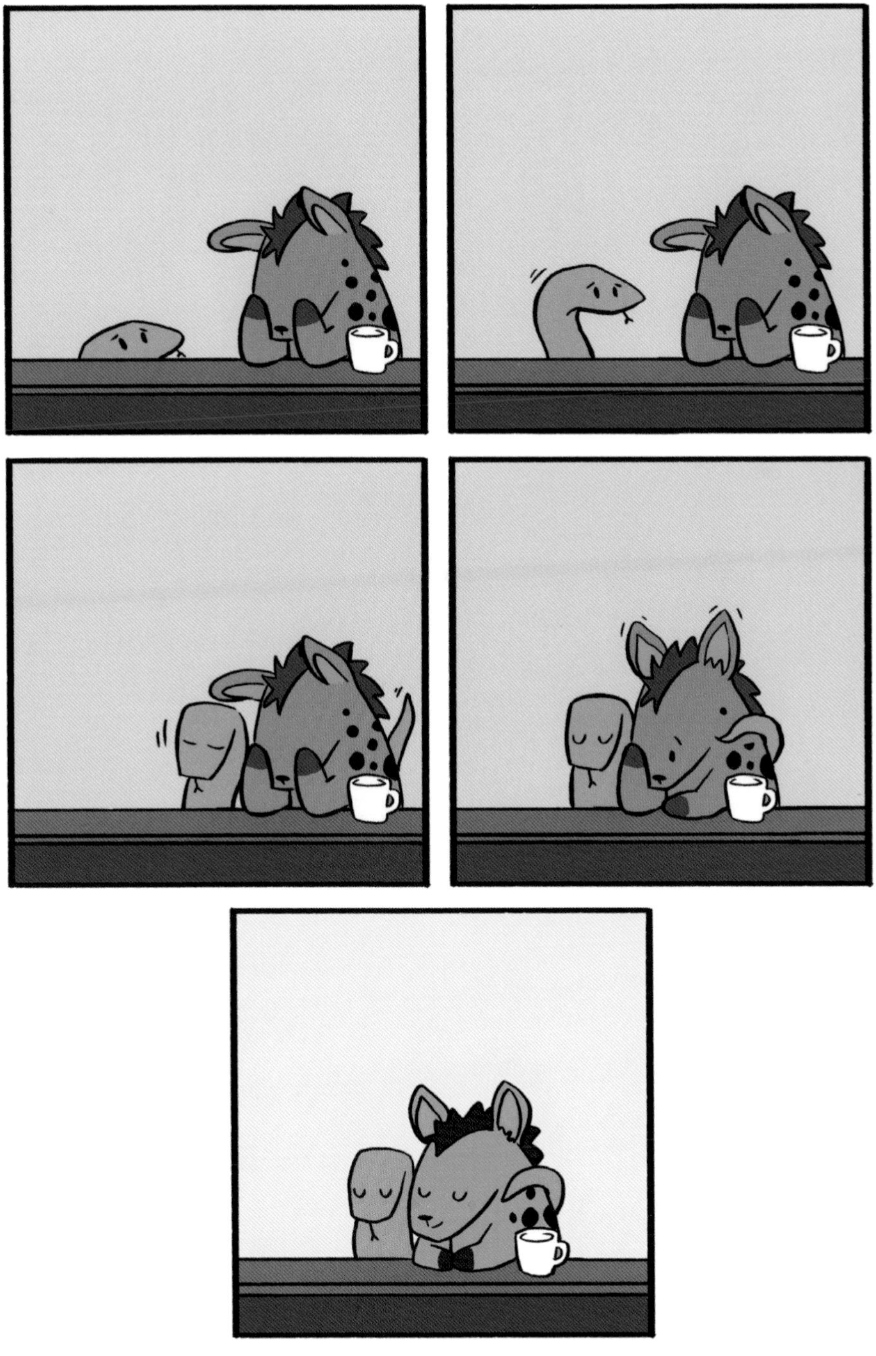

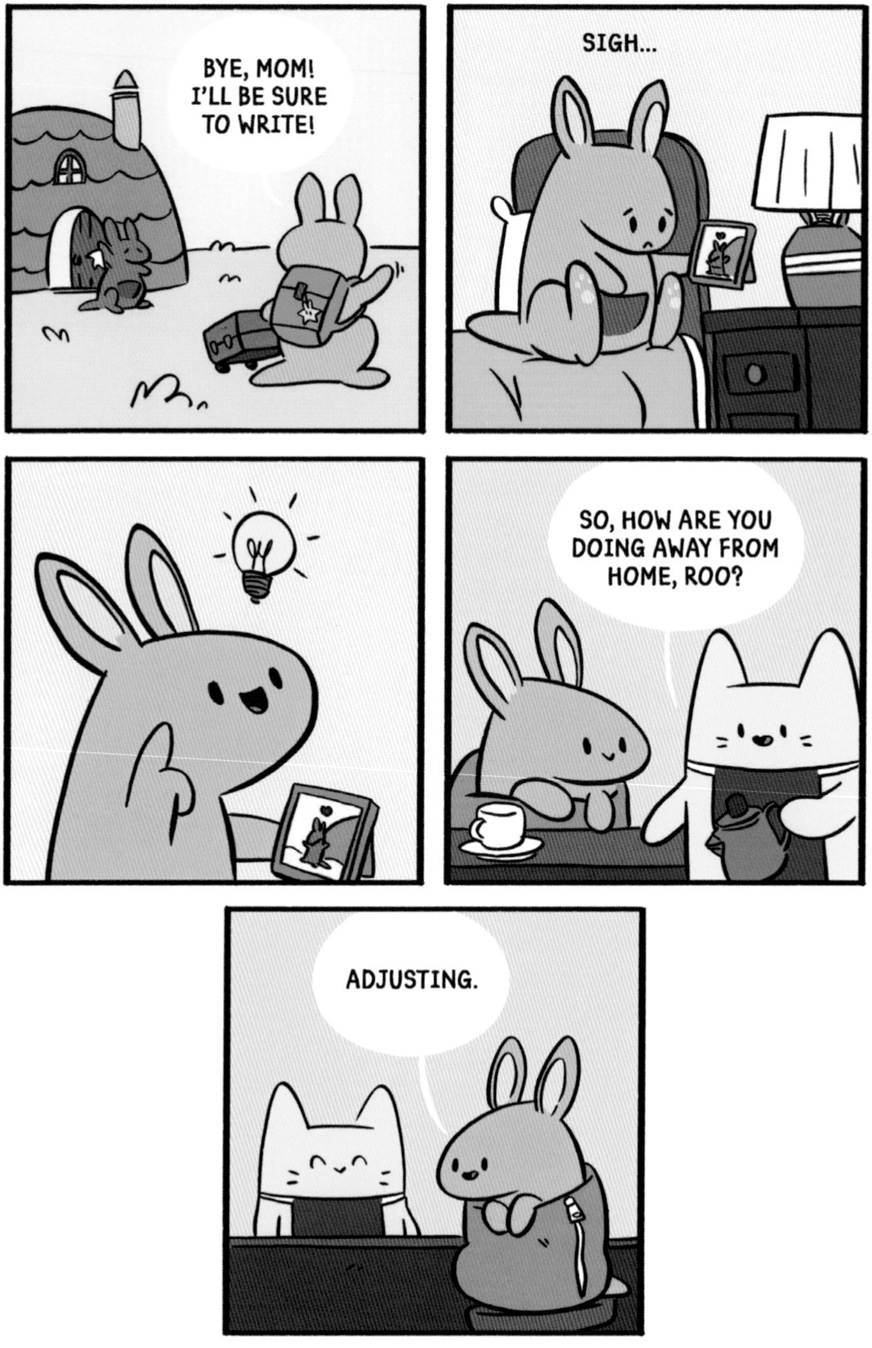
BYE, MOM! I'LL BE SURE TO WRITE!
SIGH...
SO, HOW ARE YOU DOING AWAY FROM HOME, ROO?
ADJUSTING.

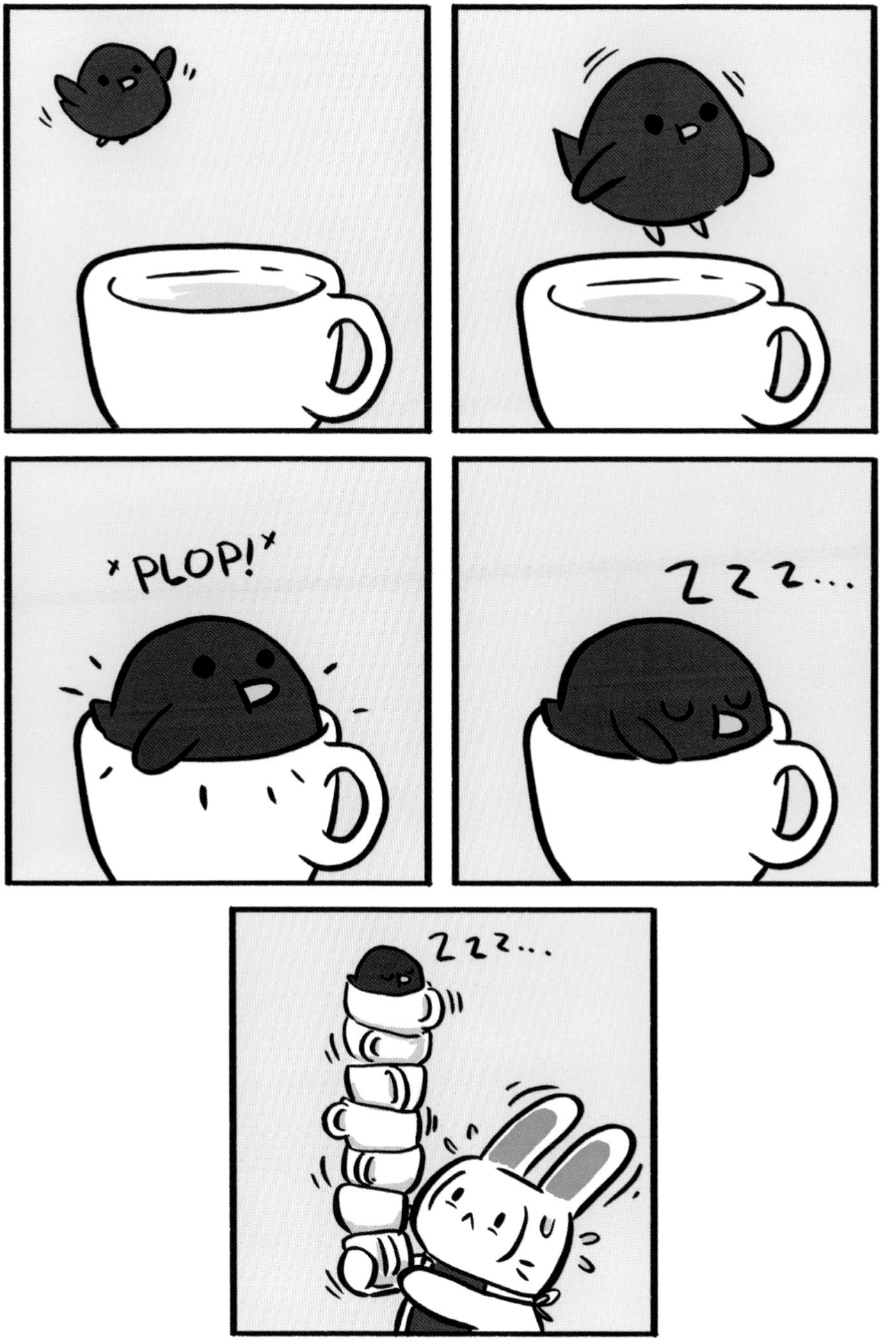
PLOP!
ZZZ...
ZZZ...

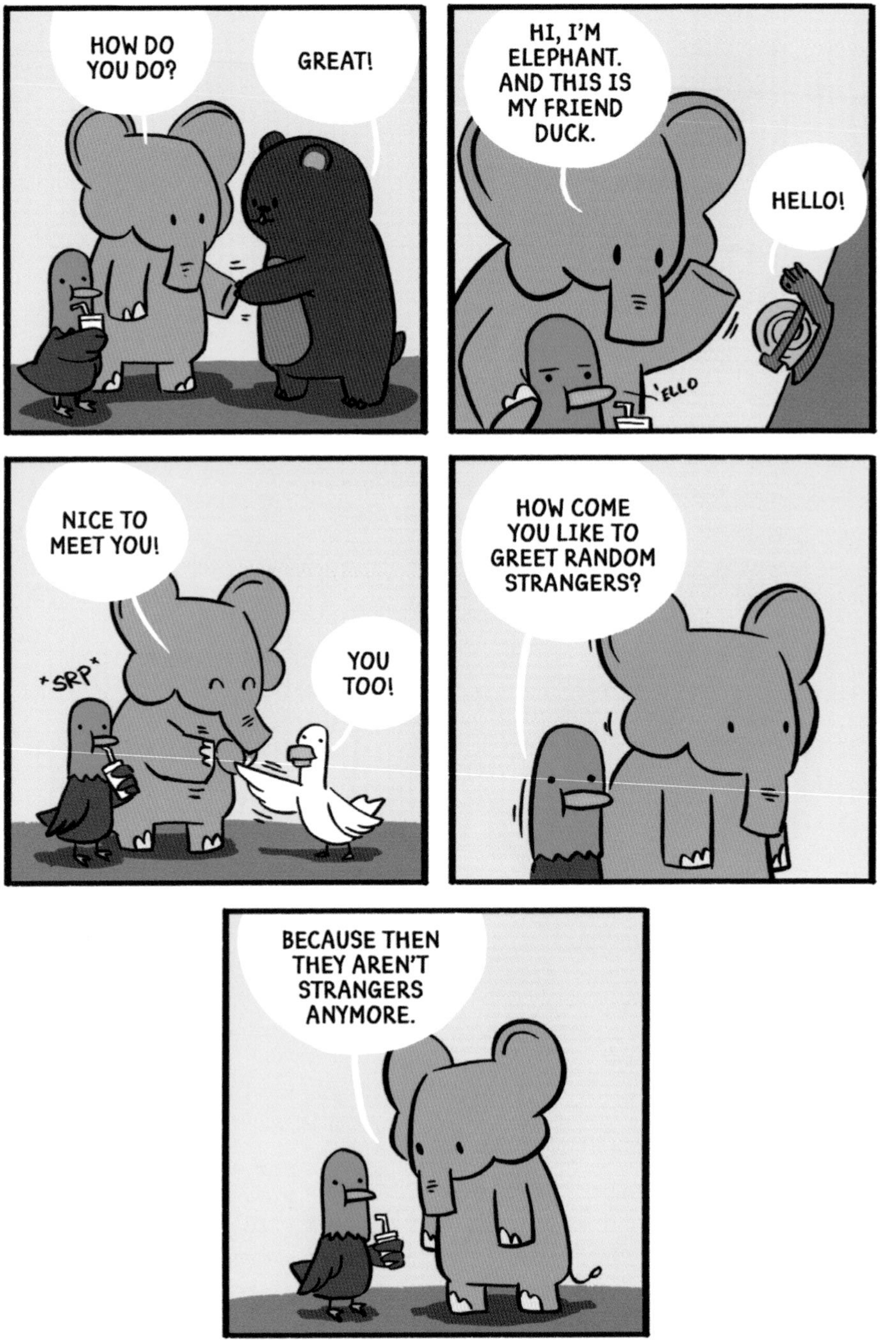
HOW DO YOU DO?
GREAT!
HI, I'M ELEPHANT. AND THIS IS MY FRIEND DUCK.
HELLO!
'ELLO
NICE TO MEET YOU!
SRP
YOU TOO!
HOW COME YOU LIKE TO GREET RANDOM STRANGERS?
BECAUSE THEN THEY AREN'T STRANGERS ANYMORE.

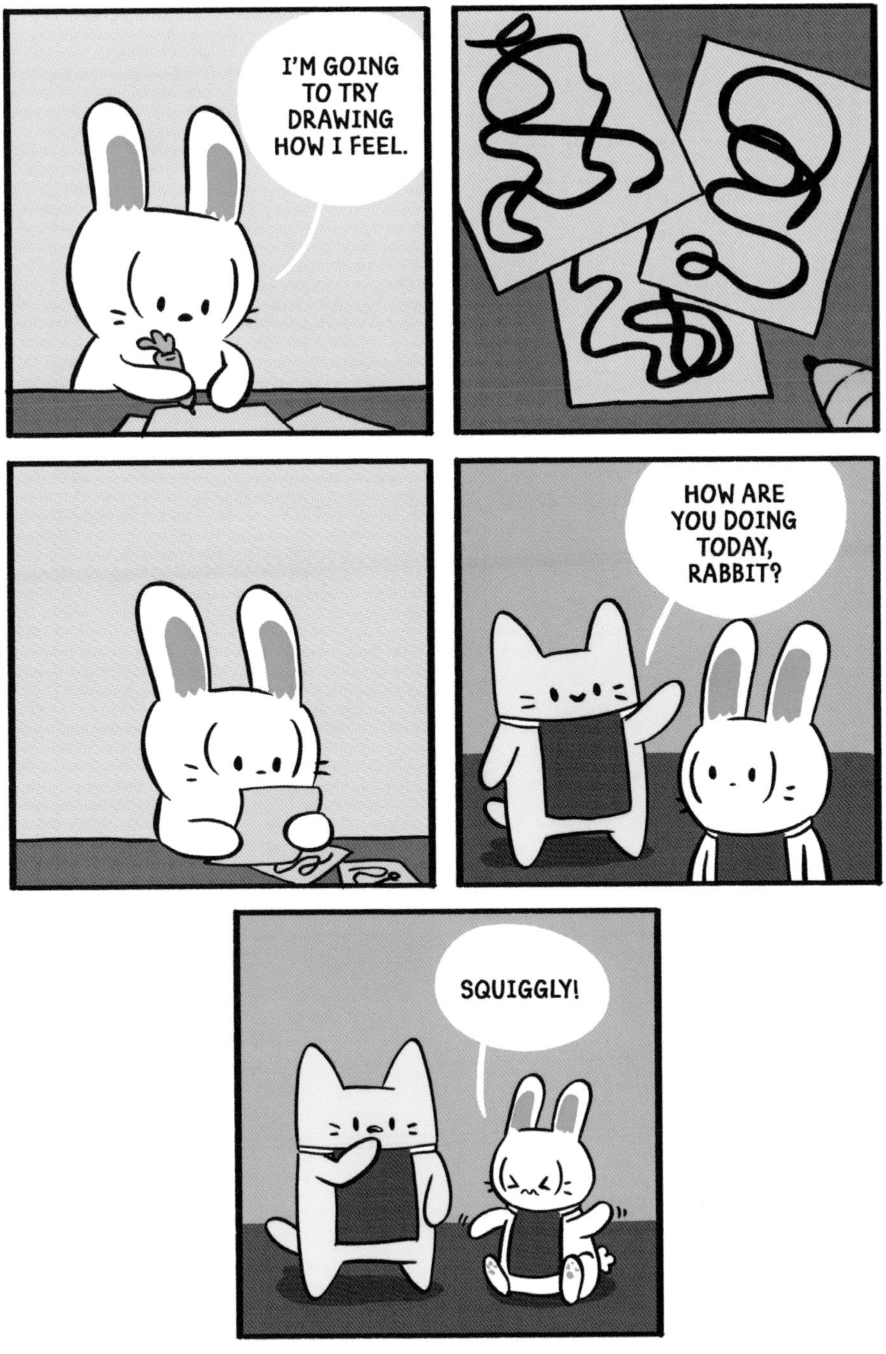
I'M GOING TO TRY DRAWING HOW I FEEL.
HOW ARE YOU DOING TODAY, RABBIT?
SQUIGGLY!

WHAT MAKES YOU HAPPY?

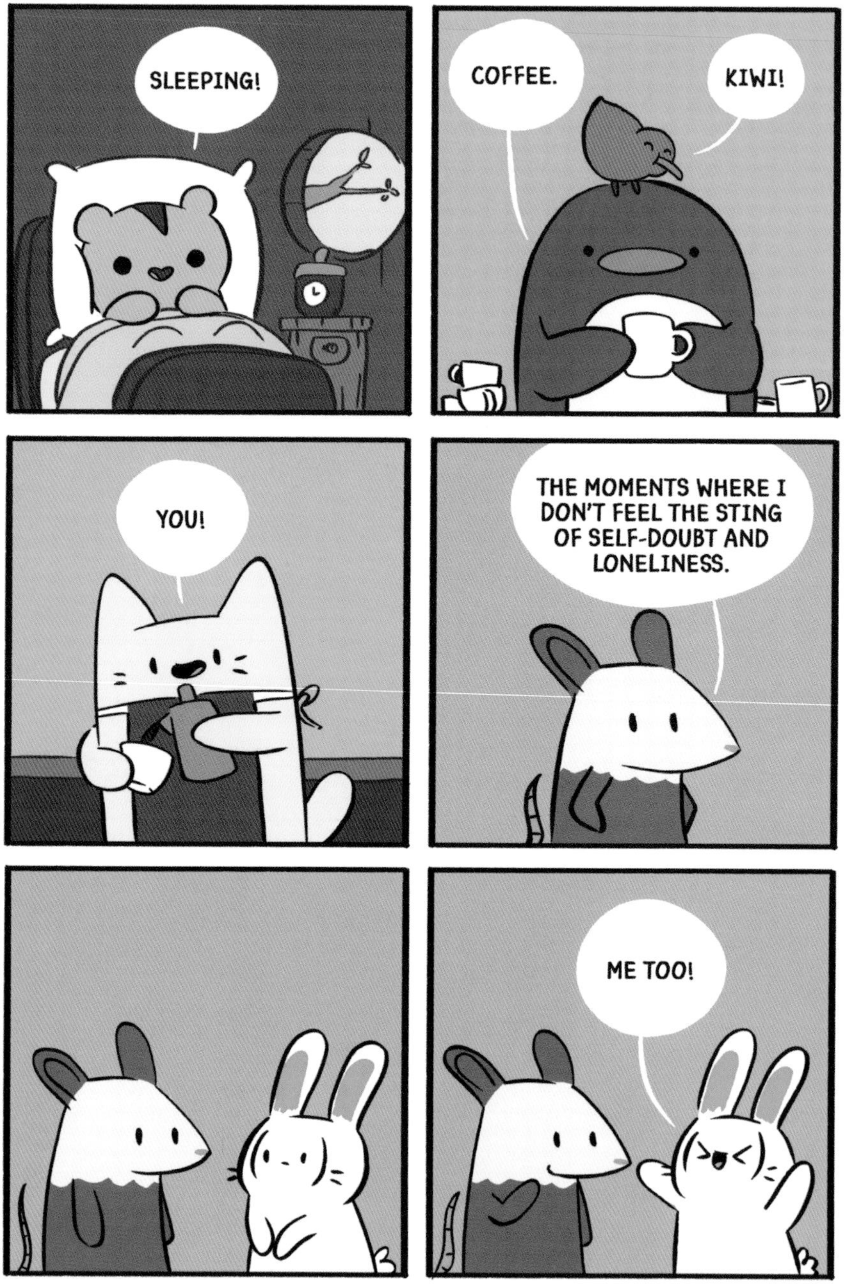
SLEEPING!
COFFEE.
KIWI!
YOU!
THE MOMENTS WHERE I DON'T FEEL THE STING OF SELF-DOUBT AND LONELINESS.
ME TOO!

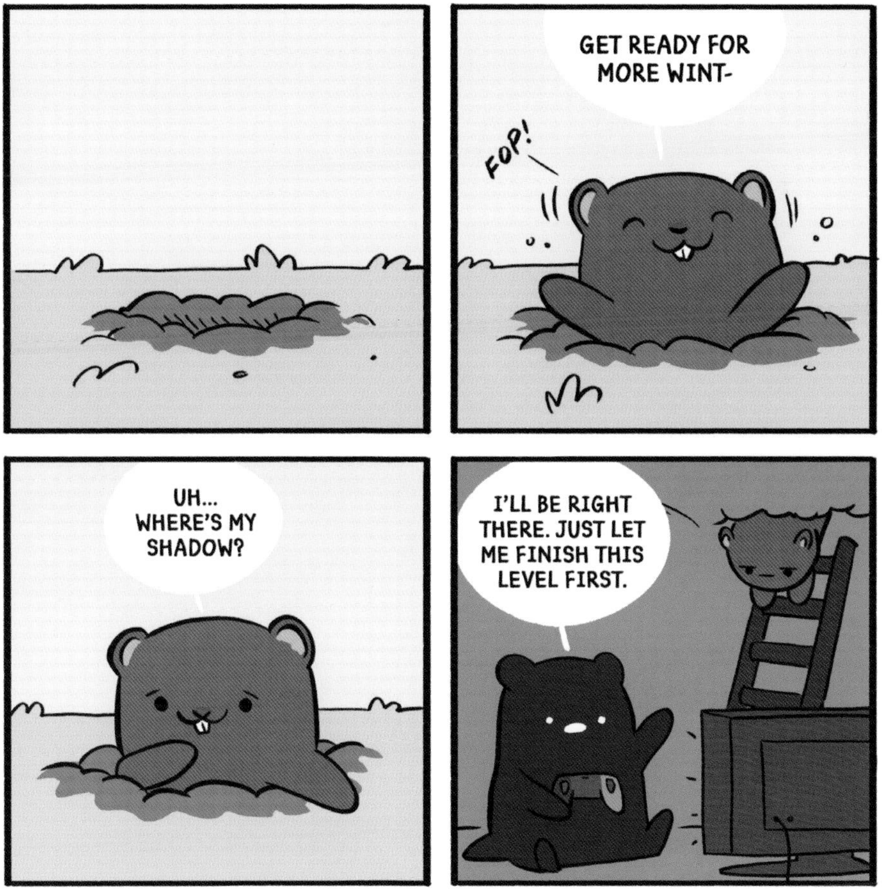
GET READY FOR MORE WINT-
FOP!
UH... WHERE'S MY SHADOW?
I'LL BE RIGHT THERE. JUST LET ME FINISH THIS LEVEL FIRST.

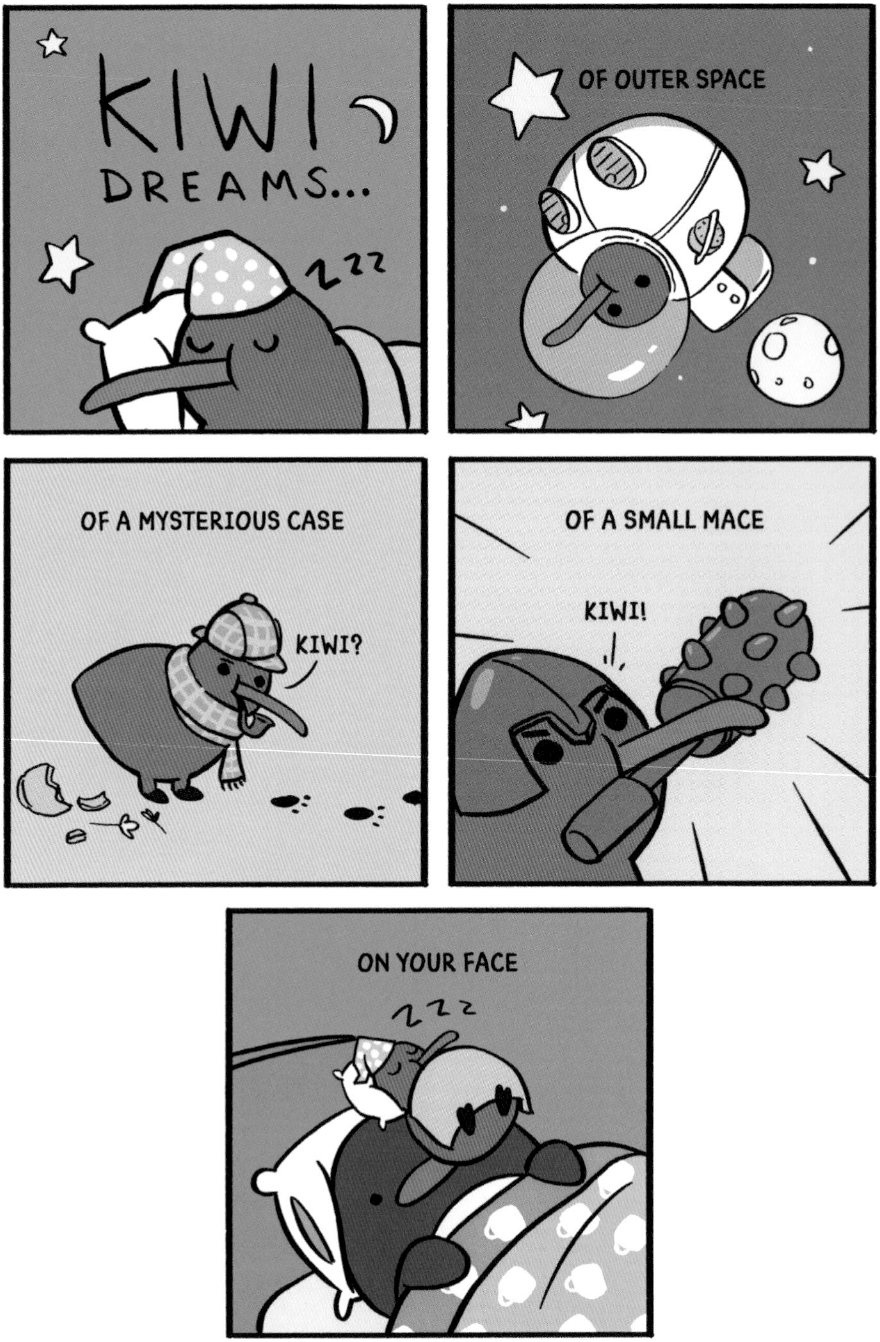
KIWI DREAMS...
ZZZ
OF OUTER SPACE
OF A MYSTERIOUS CASE
KIWI?
OF A SMALL MACE
KIWI!
ON YOUR FACE
ZZZ

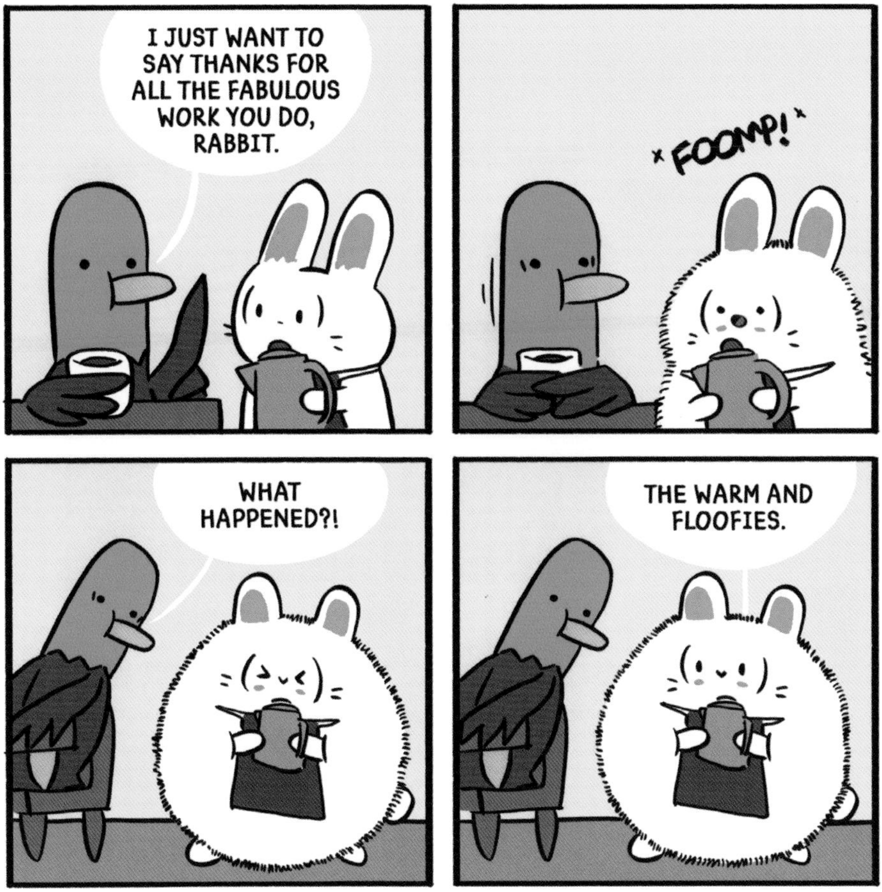
I JUST WANT TO SAY THANKS FOR ALL THE FABULOUS WORK YOU DO, RABBIT.
FOOMP!
WHAT HAPPENED?!
THE WARM AND FLOOFIES.

CELEBRATE YOUR WINS!

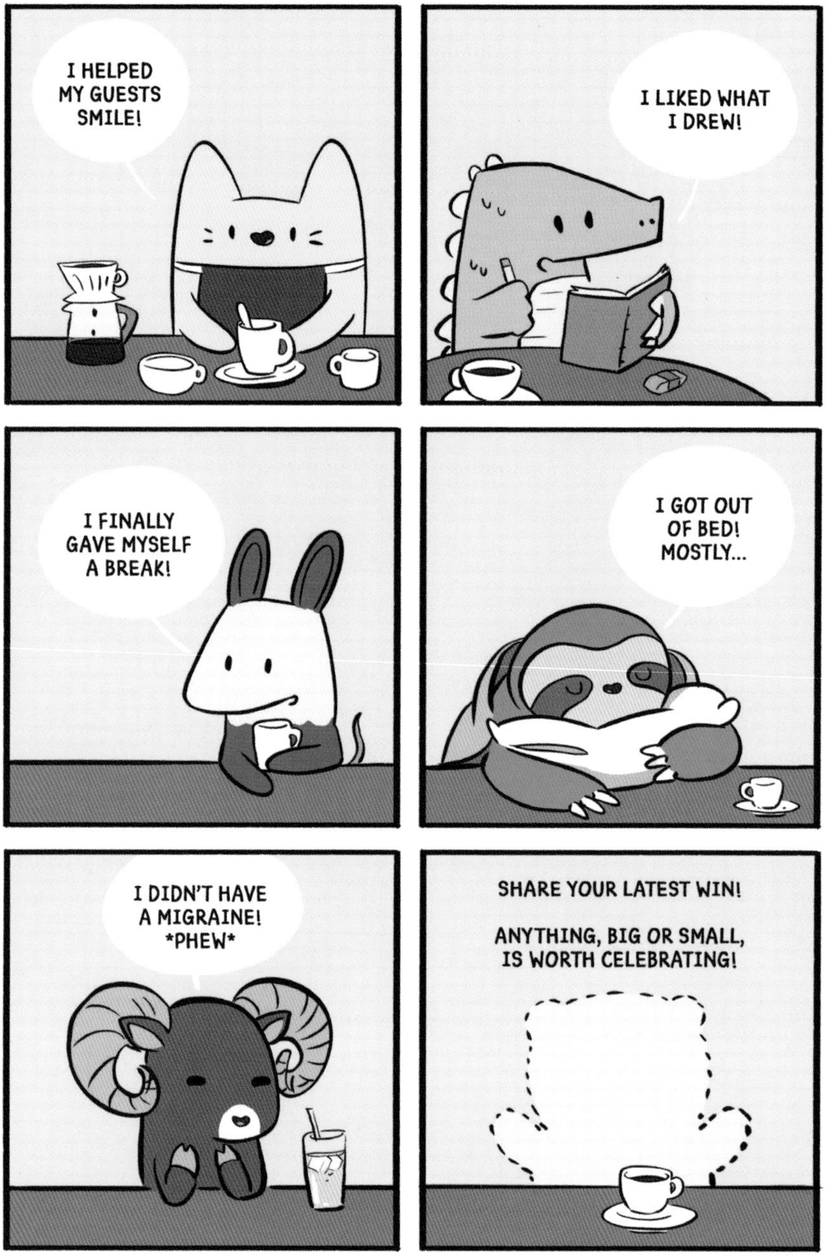

I HELPED MY GUESTS SMILE!
I LIKED WHAT I DREW!
I FINALLY GAVE MYSELF A BREAK!
I GOT OUT OF BED! MOSTLY...
I DIDN'T HAVE A MIGRAINE! *PHEW*
SHARE YOUR LATEST WIN!
ANYTHING, BIG OR SMALL, IS WORTH CELEBRATING!

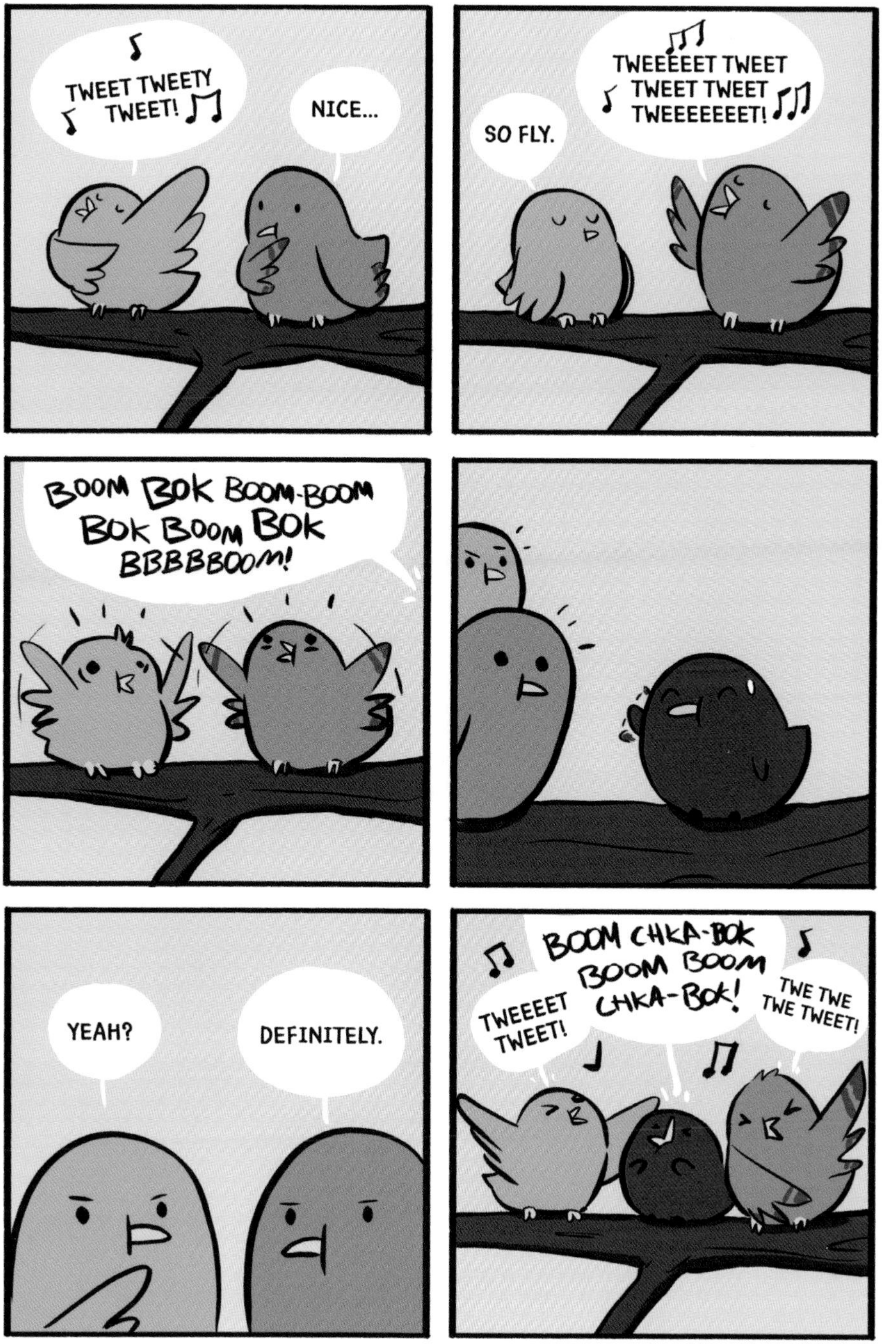
TWEET TWEETY TWEET!
NICE...
TWEEEEET TWEET TWEET TWEET TWEEEEEEET!
SO FLY.
BOOM BOK BOOM-BOOM BOK BOOM BOK BBBBBOOM!
YEAH?
DEFINITELY.
BOOM CHKA-BOK BOOM BOOM CHKA-BOK!
TWEEEET TWEET!
TWE TWE TWE TWEET!

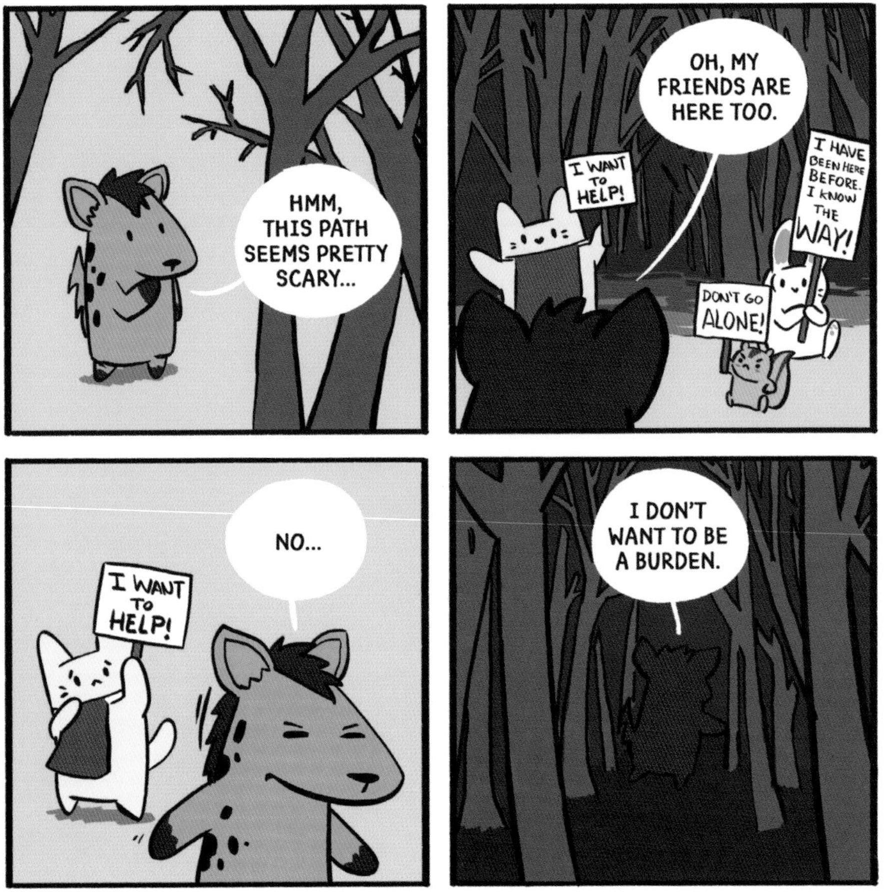
HMM, THIS PATH SEEMS PRETTY SCARY...
OH, MY FRIENDS ARE HERE TOO.
I WANT TO HELP!
I HAVE BEEN HERE BEFORE. I KNOW THE WAY!
DON'T GO ALONE!
I WANT TO HELP!
NO...
I DON'T WANT TO BE A BURDEN.

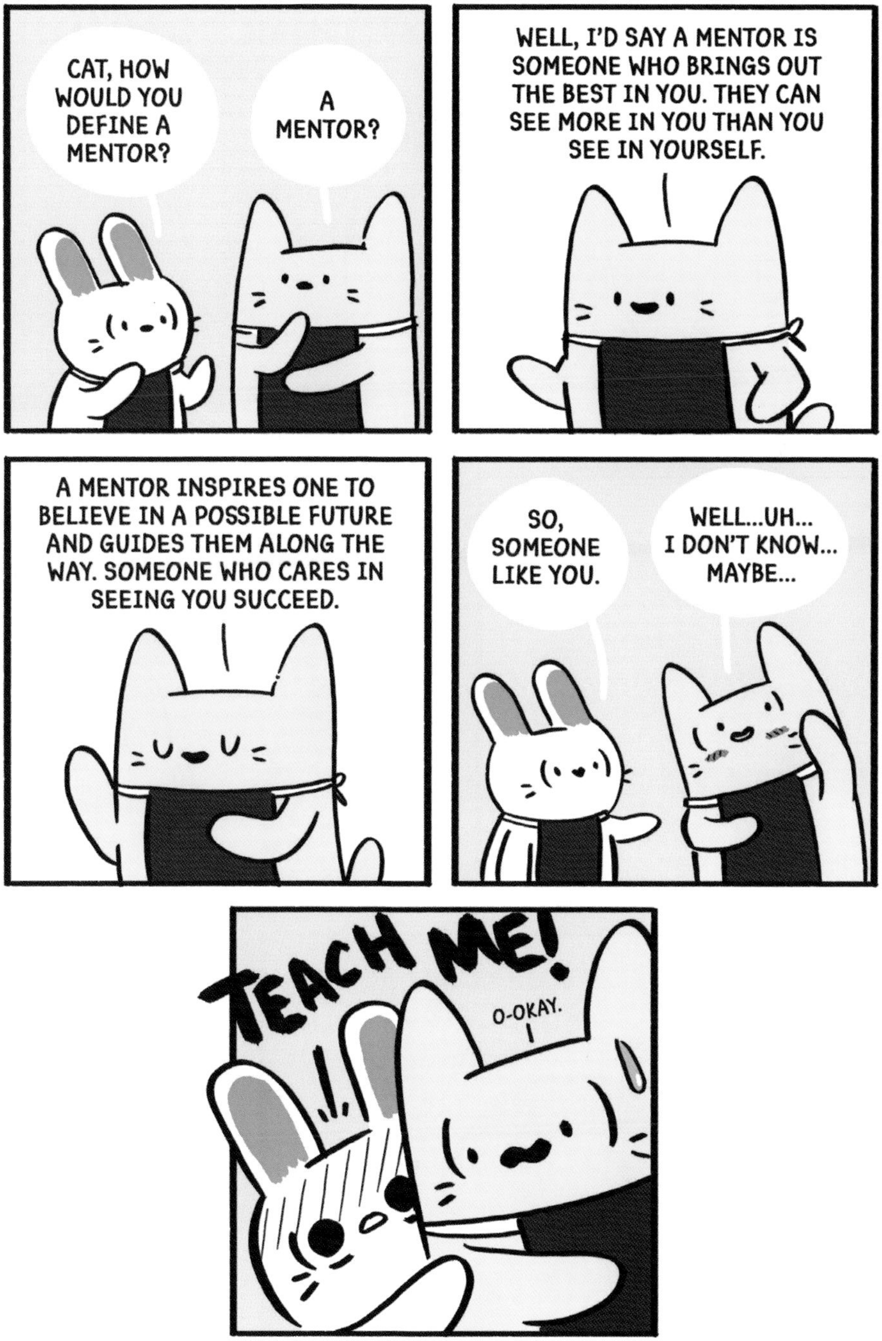
CAT, HOW WOULD YOU DEFINE A MENTOR?
A MENTOR?
WELL, I'D SAY A MENTOR IS SOMEONE WHO BRINGS OUT THE BEST IN YOU. THEY CAN SEE MORE IN YOU THAN YOU SEE IN YOURSELF.
A MENTOR INSPIRES ONE TO BELIEVE IN A POSSIBLE FUTURE AND GUIDES THEM ALONG THE WAY. SOMEONE WHO CARES IN SEEING YOU SUCCEED.
SO, SOMEONE LIKE YOU.
WELL...UH... I DON'T KNOW... MAYBE...
TEACH ME!
O-OKAY.

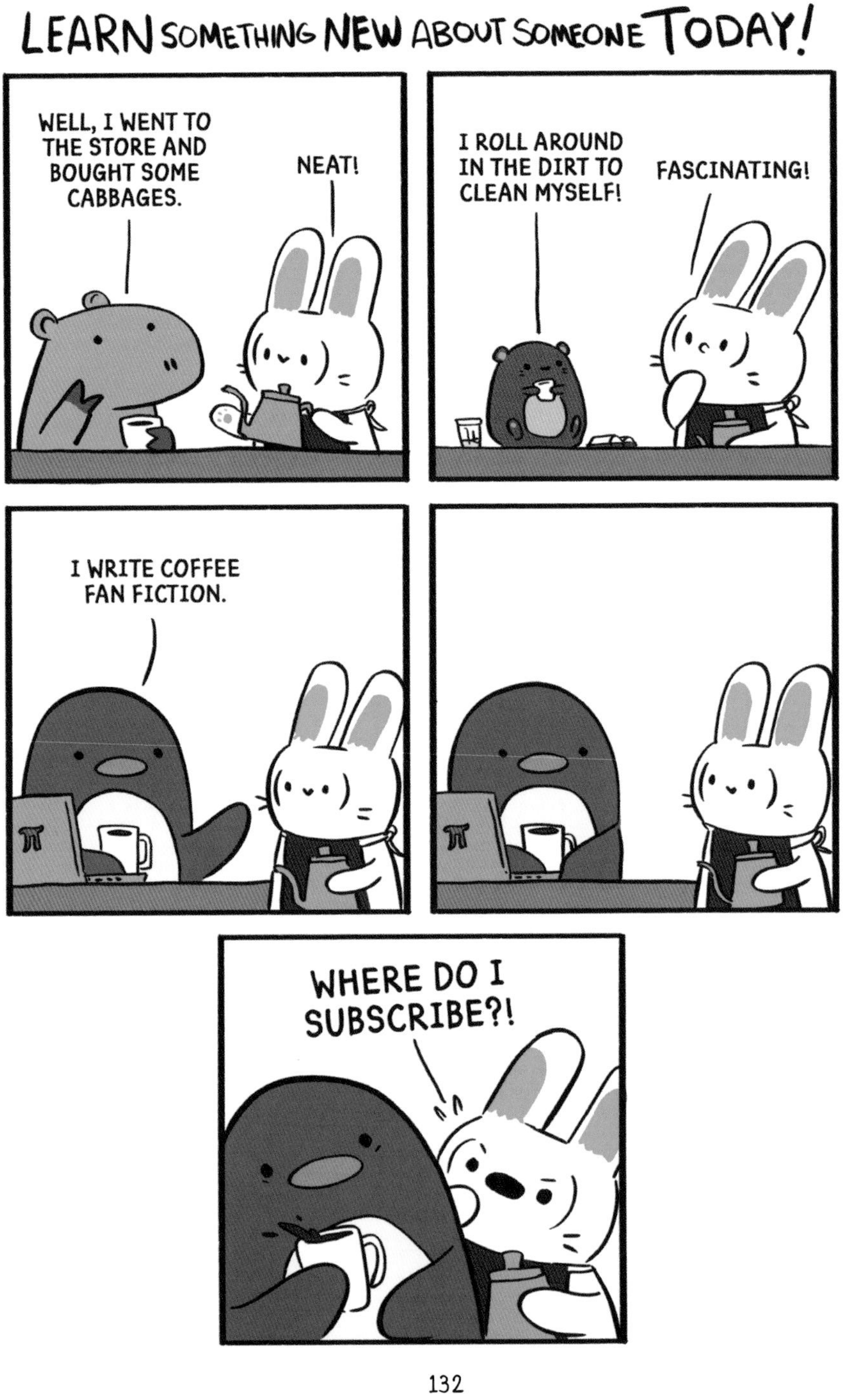
LEARN SOMETHING NEW ABOUT SOMEONE TODAY!
WELL, I WENT TO THE STORE AND BOUGHT SOME CABBAGES.
NEAT!
I ROLL AROUND IN THE DIRT TO CLEAN MYSELF!
FASCINATING!
I WRITE COFFEE FAN FICTION.
WHERE DO I SUBSCRIBE?!

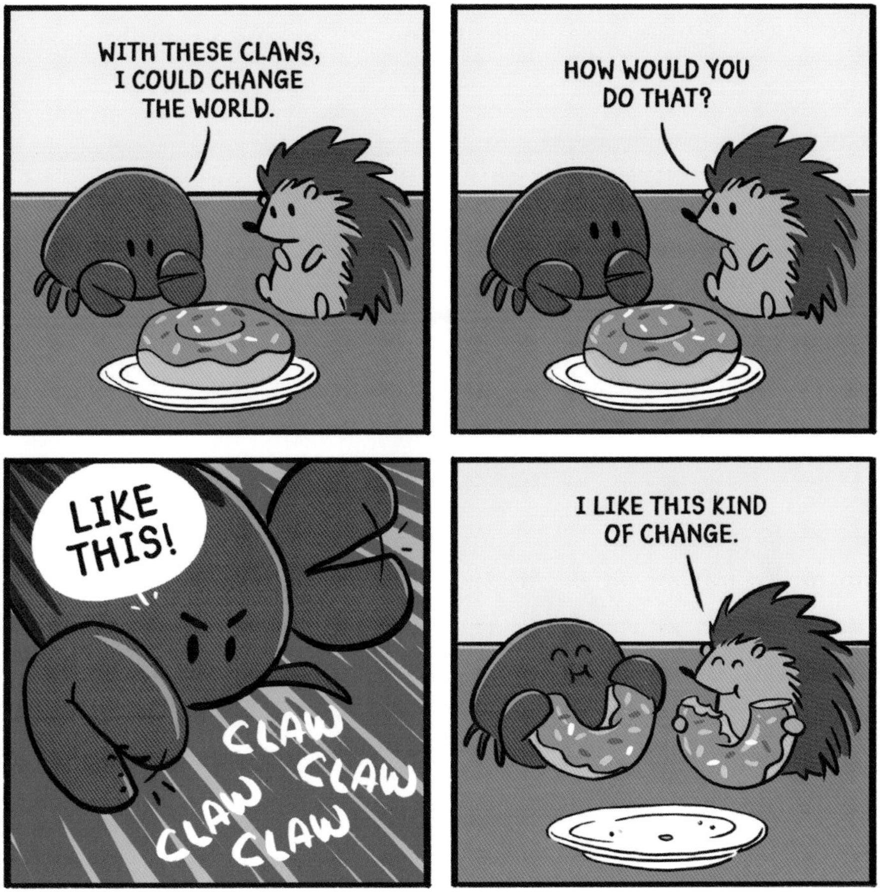
WITH THESE CLAWS, I COULD CHANGE THE WORLD.
HOW WOULD YOU DO THAT?
LIKE THIS!
CLAW CLAW CLAW CLAW CLAW
I LIKE THIS KIND OF CHANGE.

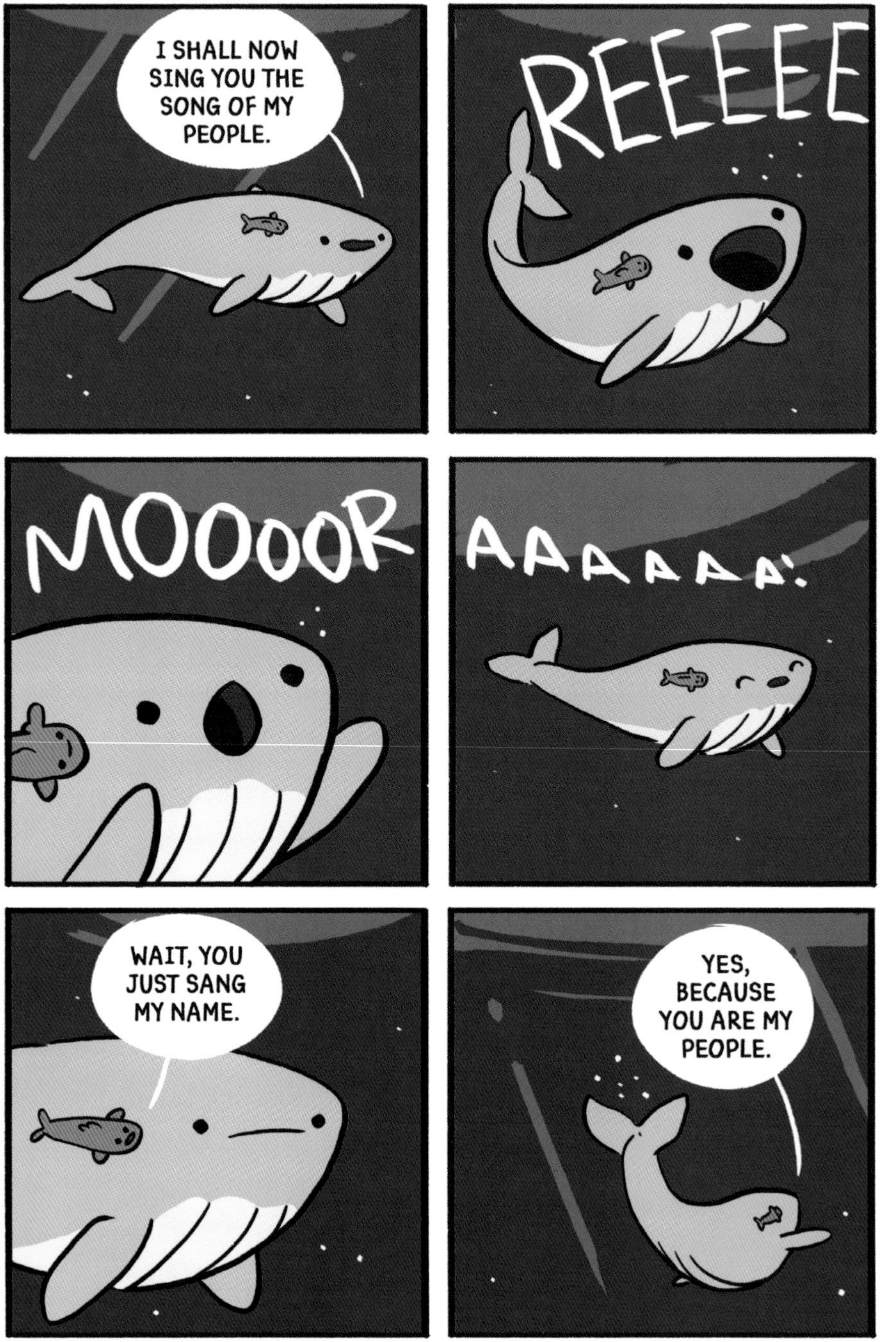
I SHALL NOW SING YOU THE SONG OF MY PEOPLE.
REEEEE
MOOOOR
AAAAAA!
WAIT, YOU JUST SANG MY NAME.
YES, BECAUSE YOU ARE MY PEOPLE.

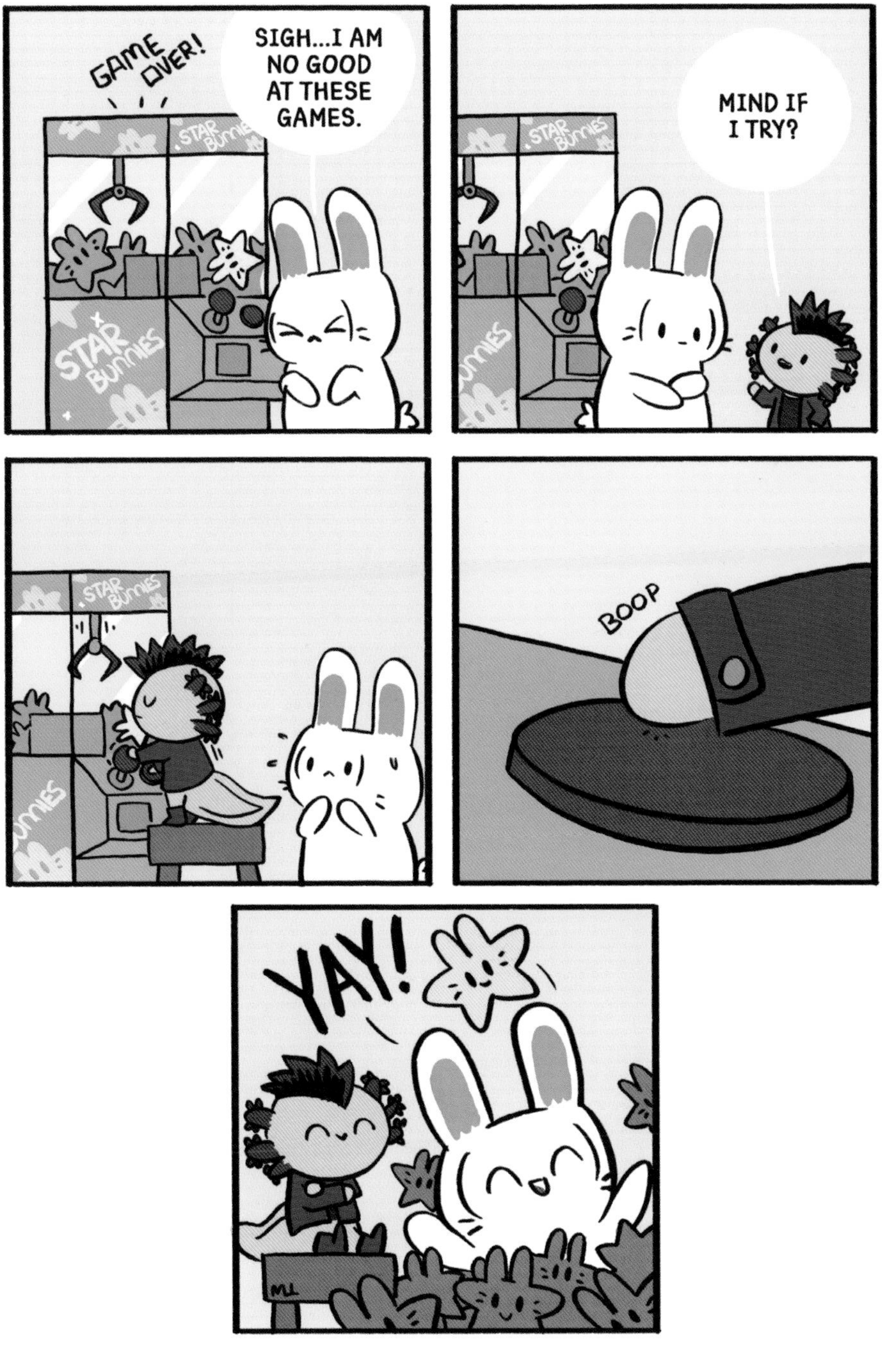
GAME OVER!
SIGH...I AM NO GOOD AT THESE GAMES.
STAR BUNNIES
MIND IF I TRY?
BOOP
YAY!

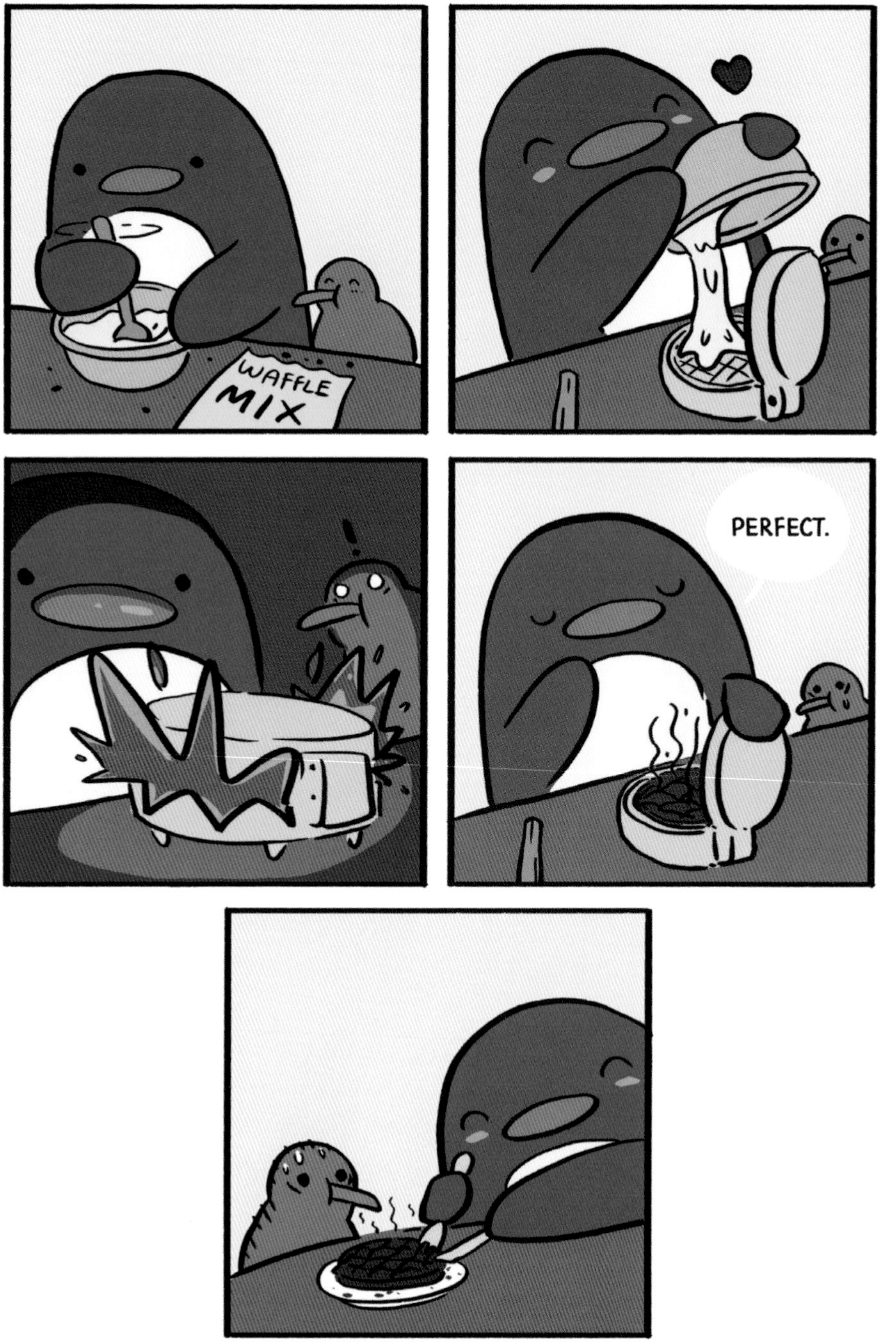
WAFFLE MIX
!
PERFECT.

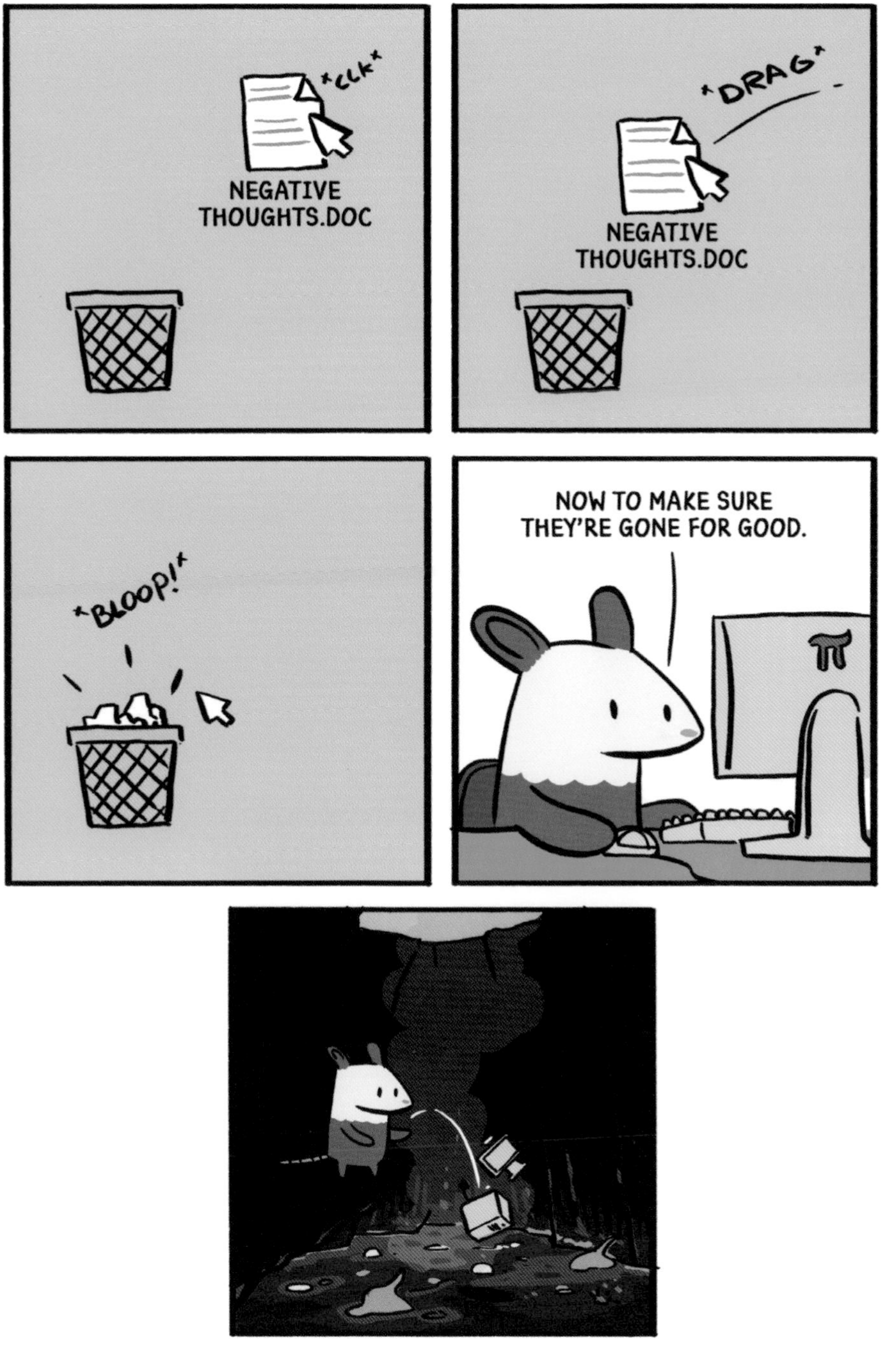
CLK
NEGATIVE THOUGHTS.DOC
DRAG
NEGATIVE THOUGHTS.DOC
BLOOP!
NOW TO MAKE SURE THEY'RE GONE FOR GOOD.

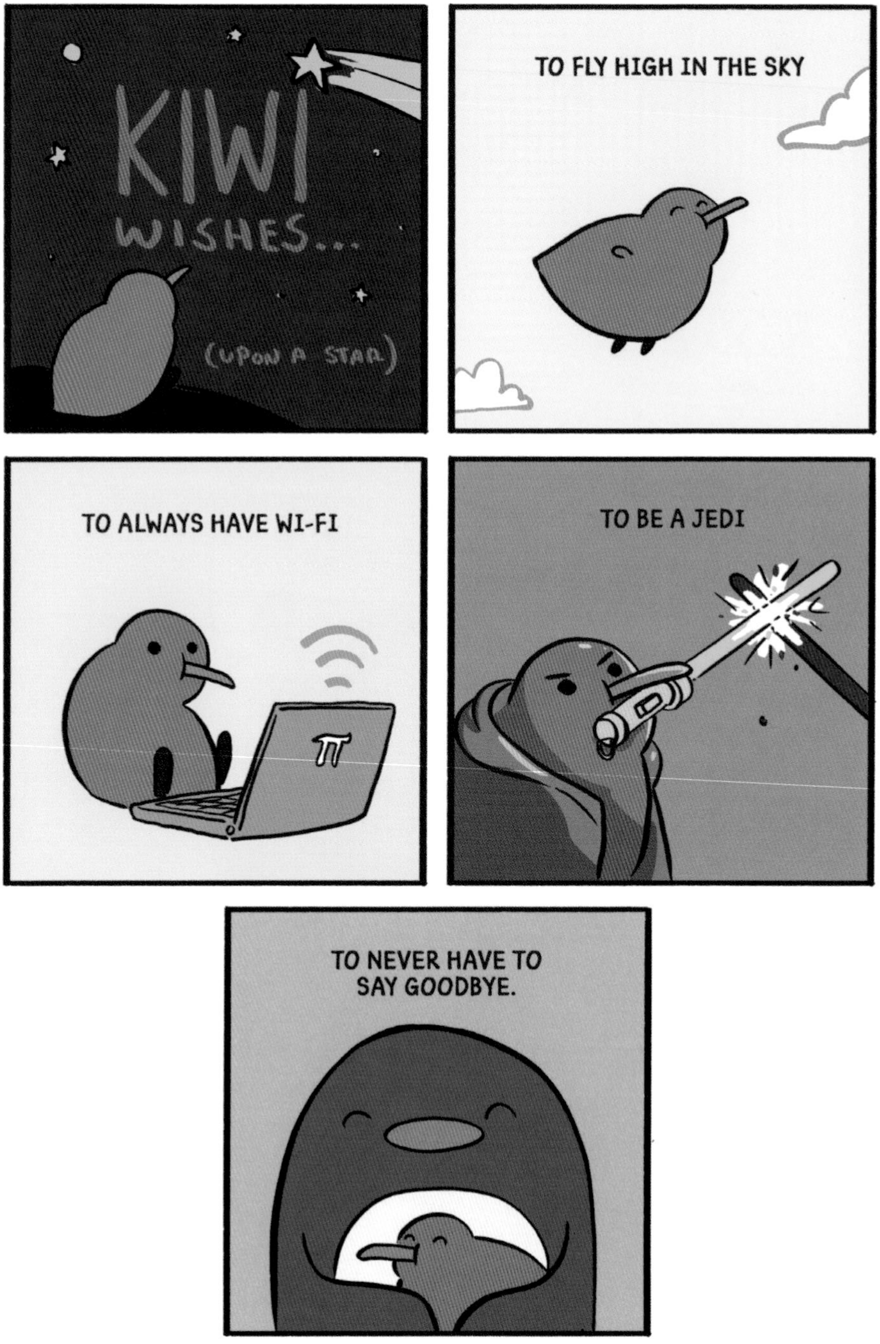
KIWI WISHES...
(UPON A STAR)
TO FLY HIGH IN THE SKY
TO ALWAYS HAVE WI-FI
π
TO BE A JEDI
TO NEVER HAVE TO SAY GOODBYE.

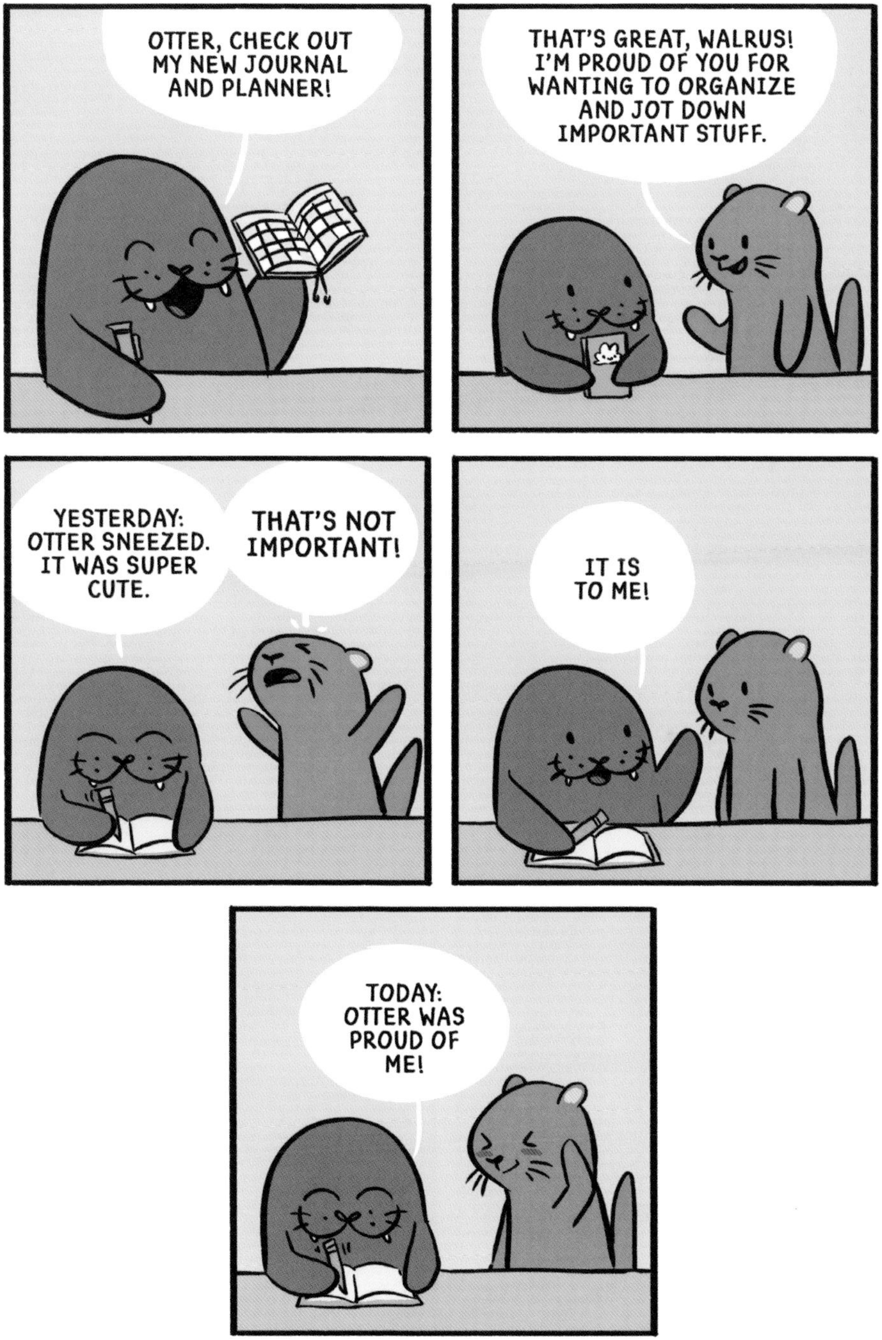
OTTER, CHECK OUT MY NEW JOURNAL AND PLANNER!
THAT'S GREAT, WALRUS! I'M PROUD OF YOU FOR WANTING TO ORGANIZE AND JOT DOWN IMPORTANT STUFF.
YESTERDAY: OTTER SNEEZED. IT WAS SUPER CUTE.
THAT'S NOT IMPORTANT!
IT IS TO ME!
TODAY: OTTER WAS PROUD OF ME!

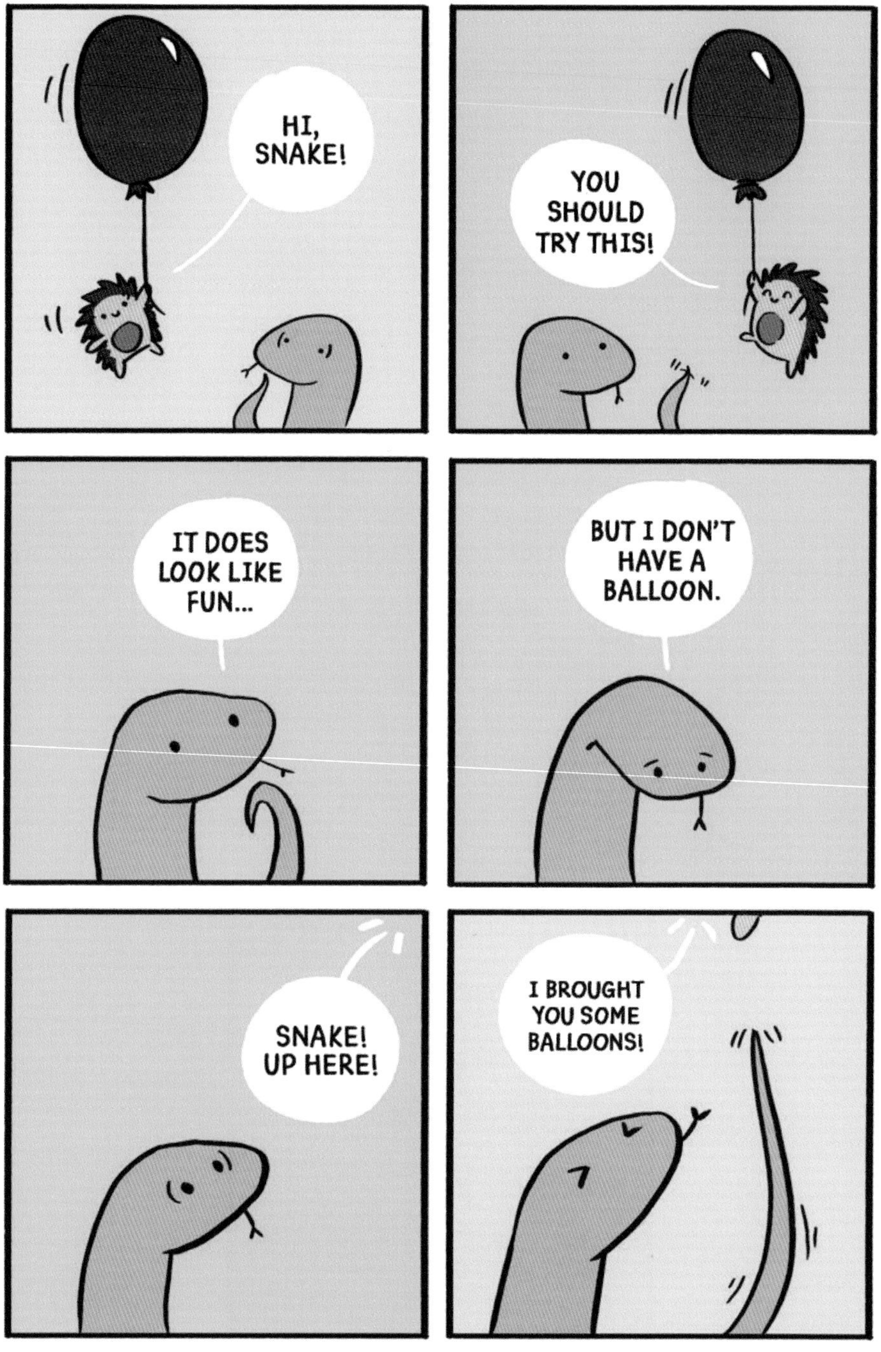
HI, SNAKE!
YOU SHOULD TRY THIS!
IT DOES LOOK LIKE FUN...
BUT I DON'T HAVE A BALLOON.
SNAKE! UP HERE!
I BROUGHT YOU SOME BALLOONS!

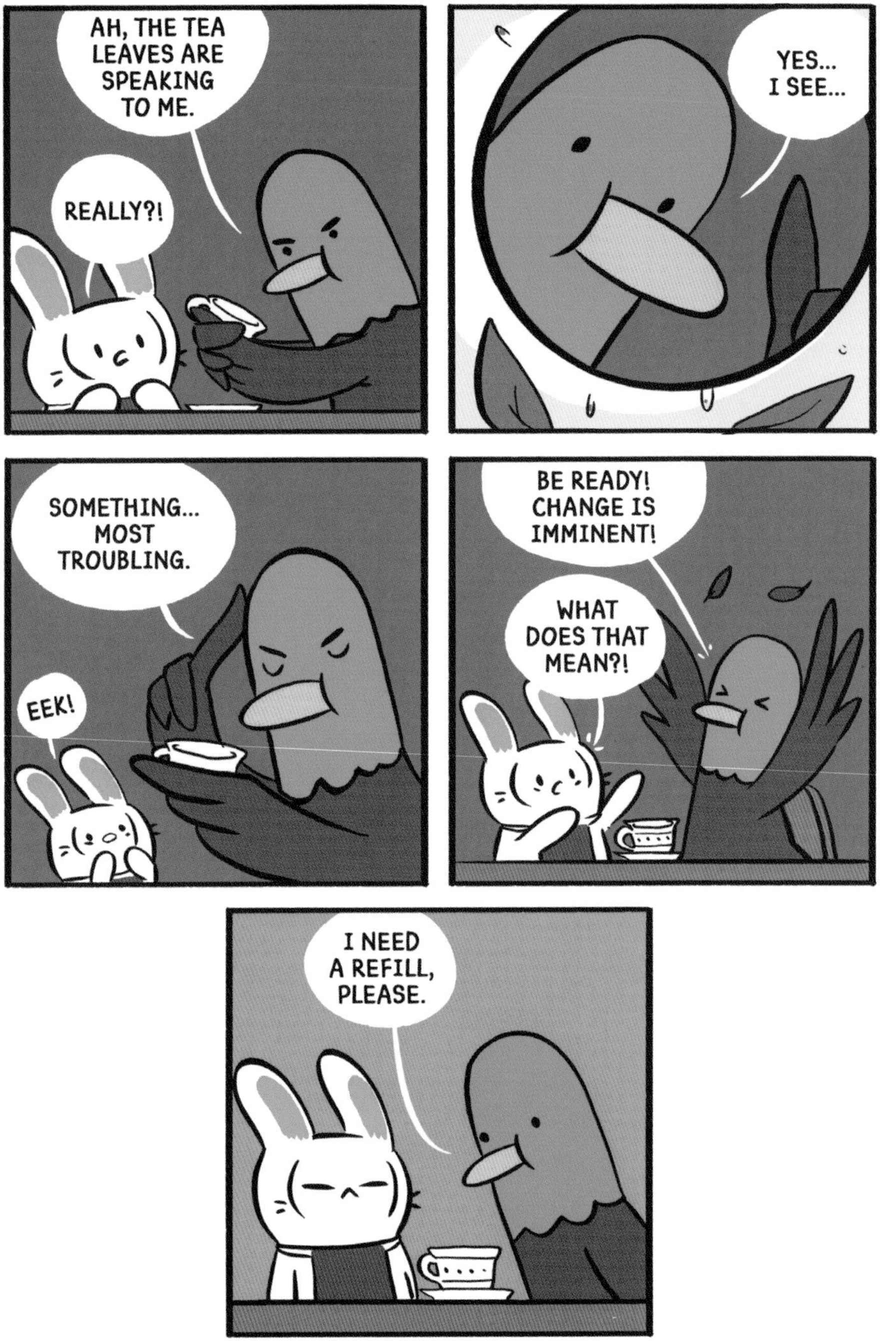
AH, THE TEA LEAVES ARE SPEAKING TO ME.
REALLY?!
YES... I SEE...
SOMETHING... MOST TROUBLING.
EEK!
BE READY! CHANGE IS IMMINENT!
WHAT DOES THAT MEAN?!
I NEED A REFILL, PLEASE.

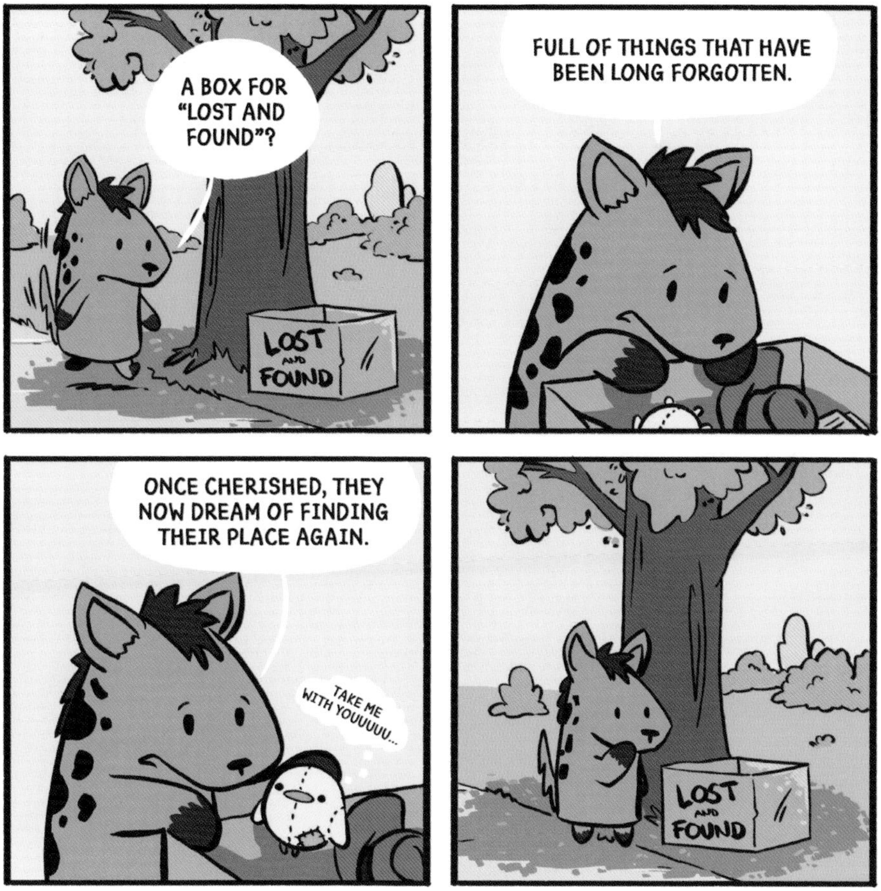
A BOX FOR "LOST AND FOUND"?
LOST AND FOUND
FULL OF THINGS THAT HAVE BEEN LONG FORGOTTEN.
ONCE CHERISHED, THEY NOW DREAM OF FINDING THEIR PLACE AGAIN.
TAKE ME WITH YOUUUUU...
LOST AND FOUND

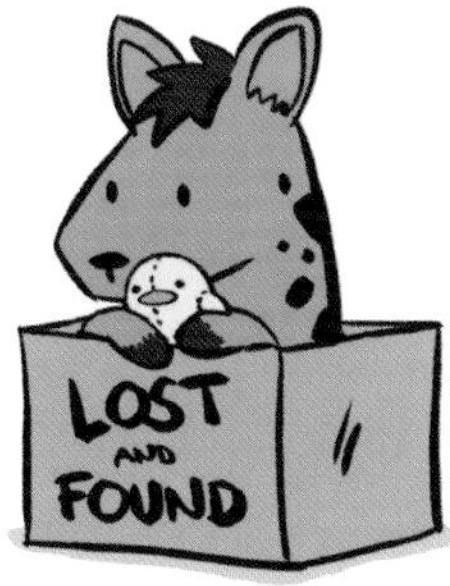
LOST AND FOUND

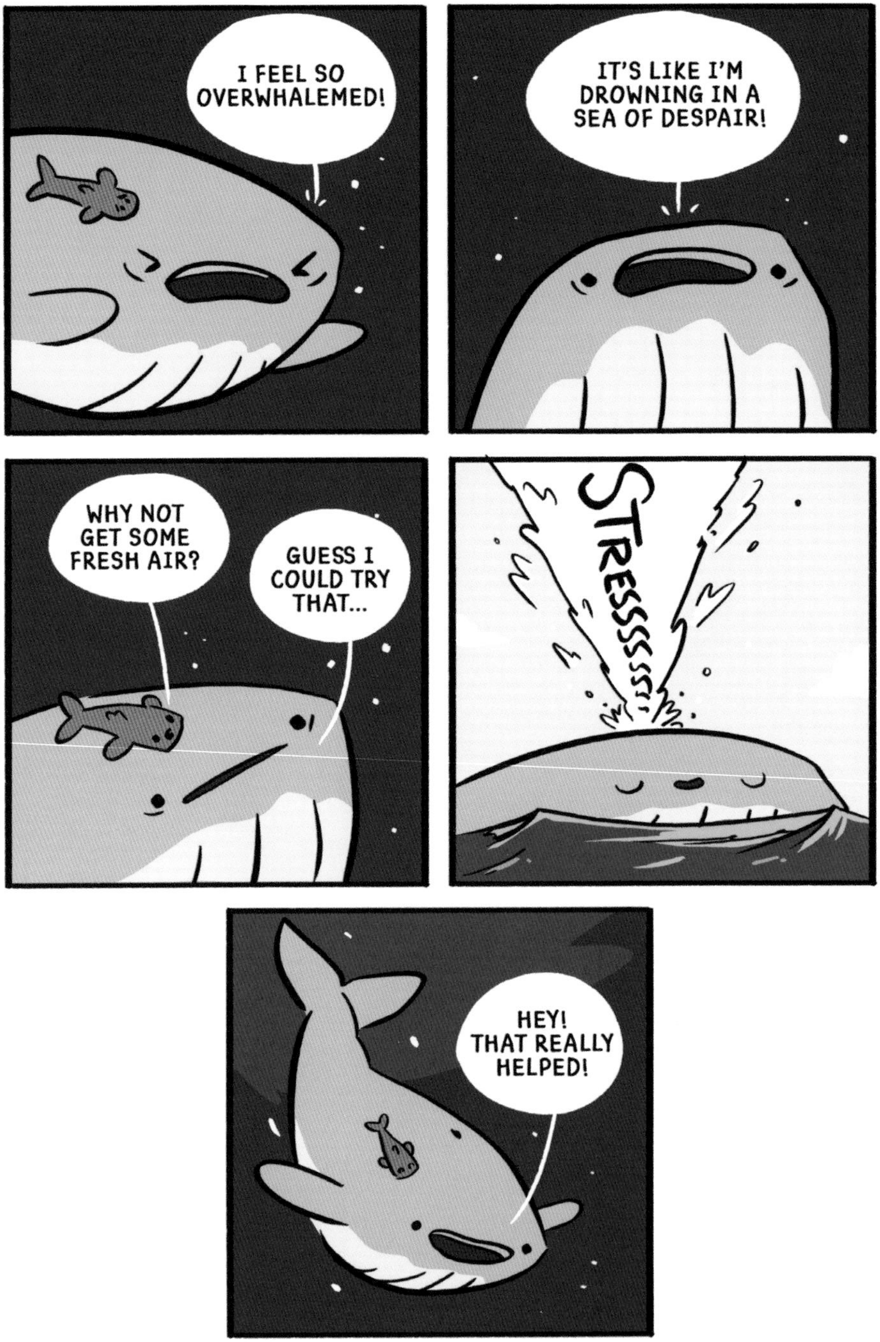
I FEEL SO OVERWHALEMED!
IT'S LIKE I'M DROWNING IN A SEA OF DESPAIR!
WHY NOT GET SOME FRESH AIR?
GUESS I COULD TRY THAT...
STRESSSSSSS
HEY! THAT REALLY HELPED!

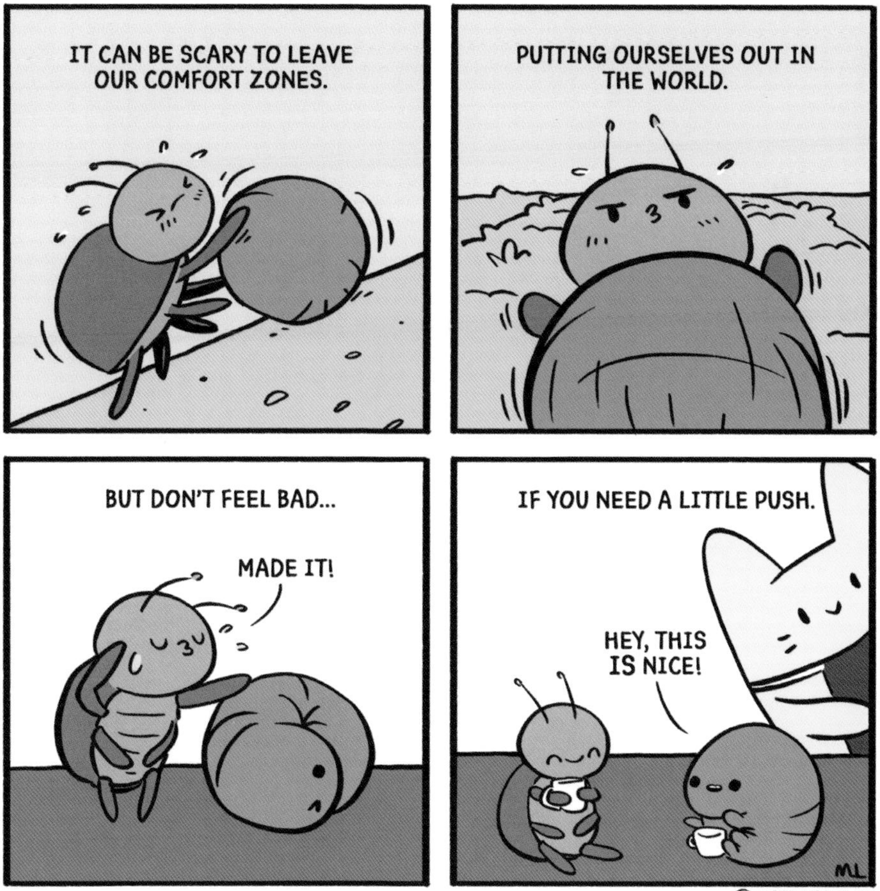
IT CAN BE SCARY TO LEAVE OUR COMFORT ZONES.
PUTTING OURSELVES OUT IN THE WORLD.
BUT DON'T FEEL BAD...
MADE IT!
IF YOU NEED A LITTLE PUSH.
HEY, THIS IS NICE!
ML

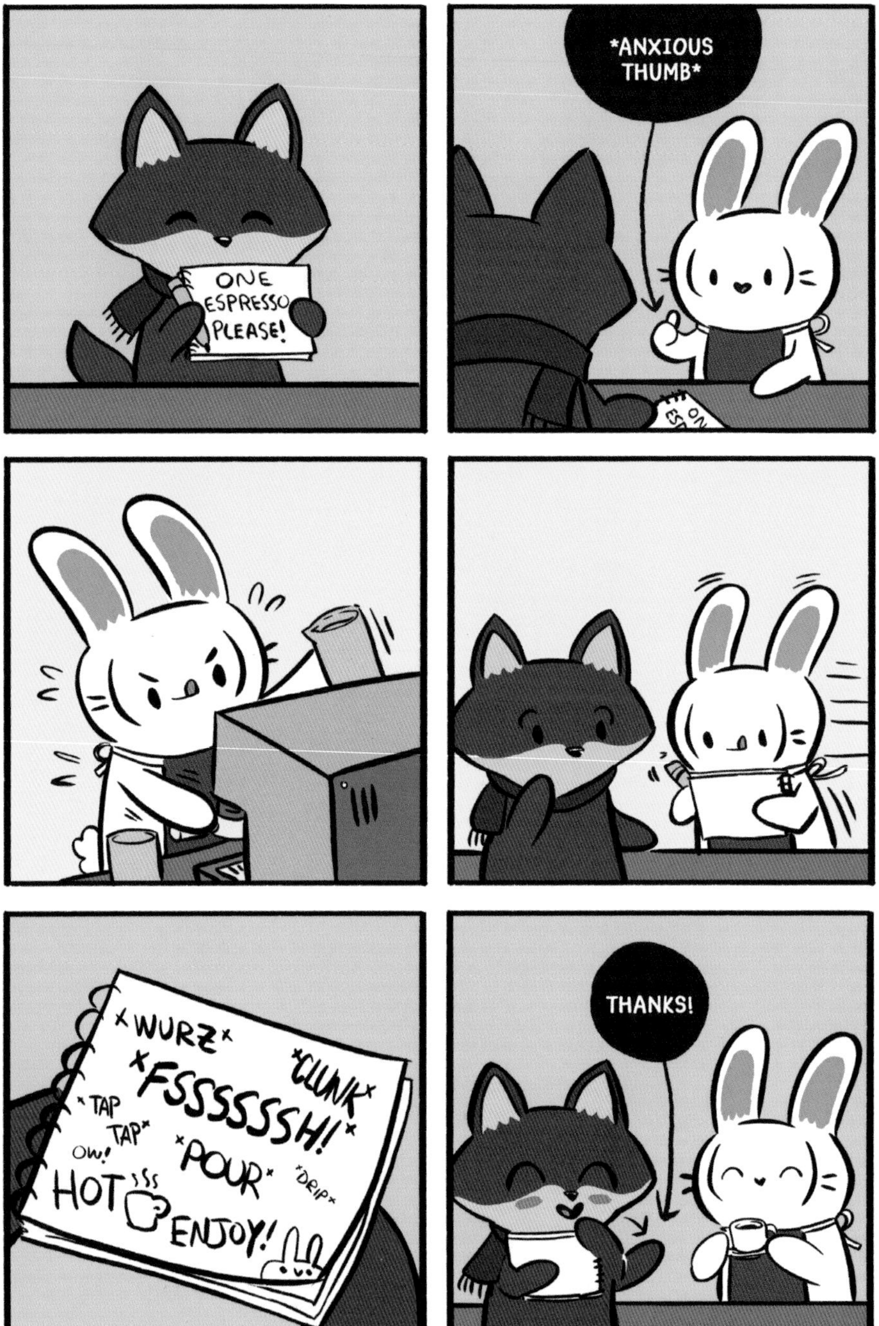
ONE ESPRESSO PLEASE!
ANXIOUS THUMB
ONE ESP
WURZ
FSSSSSSH!
CLUNK
TAP TAP
OW!
POUR
DRIP
HOT
ENJOY!
THANKS!

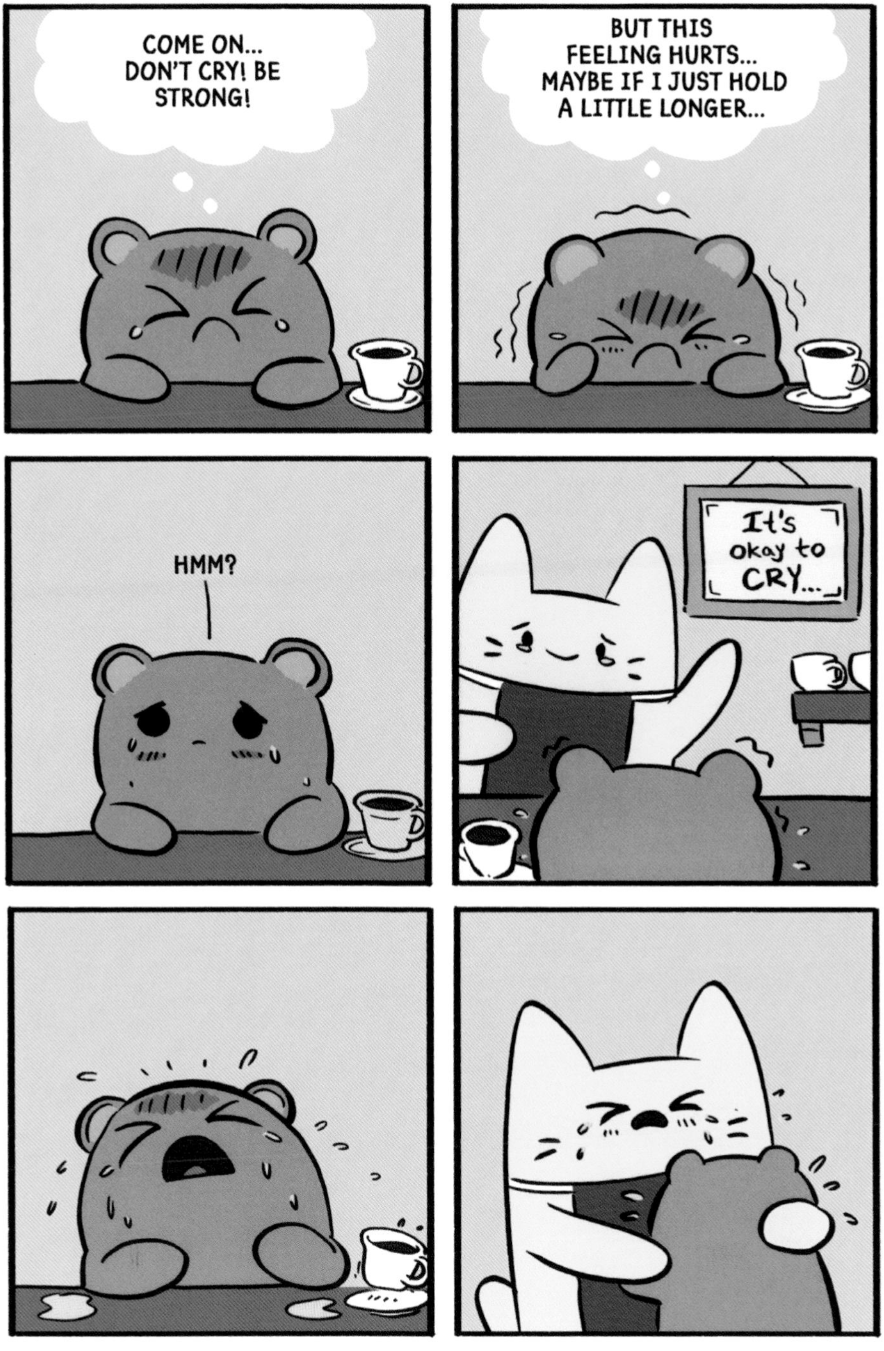
COME ON... DON'T CRY! BE STRONG!
BUT THIS FEELING HURTS... MAYBE IF I JUST HOLD A LITTLE LONGER...
HMM?
It's okay to CRY...

HOW DO YOU COPE WITH STRESS?

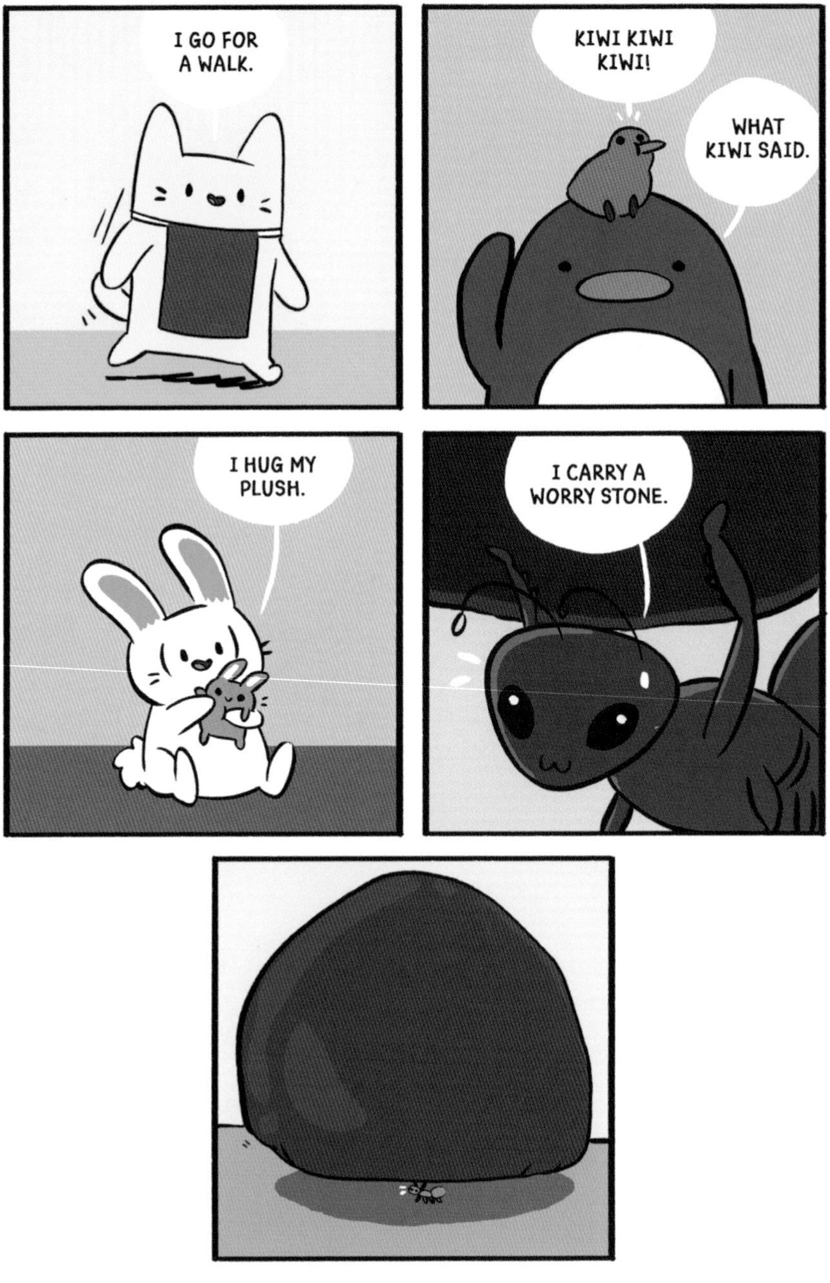
I GO FOR A WALK.
KIWI KIWI KIWI!
WHAT KIWI SAID.
I HUG MY PLUSH.
I CARRY A WORRY STONE.

PHASES OF THE MOOD

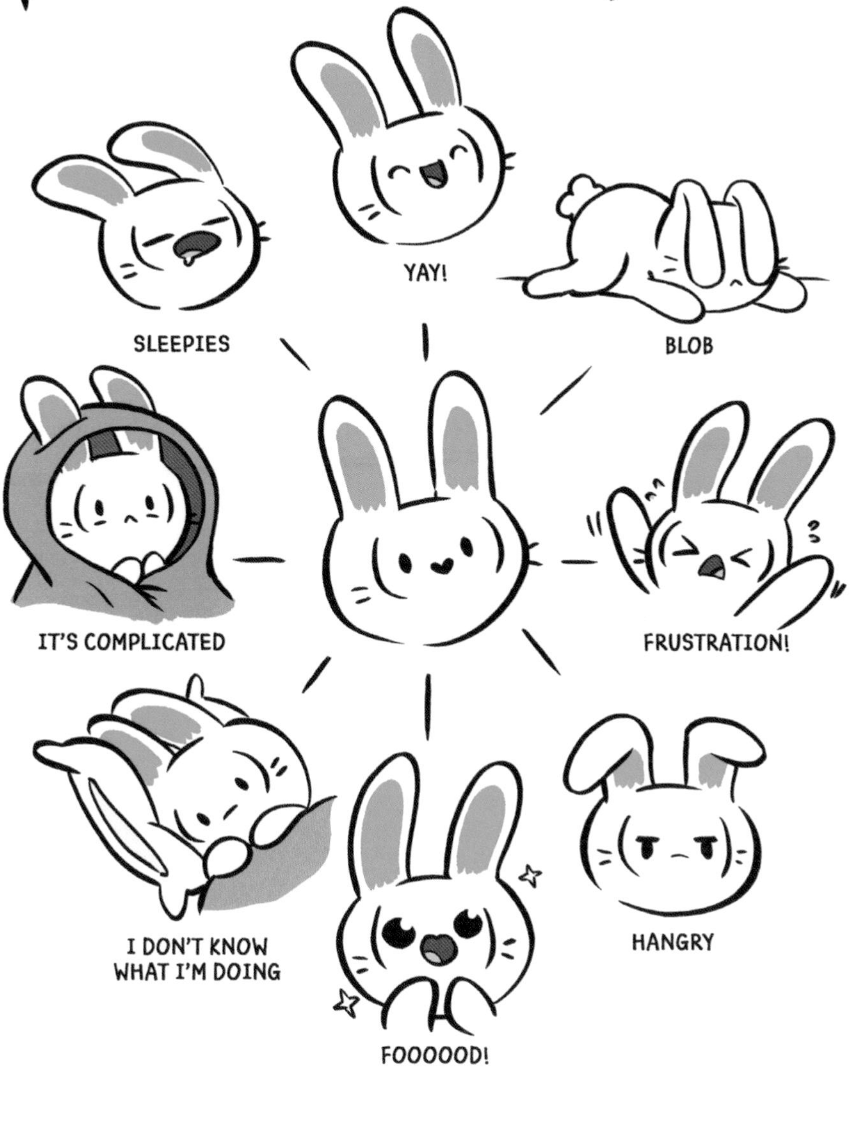
YAY!
SLEEPIES
BLOB
IT'S COMPLICATED
FRUSTRATION!
I DON'T KNOW WHAT I'M DOING
HANGRY
FOOOOOD!

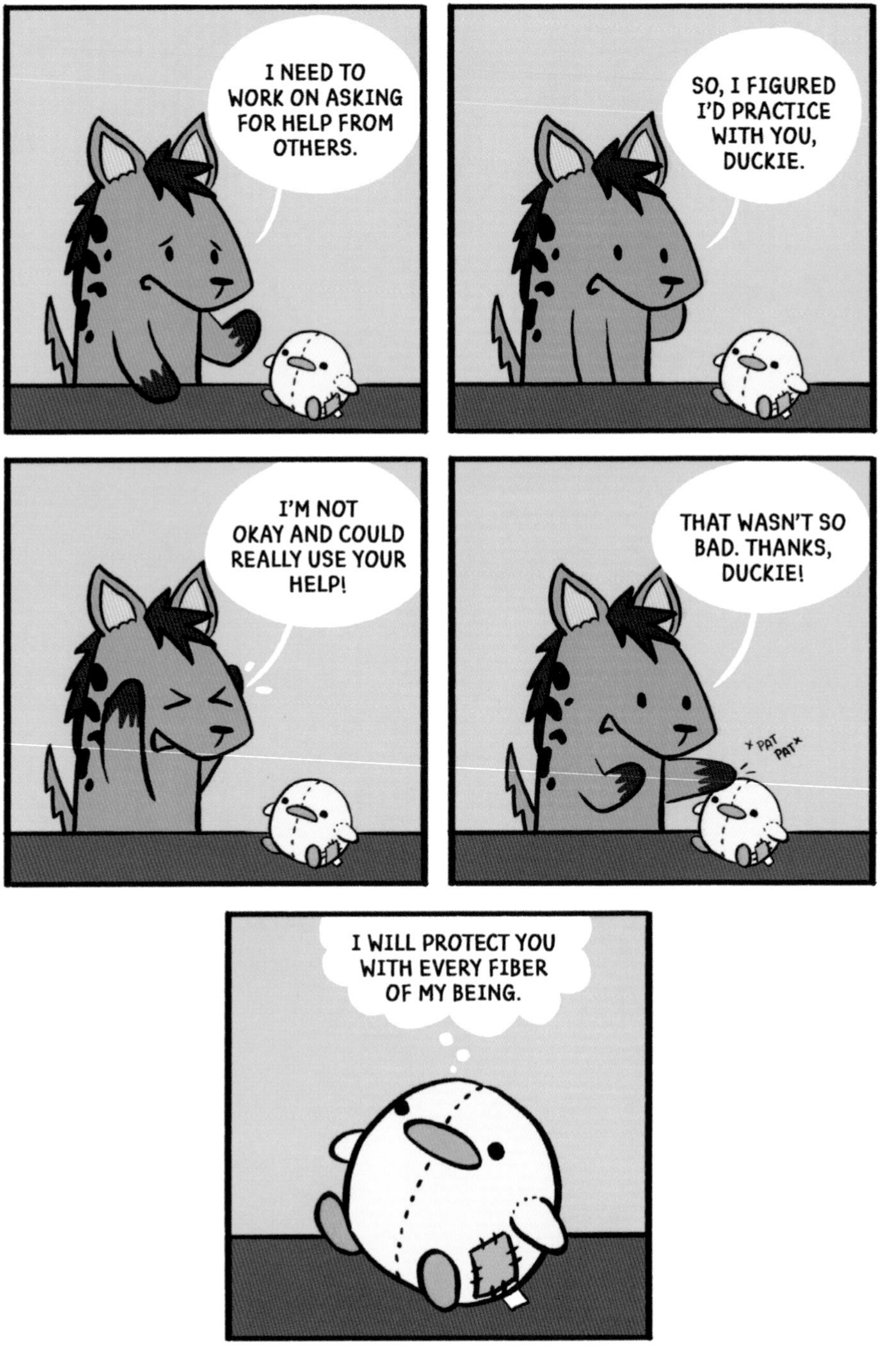
I NEED TO WORK ON ASKING FOR HELP FROM OTHERS.
SO, I FIGURED I'D PRACTICE WITH YOU, DUCKIE.
I'M NOT OKAY AND COULD REALLY USE YOUR HELP!
THAT WASN'T SO BAD. THANKS, DUCKIE!
PAT PAT
I WILL PROTECT YOU WITH EVERY FIBER OF MY BEING.

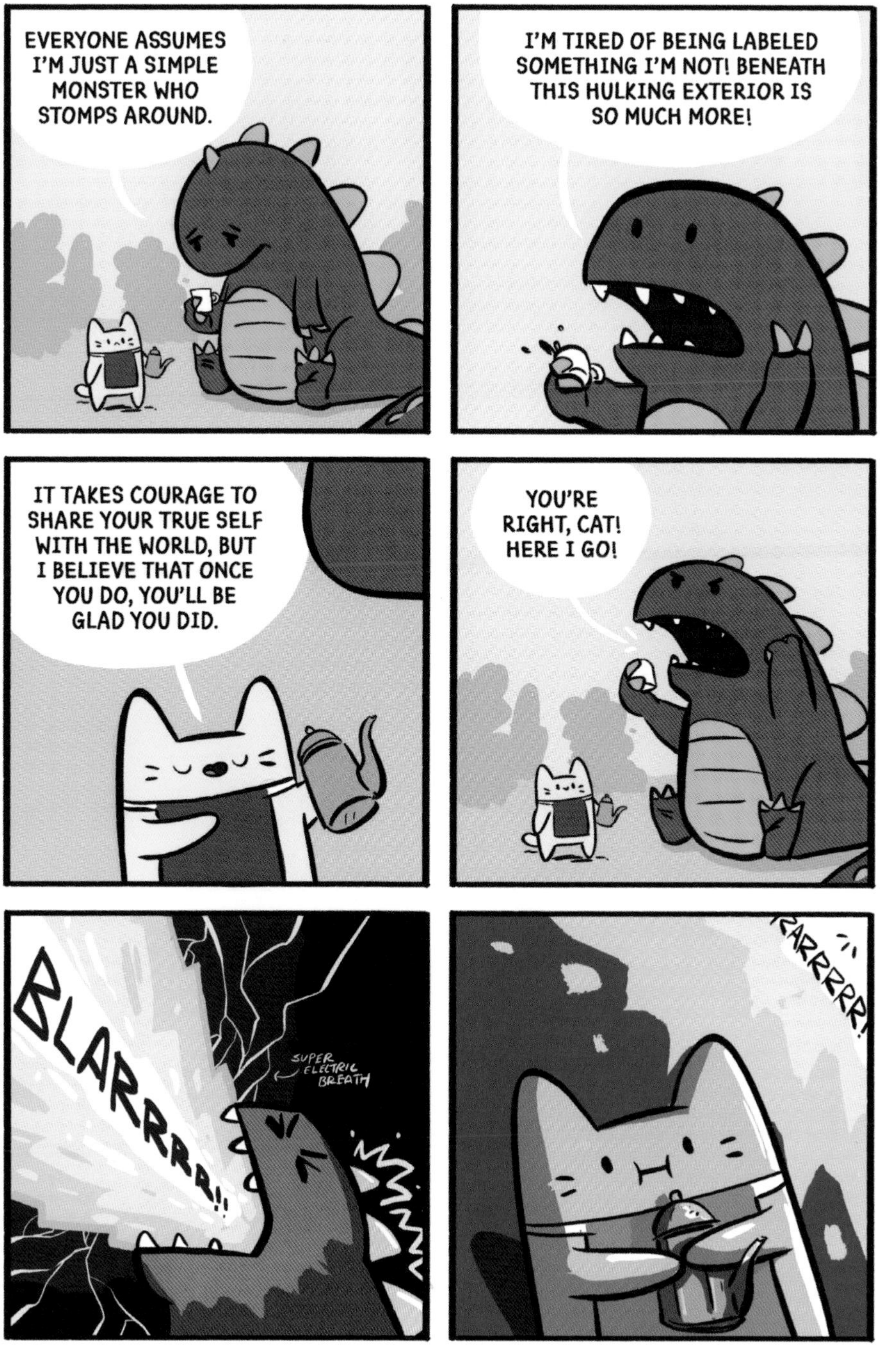
EVERYONE ASSUMES I'M JUST A SIMPLE MONSTER WHO STOMPS AROUND.
I'M TIRED OF BEING LABELED SOMETHING I'M NOT! BENEATH THIS HULKING EXTERIOR IS SO MUCH MORE!
IT TAKES COURAGE TO SHARE YOUR TRUE SELF WITH THE WORLD, BUT I BELIEVE THAT ONCE YOU DO, YOU'LL BE GLAD YOU DID.
YOU'RE RIGHT, CAT! HERE I GO!
BLARRRRR!!
SUPER ELECTRIC BREATH
RARRRRR!

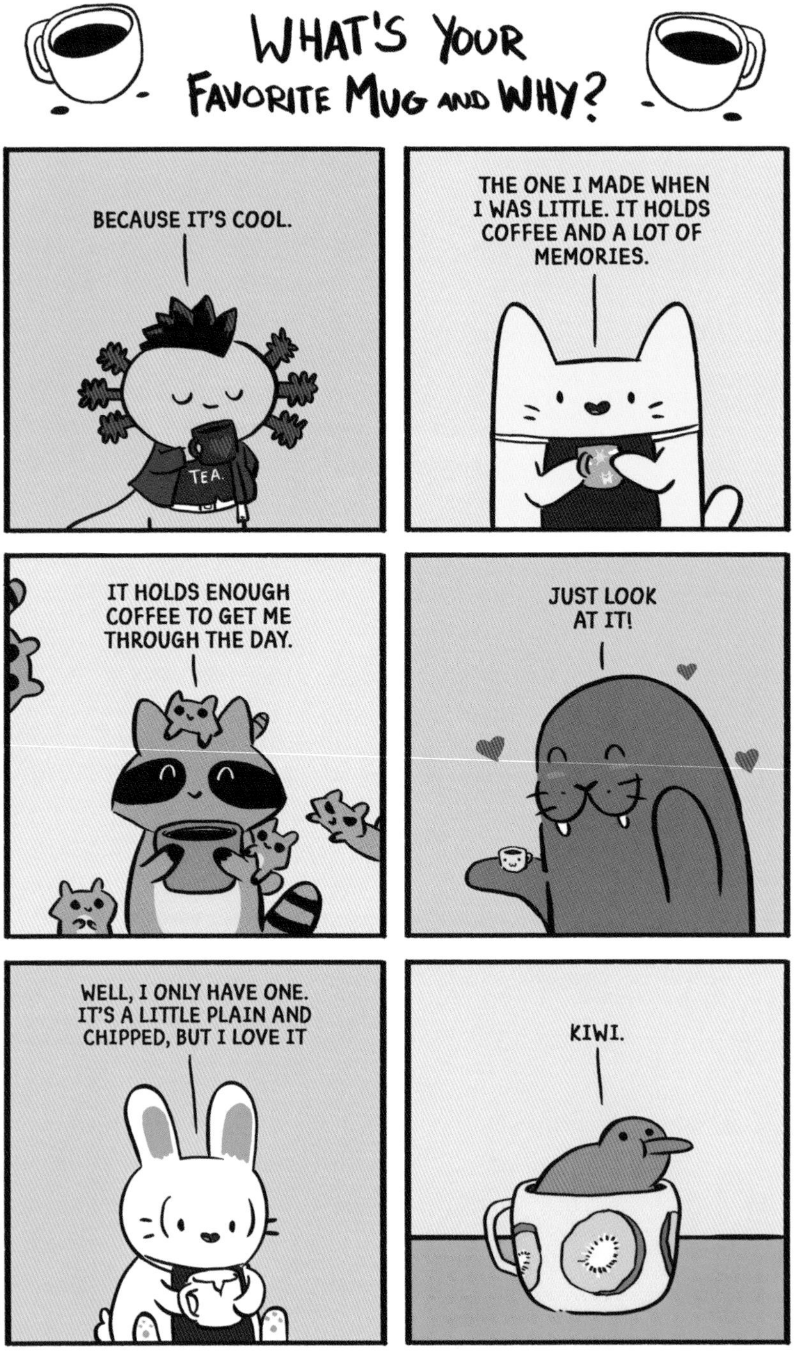
WHAT'S YOUR FAVORITE MUG AND WHY?
BECAUSE IT'S COOL.
TEA.
THE ONE I MADE WHEN I WAS LITTLE. IT HOLDS COFFEE AND A LOT OF MEMORIES.
IT HOLDS ENOUGH COFFEE TO GET ME THROUGH THE DAY.
JUST LOOK AT IT!
WELL, I ONLY HAVE ONE. IT'S A LITTLE PLAIN AND CHIPPED, BUT I LOVE IT
KIWI.

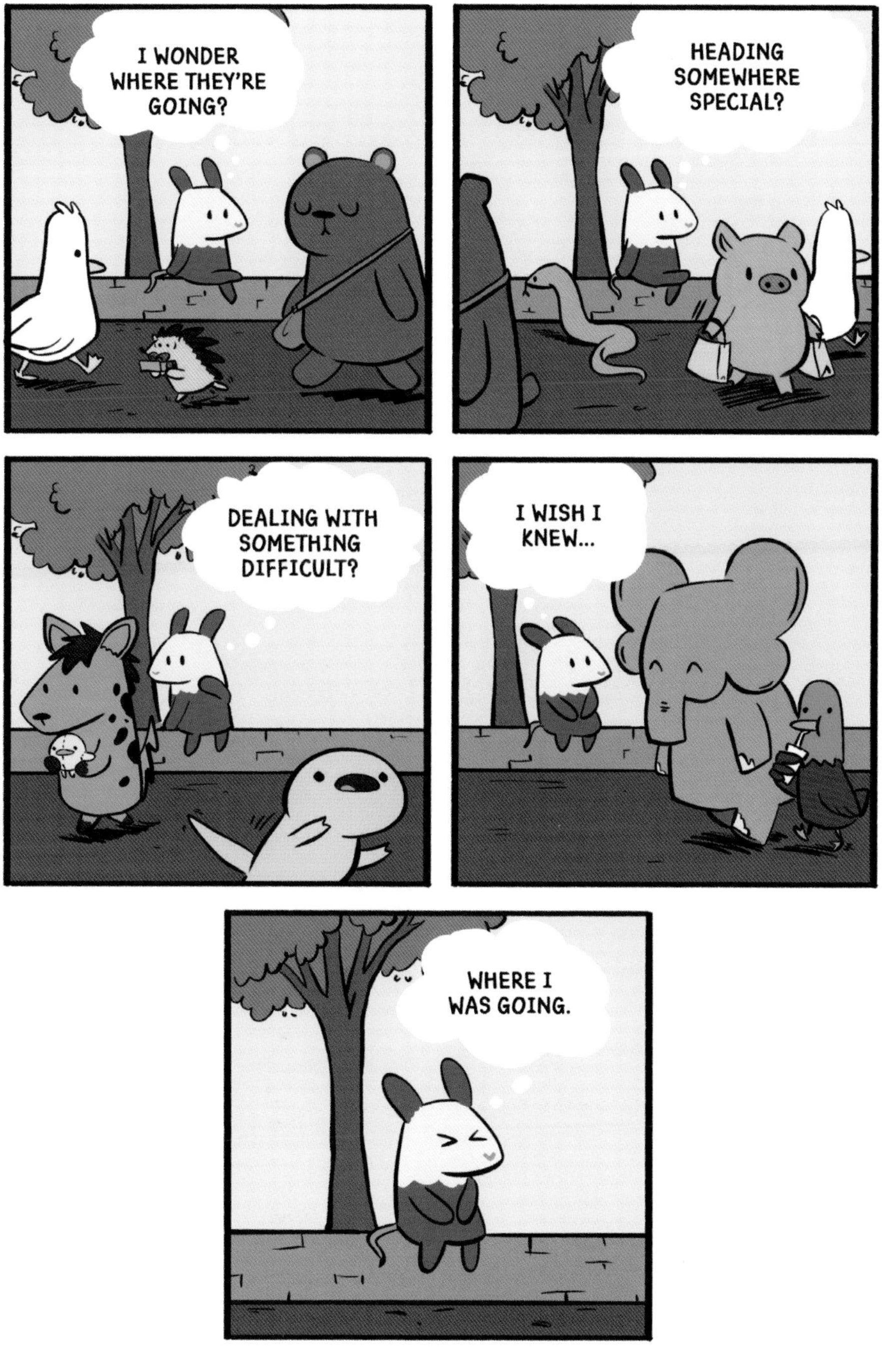
I WONDER WHERE THEY'RE GOING?
HEADING SOMEWHERE SPECIAL?
DEALING WITH SOMETHING DIFFICULT?
I WISH I KNEW...
WHERE I WAS GOING.

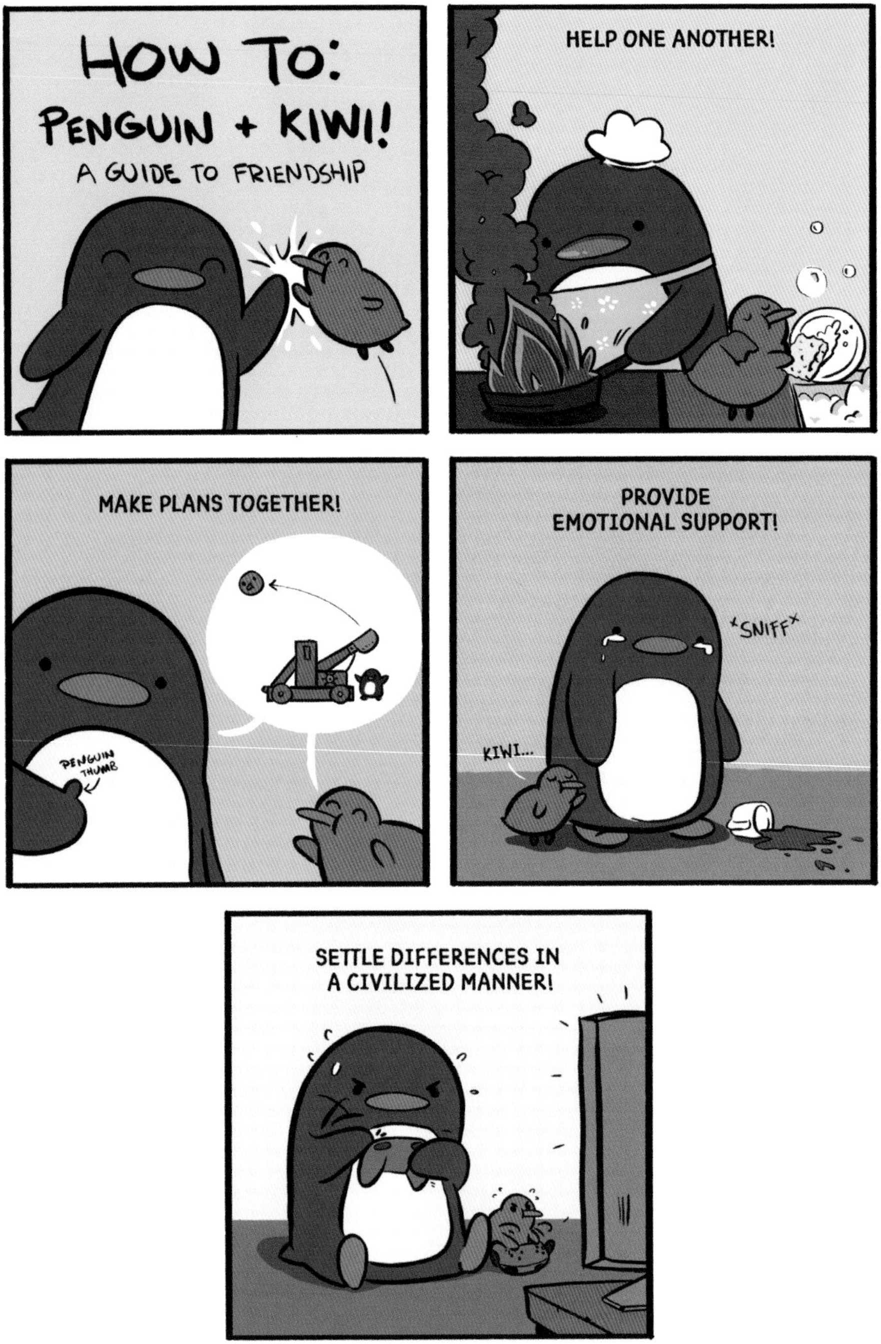
HOW TO:
PENGUIN + KIWI!
A GUIDE TO FRIENDSHIP
HELP ONE ANOTHER!
MAKE PLANS TOGETHER!
PENGUIN THUMB
PROVIDE EMOTIONAL SUPPORT!
SNIFF
KIWI...
SETTLE DIFFERENCES IN A CIVILIZED MANNER!

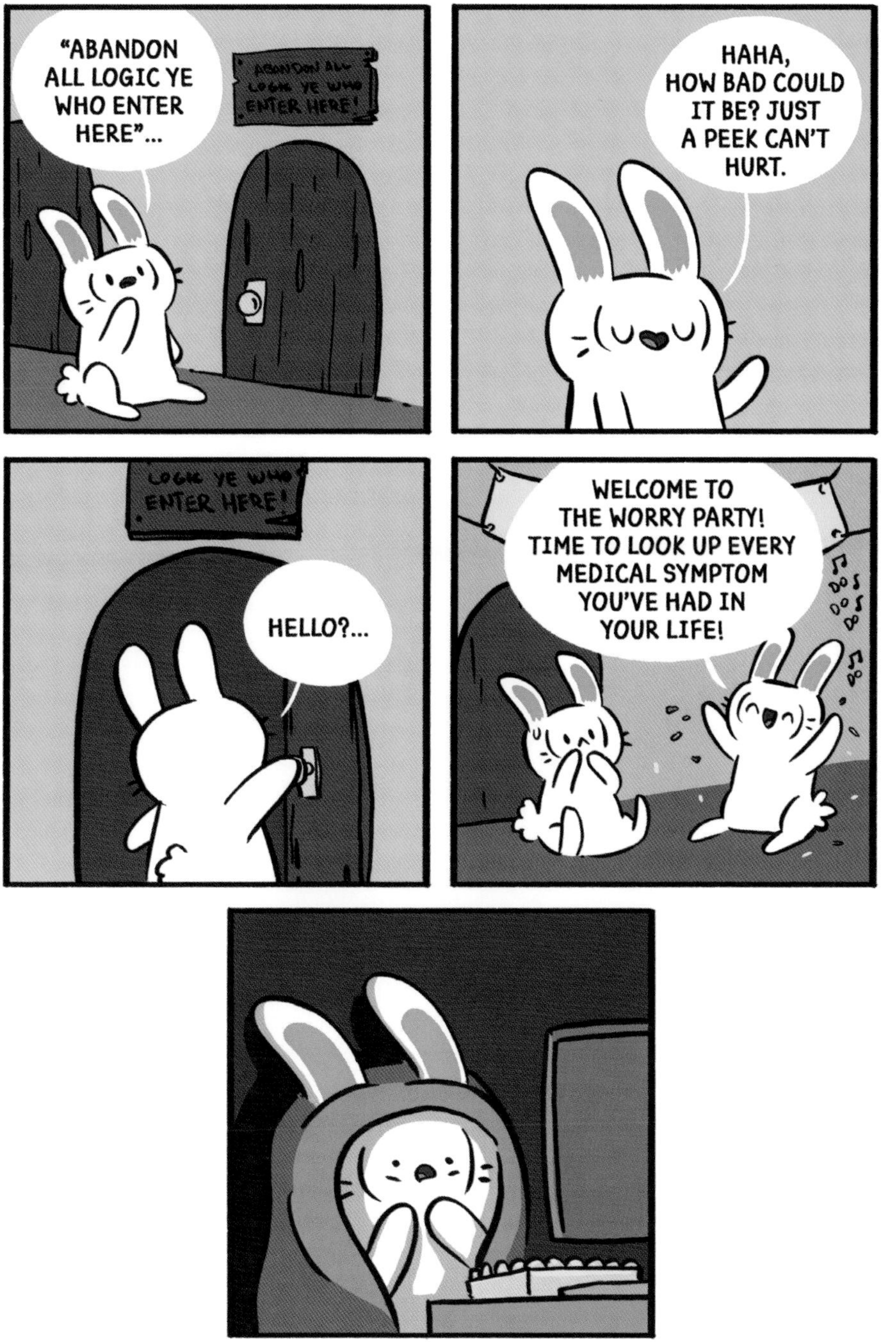
"ABANDON ALL LOGIC YE WHO ENTER HERE"...
ABANDON ALL LOGIC YE WHO ENTER HERE!
HAHA, HOW BAD COULD IT BE? JUST A PEEK CAN'T HURT.
LOGIC YE WHO ENTER HERE!
HELLO?...
WELCOME TO THE WORRY PARTY! TIME TO LOOK UP EVERY MEDICAL SYMPTOM YOU'VE HAD IN YOUR LIFE!

KIWI'S SELF-IMPROVEMENT TIPS

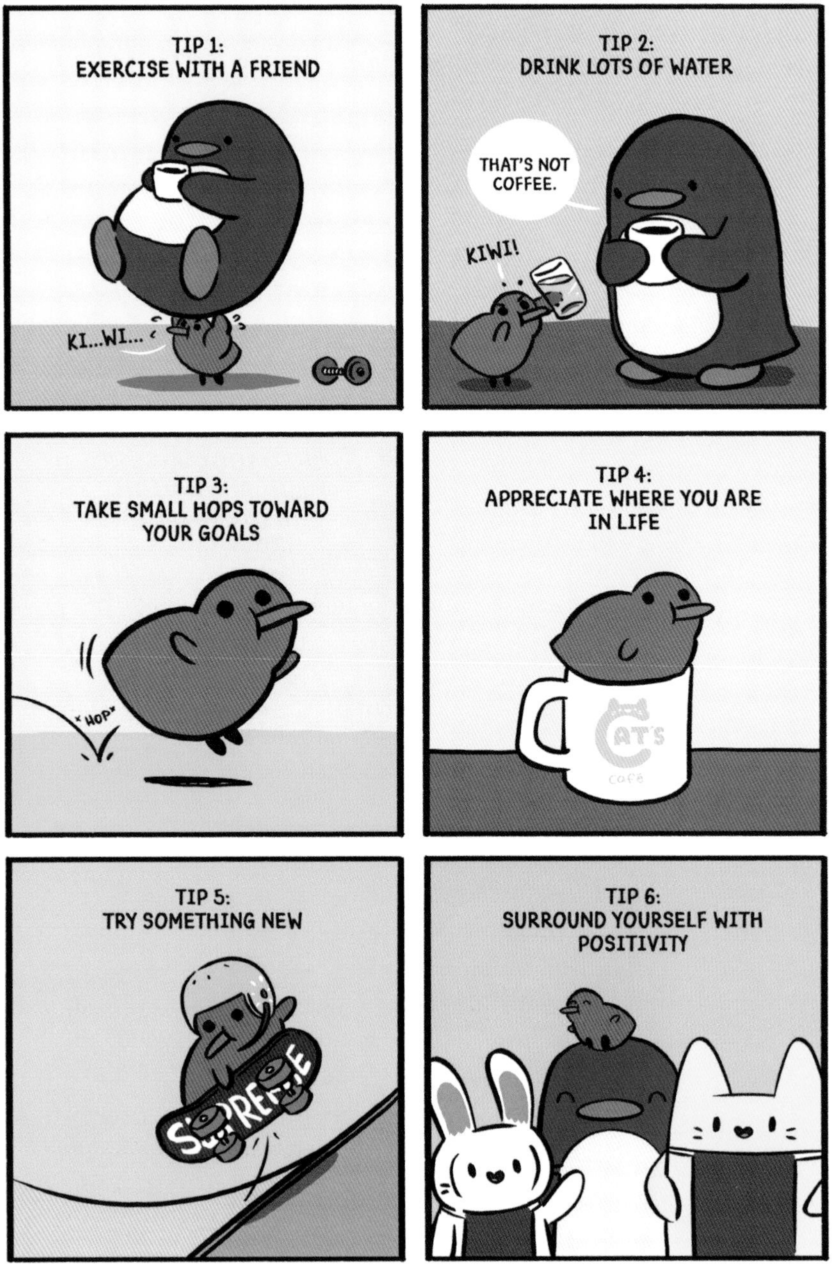
TIP 1:
EXERCISE WITH A FRIEND
KI...WI...
TIP 2:
DRINK LOTS OF WATER
THAT'S NOT COFFEE.
KIWI!
TIP 3:
TAKE SMALL HOPS TOWARD YOUR GOALS
HOP
TIP 4:
APPRECIATE WHERE YOU ARE IN LIFE
CAT'S
café
TIP 5:
TRY SOMETHING NEW
TIP 6:
SURROUND YOURSELF WITH POSITIVITY

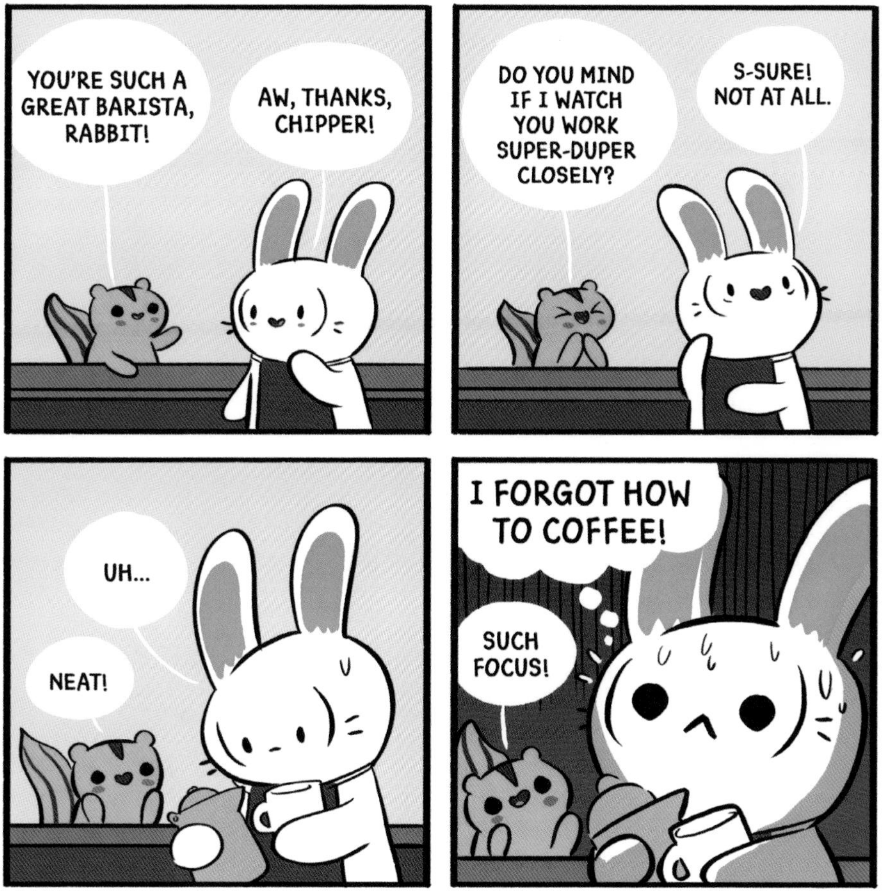
YOU'RE SUCH A GREAT BARISTA, RABBIT!
AW, THANKS, CHIPPER!
DO YOU MIND IF I WATCH YOU WORK SUPER-DUPER CLOSELY?
S-SURE! NOT AT ALL.
UH...
NEAT!
I FORGOT HOW TO COFFEE!
SUCH FOCUS!

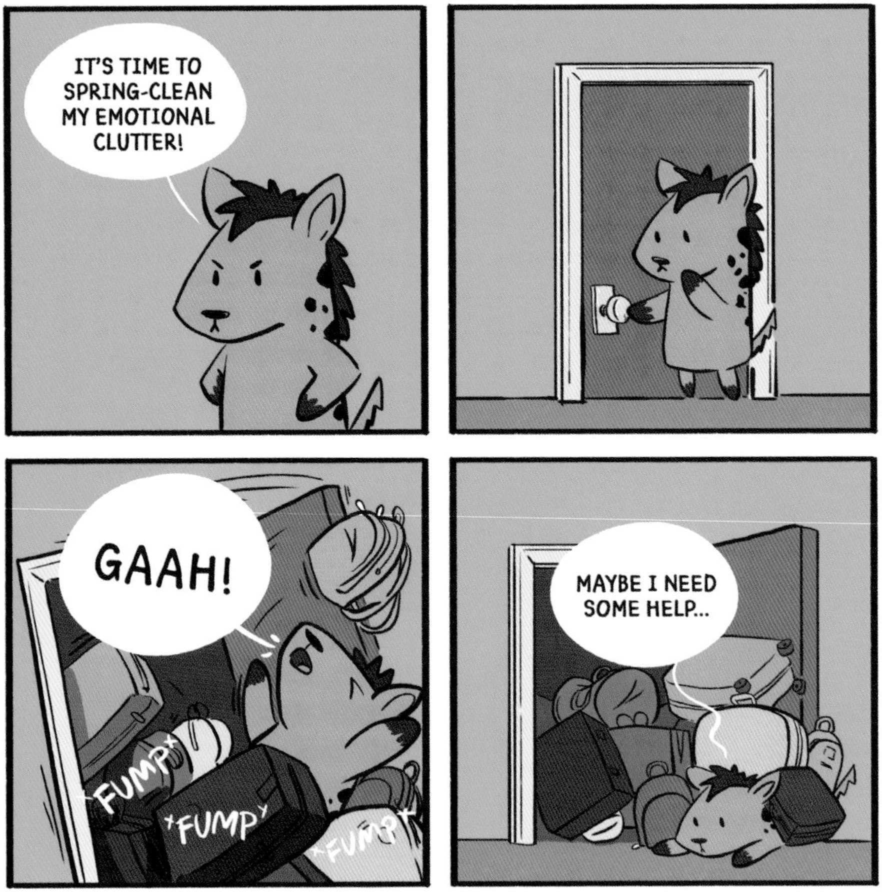
IT'S TIME TO SPRING-CLEAN MY EMOTIONAL CLUTTER!
GAAH!
FUMP
FUMP
FUMP
MAYBE I NEED SOME HELP...

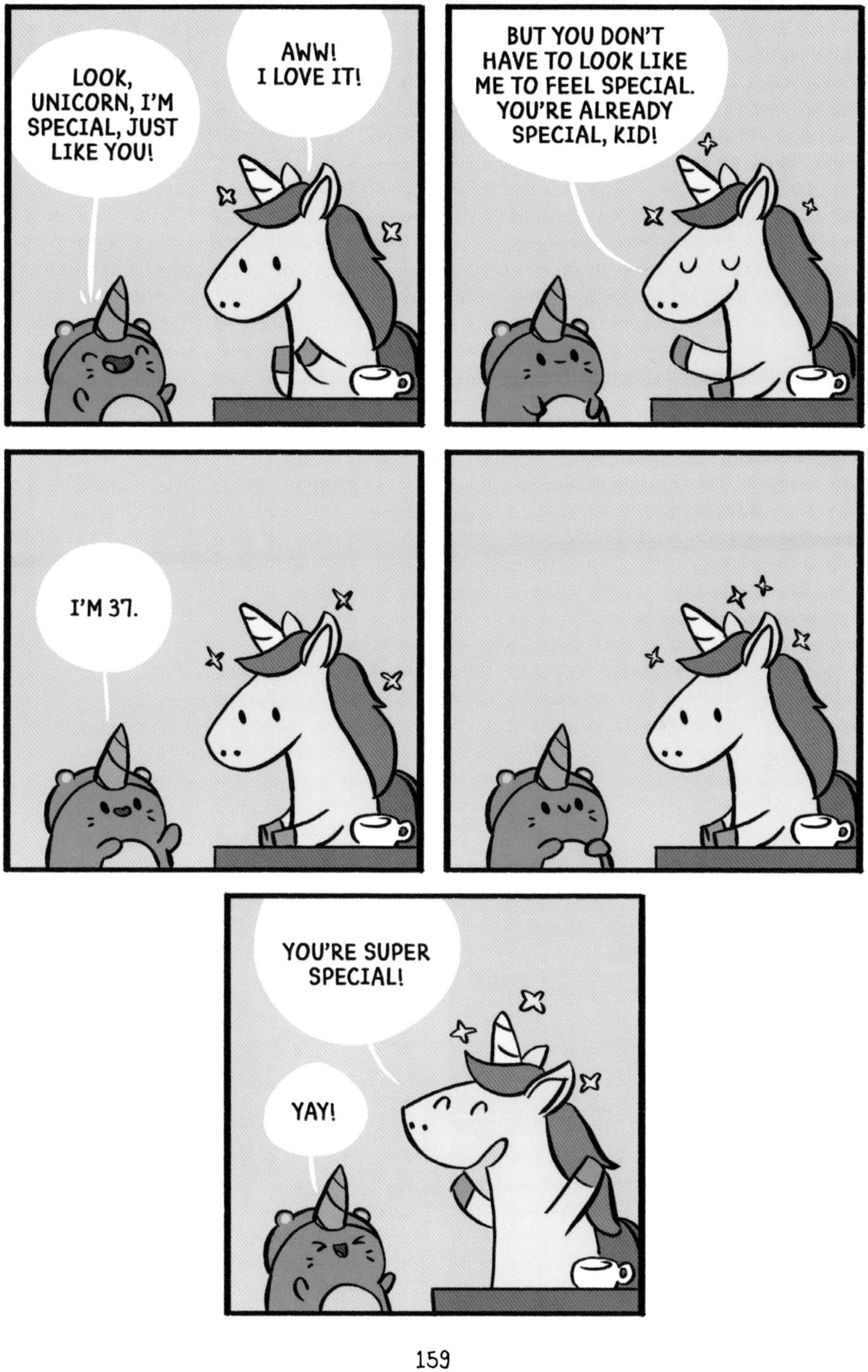
LOOK, UNICORN, I'M SPECIAL, JUST LIKE YOU!
AWW! I LOVE IT!
BUT YOU DON'T HAVE TO LOOK LIKE ME TO FEEL SPECIAL. YOU'RE ALREADY SPECIAL, KID!
I'M 37.
YOU'RE SUPER SPECIAL!
YAY!

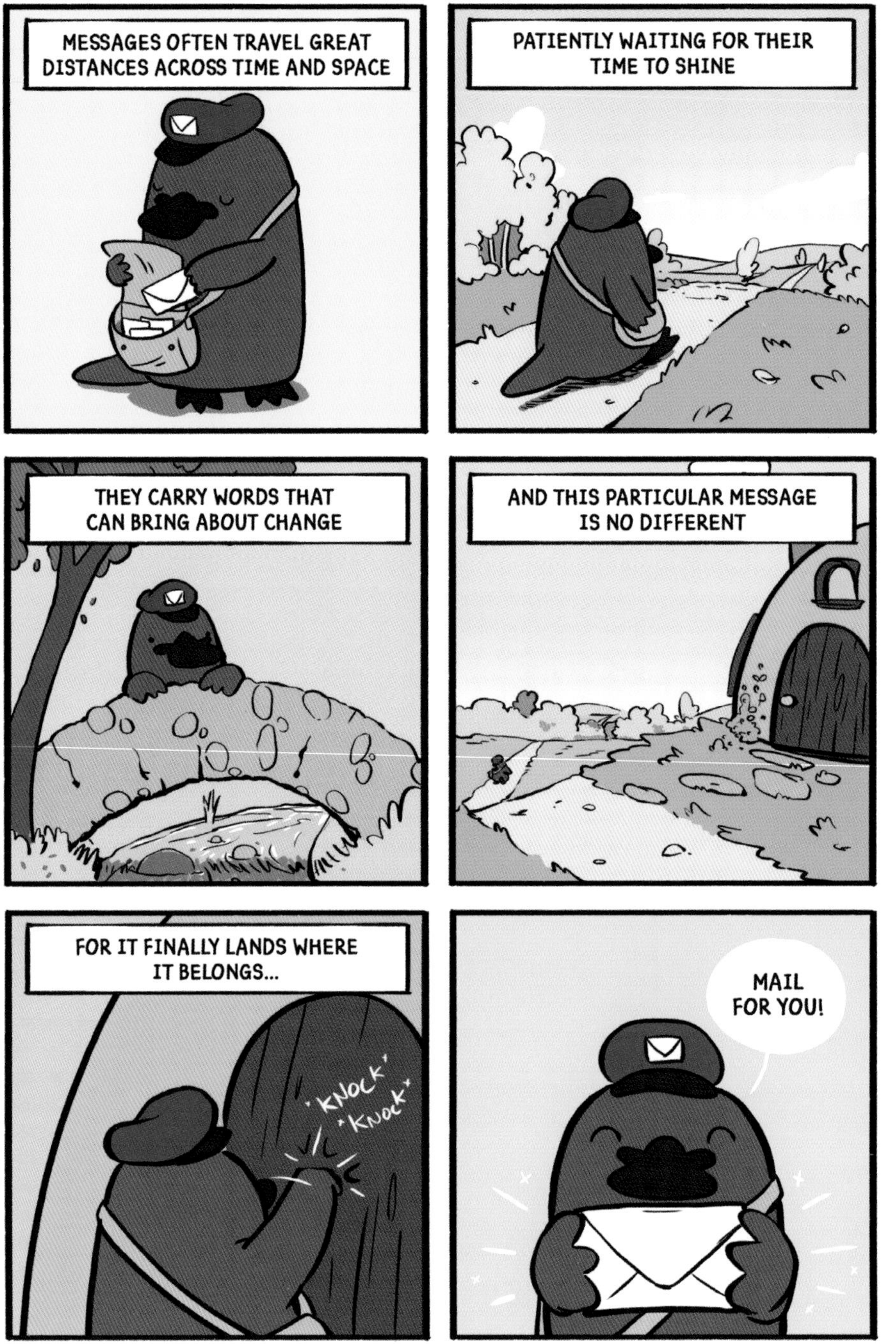
MESSAGES OFTEN TRAVEL GREAT DISTANCES ACROSS TIME AND SPACE
PATIENTLY WAITING FOR THEIR TIME TO SHINE
THEY CARRY WORDS THAT CAN BRING ABOUT CHANGE
AND THIS PARTICULAR MESSAGE IS NO DIFFERENT
FOR IT FINALLY LANDS WHERE IT BELONGS...
KNOCK KNOCK
MAIL FOR YOU!

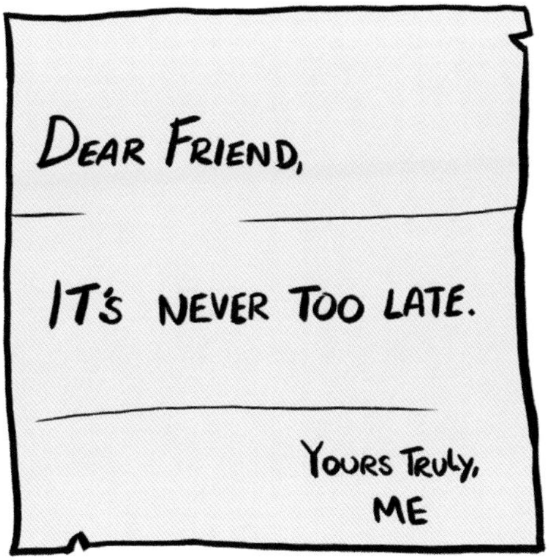

DEAR FRIEND,
IT'S NEVER TOO LATE.
YOURS TRULY,
ME

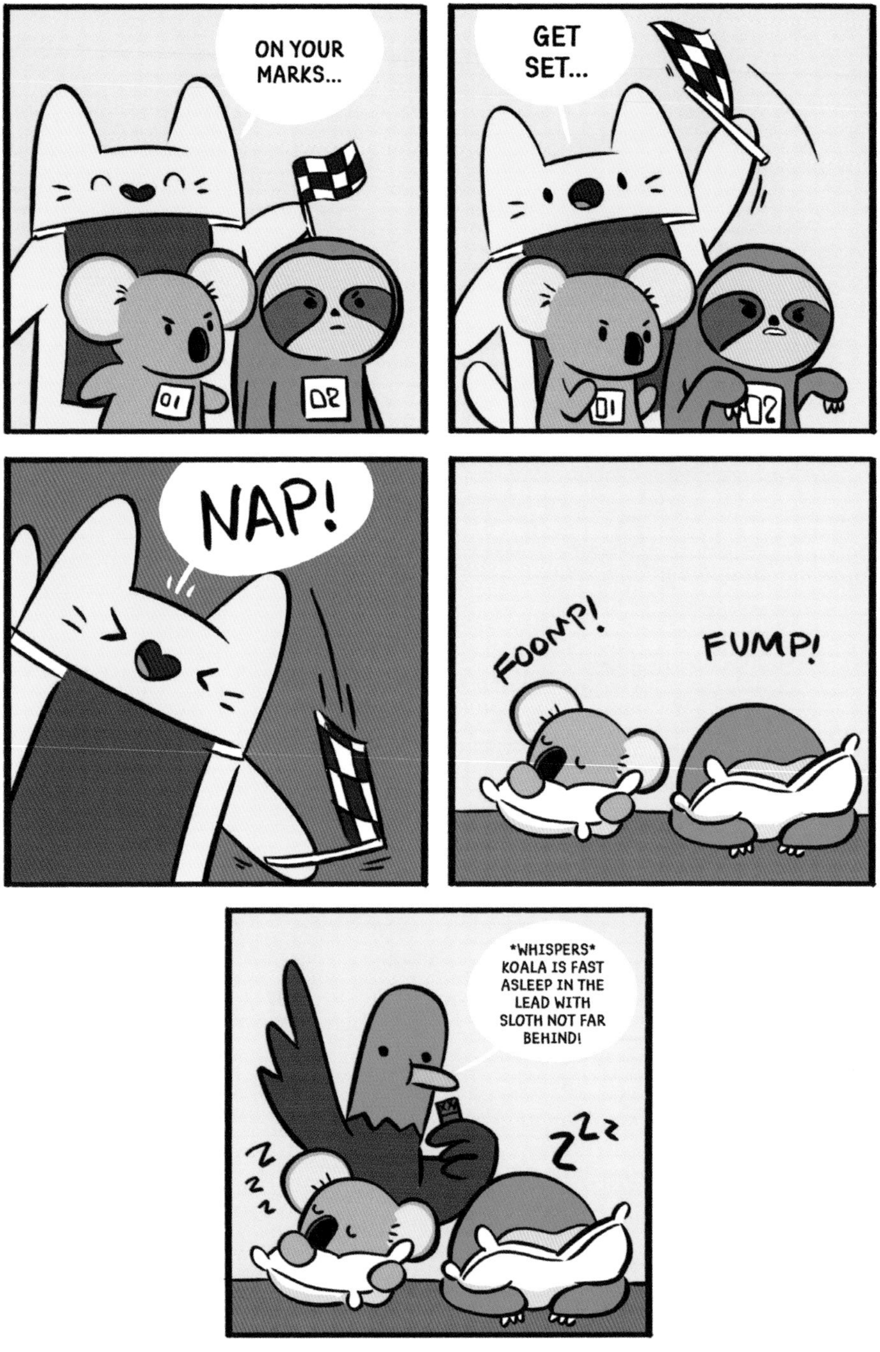

ON YOUR MARKS...
01
02
GET SET...
01
02
NAP!
FOOMP!
FUMP!
WHISPERS KOALA IS FAST ASLEEP IN THE LEAD WITH SLOTH NOT FAR BEHIND!

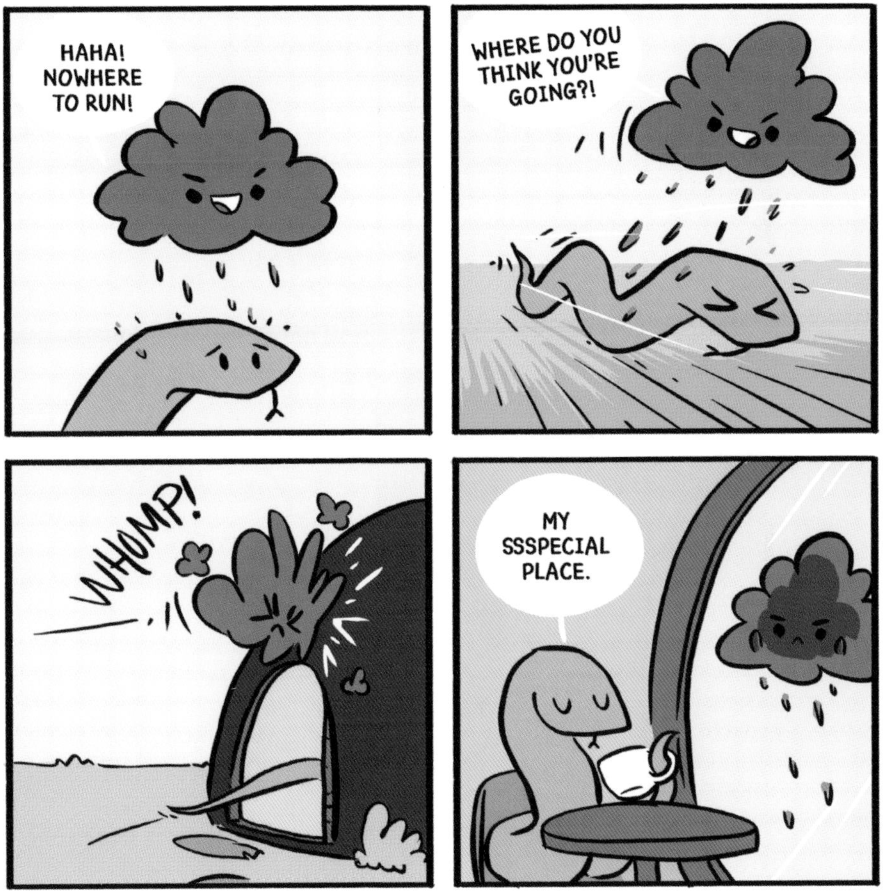
HAHA! NOWHERE TO RUN!
WHERE DO YOU THINK YOU'RE GOING?!
WHOMP!
MY SSSPECIAL PLACE.

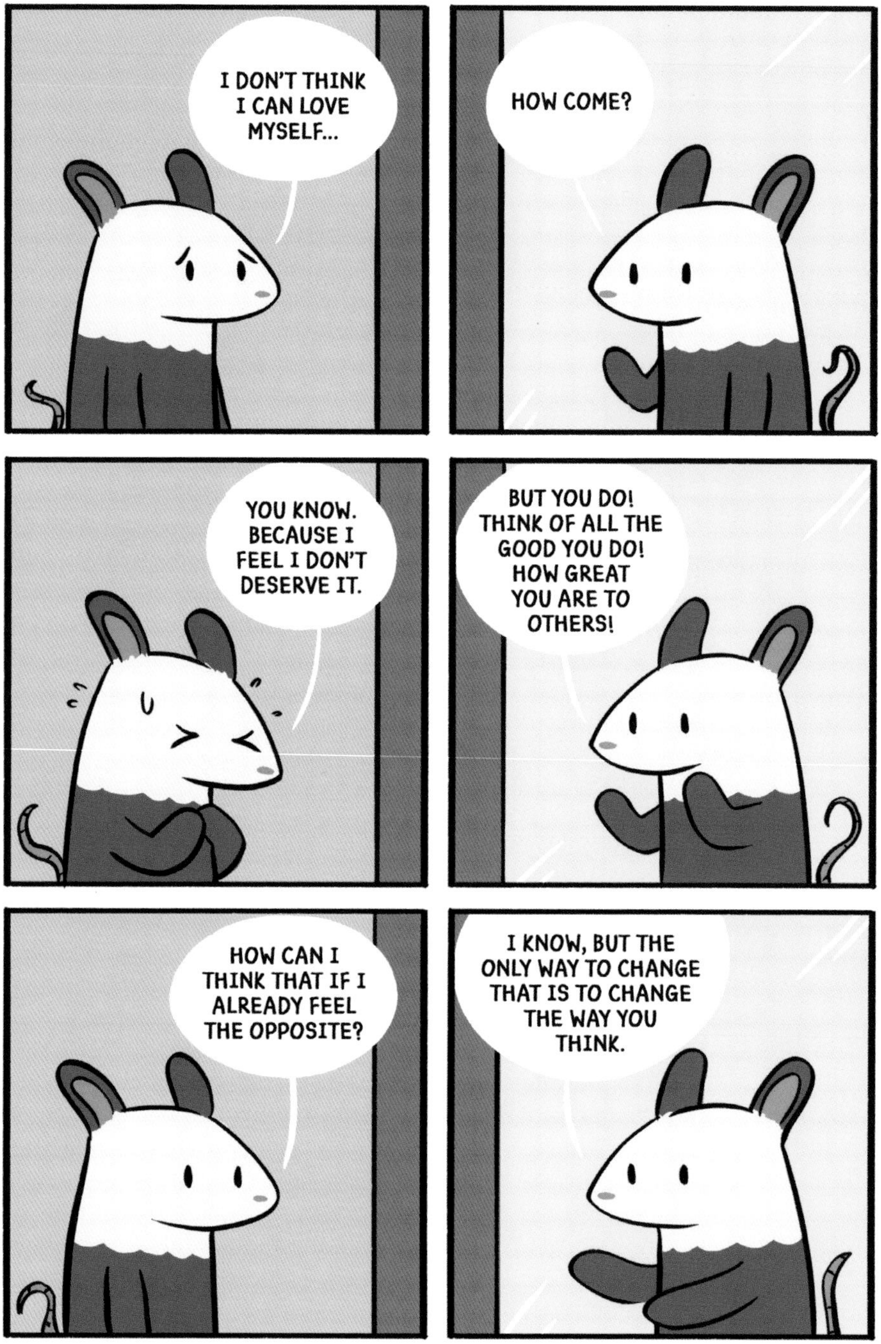
I DON'T THINK I CAN LOVE MYSELF...
HOW COME?
YOU KNOW. BECAUSE I FEEL I DON'T DESERVE IT.
BUT YOU DO! THINK OF ALL THE GOOD YOU DO! HOW GREAT YOU ARE TO OTHERS!
HOW CAN I THINK THAT IF I ALREADY FEEL THE OPPOSITE?
I KNOW, BUT THE ONLY WAY TO CHANGE THAT IS TO CHANGE THE WAY YOU THINK.

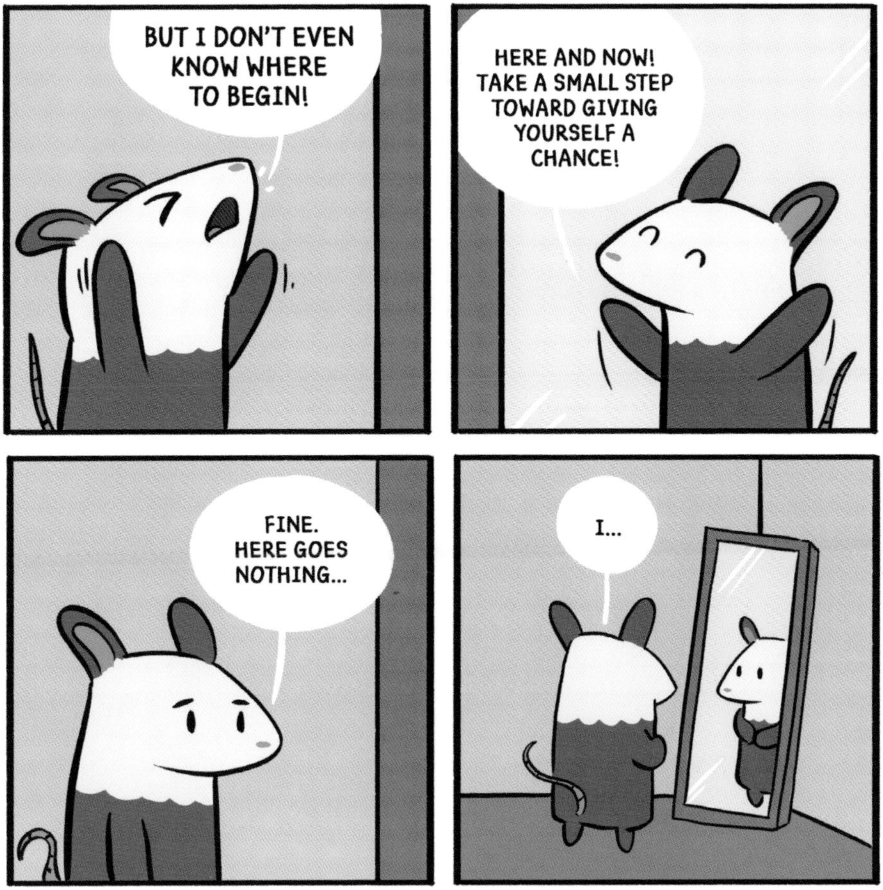
BUT I DON'T EVEN KNOW WHERE TO BEGIN!
HERE AND NOW! TAKE A SMALL STEP TOWARD GIVING YOURSELF A CHANCE!
FINE. HERE GOES NOTHING...
I...

OPOSSUM NEEDS YOUR HELP TO SAY WHAT NEEDS TO BE SAID!

WRITE DOWN ON THE NOTE PAGE ON PAGE 167 WHAT YOU'D WANT OPOSSUM TO SAY, STARTING WITH, "I..."

BY HELPING OPOSSUM, WHO KNOWS WHO ELSE YOU MIGHT HELP...

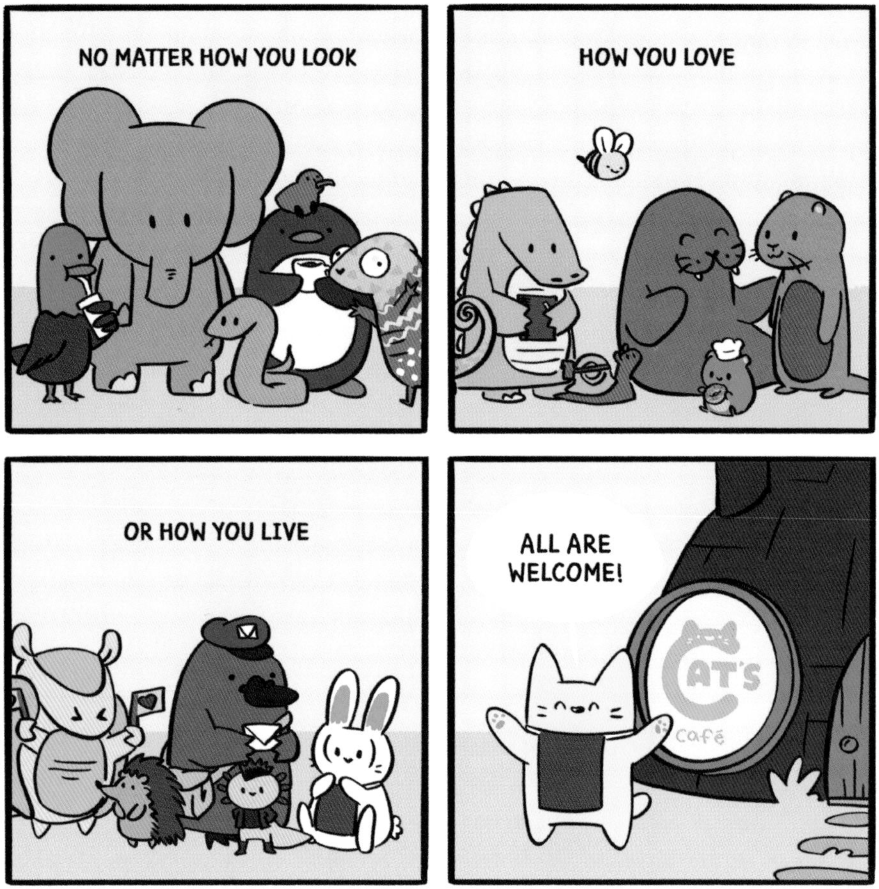
NO MATTER HOW YOU LOOK
HOW YOU LOVE
OR HOW YOU LIVE
ALL ARE WELCOME!
CAT'S
café

Andrews McMeel Publishing
a division of Andrews McMeel Universal
1130 Walnut Street, Kansas City, Missouri 64106

www.andrewsmcmeel.com

www.catscafecomics.com

20 21 22 23 24 TEN 10 9 8 7 6 5 4 3 2 1

ISBN: 978-1-5248-5504-8

Library of Congress Control Number: 2019950510

Editor: Allison Adler
Art Director: Tiffany Meairs
Production Editor: Elizabeth A. Garcia
Production Manager: Carol Coe

ATTENTION: SCHOOLS AND BUSINESSES
Andrews McMeel books are available at quantity discounts with bulk purchase for educational, business, or sales promotional use. For information, please e-mail the Andrews McMeel Publishing Special Sales Department: specialsales@amuniversal.com.